Peoples Library Movement: Myths and Truths

Peoples Library Movement: Myths and Truths

Neelesh Kashyap

RANDOM PUBLICATIONS
NEW DELHI (INDIA)

Peoples Library Movement: Myths and Truths

ISBN 978-93-5111-854-1

Published in 2016 in India by

RANDOM PUBLICATIONS

4376-A/4B, Gali Murari Lal, Ansari Road
New Delhi-110 002
Phone : +9111-43580356, 011-23289044, 011-43142548
e-mail: sales@randompublications.com,
info@randompublications.com, randomexports@gmail.com

Reprint 2021

Type Setting by : Friends Media, Delhi-110089
Digitally Printed at : Replika Press Pvt. Ltd.

Preface

A public library is a library that is accessible by the general public and is generally funded from public sources, such as taxes. It is operated by librarians and library paraprofessionals, who are also civil servants. There are five fundamental characteristics shared by public libraries. The first is that they are generally supported by taxes; they are governed by a board to serve the public interest; they are open to all, and every community member can access the collection; they are entirely voluntary in that no one is ever forced to use the services provided; and public libraries provide basic services without charge.

The first libraries were only partly libraries, and stored most of the unpublished records, which are usually viewed as archives. The archeological as well as literary evidence make it clear that writing and reading of manuscripts were regularly practiced in ancient period since the fourth century B.C. to the sixth century after Christ. This must have led to the growth and development of collection of manuscripts in important centers of learning. The important library of that period was that of Nalanda University of Bihar in the fourth century AD. The library was said to be in three grandest buildings, the area of which was called "Drama Ganja" meaning mast of religion. The other important academic library of that period was Vikramsila, Odantapuri, Somapuri, Jaggadal, Mithila, Vallabhi, Kanheri, etc. During that period there was a considerable activity in South India too, and there was a tradition about the libraries in that period known as sangam age. The Buddhist of India laid special emphasis on the writing of manuscripts and maintaining their collection. The Jains and Hindus also made immense contribution in the field of learning. They patronized education and literary activities, established innumerable institution called Upasrayas and Temple College. Acharya Nagarjuna, the founder of Mahayana Buddhism is known to have maintained a library on the top floor of the university building. It was also said that Taxila has a rich library.

– ***Author***

Contents

1

Library and Society

THE ROLE OF LIBRARIES IN MODERN SOCIETY

First, the general development of the information society is pushing to re-evaluation of all the institutions which work with information, data, and knowledge-indirectly also with culture. In this connection the roles of education and media have been discussed already quite largely also in the European Union. But libraries-as well as other memory institutions like archives and museums-have not been considered.

Still, there is a clear need in the information society to maintain an institution which is concentrating in collecting and organizing information and offering general access to it. Until now, this work has been underestimated, but I argue the situation will change!

Libraries are especially important now when the whole idea of education is stressing more and more independent learning and acting. All citizens must be able to find and use information. It is the key raw material-but it is a zero resource, if there are no access points to it and if documents are in chaotic order.

Here we can see libraries enter the stage:

- The unique function of libraries is to acquire, organize, offer for use and preserve publicly available material irrespective of the form in which it is packaged in such a way that, when it is needed, it can be found and put to use. No other institution carries out this long-term, systematic work. Culture must be nominated especially: it has an important and unique role in mobilizing resources of human beings. It has been described: To some extent, culture makes its influence felt more indirectly than knowledge, but it is impossible to imagine how people's creative powers could be fully activated without the impact of culture, which extends into the depths of the mind.

The challenge to modern societies is that the basic resource, knowledge, is developing from information in very individual, capricious and unpredictable process. It cannot be commanded. Still, societies can support this development, *e.g.* by offering access to cultural and knowledge treasures. This can even be translated into economic language: to get out the best from the human resources in Europe, this resource must be feeded up with rich and various cultural and infor-mation contents! I would like to stress especially the idea of organizing information by libraries.

It is often shadowed by the second important side of library work: offering access. But in the life-long learning and new technology context just all forms of organizing documents are getting more to the focus. This is clear to anybody who has tried to find something from not-so-often-used Internet websites.

NEW LINES IN THE EU AND IN THE UNITED STATES

In accordance with these phenomenons, there are new political lines in the European Union: The Maastricht Treaty in 1992 launched the cultural aspects. This was only after a long discussion, which made it clear that we have to remember to separate the national view and the European view. The Amsterdam Treaty in 1997 declared citizenship as an important theme.

A significant part of this are a.o. granting information skills and access to information to every European. In addition to this, the European future strategies need to meet the democratic aspects of the information society development. One of the crucial points is again general access to information. Libraries, especially public libraries, are a good tool in all of these new areas. But the European union does not support whichever cultural or citizen concentrated projects in Europe.

In the interests of the European Union there is always to find the European element. So, what can be done in library policy on the European level, taking in account that libraries are primarily a part of national education and cultural policies? The own-initiative report "The role of libraries in modern societies," adopted by the European Parliament in October 1998, is the first effort to answer these questions.

The same topics have been discussed in the United States. They have reached the point where especially the problems of those lacking access to digital resources have been studied. The report Falling Through the Net: Defining the Digital Divide by the U.S. Department of Commerce was released earlier in July 1999.

The report finds that minorities, low-income persons, the less educated, and children of single parent households, particularly when they reside in rural areas or central cities, are risk groups. The report calls for public policies and private initiatives to expand affordable access to critical information resources.

But it also shows, for the first time as far as I know, that libraries and community centres really can diminish the information gap between haves and not-haves. The 1998 data from the U.S. demonstrate very clearly that community access centres, primarily public libraries, are particularly well used by those groups who lack access at home or at work: *e.g.* unemployed groups used Internet in libraries three times as often as an average citizen.

EARLIER ACTIONS IN EU

In the European Union, there have been some efforts to mobilize "the treasures of the European libraries" since the mid-80's. These discussions and resolutions led to two special library programmes under the 3rd and 4th Framework programmes of research and development. The later programme has been known as "Telematics for Libraries". They have been strongly concentrated in IT, because it has been seen as a good tool to produce better access to the existing, underused library resources.

These programmes have had a clear impact in the European library co-operation and development. Benefits of this work come to public libraries indirectly: common standards and working methods help in the end all kind of libraries. But a fact is, that nearly all the libraries active in these EU projects are national libraries or big research and university libraries. Two main exceptions are Publican, a network of European public libraries, and ECUP, which was a copyright awareness raising project, and reached public libraries as well.

A new beginning was the so called Morgan report in 1997. In this report libraries were for the first time put clearly onto the place where they belong in the information society.

As one result of the Morgan report, the European Commission informed that it will produce a Green Paper about the role of libraries in the information society.

For one or another reason, this was made quite ready but was never published. In this situation the Committee on Culture, Youth, Education and the Media in the European Parliament decided to produce an own-initiative report about libraries.

The main reason was that they wanted to influence the big issues under work in the EU, first of all the copyright directive and the 5th framework programme, which will have a direct impact to libraries. I was nominated the rapporteur of the own-initiative report. The report was adopted almost unanimously and with a very encouraging discussion in the Plenary session of the Parliament in October 1998.

DECISIONS OF THE EP CONCERNING LIBRARY POLICY

In short, when adopting the own-initiative report, the EP was calling the Commission and/or the member states to following actions:

- Libraries must be taken in account in national and EU information society strategies and in the respective budgets.
- Libraries need more resources for acquiring expensive books.
- The Green Paper on libraries by the Commission must be completed.
- The users position must be taken in account in the copyright directive process, the balance must be maintained-this was politically the most important decision in short run.
- Support to libraries was demanded from the 5th Framework programme of research and development, *e.g.* for networking, drafting standards, preserving, and transferring information; there is no more named library programme under the 5th framework programme
- A clearing-house to solve problems of long-term conservation should be founded.
- Studies concerning permanent paper should be done on European level.
- The member–states should take care of digitizing their cultural heritage for future.
- There should be studies and concrete support to libraries in licensing matters, which are–will be the next big issue in library work.
- The EU cultural and information budget should be opened to libraries as well, libraries and their co-operation should be taken in account in planning new programmes.
- Problems of legal deposit in international and multinational materials, especially in electronic materials should be solved.
- The member states should provide all types of libraries with modern equipment, particularly with Internet connections.
- Free of charge use of public libraries, in the spirit of the UNESCO Public Library Manifest, was demanded.
- Free and easy access via libraries to material produced with the aid of tax revenues was demanded.
- The members states should organize for their library professionals up-dating education and training.
- A European Union focal point for libraries should be set up
- The member states should found European information points at libraries in countries where they do not yet exist.
- Library statistics should be better and more comparable both on national and European level.
- The national Parliament libraries should be opened to the MEP's in countries where this is not yet the practice.

In addition to these, the report strongly stresses that the library financing must be re-thought in the information society. Without new resources libraries are unable to do everything they are expected to do! After the EP adoption of this report, the European Commission informed that it will next prepare a communication about actions to do. It was stated that the report had already served as a discussion paper, and so the need for the Green Paper had disappeared. The communication is in summer 1999 still under work in the Commission DGXIII/2.

TRADITIONS AND NEW FORMS OF WORK IN THE SAME HOUSE

The European Commission R&D framework programmes have concentrated in IT matters. The three cultural programmes, Caledoskope, Ariane and Raphael, have not been very useful for libraries, because their scope has been quite narrow. *E.g.* the books and reading programme Ariane has concentrated in translations.

In the coming framework programme Culture 2000 libraries will have more possibilities to get support also for their cultural actions. What then will be the fate of the traditional tasks of libraries in general? Will the information society wipe out book loaning and poems?

THE PUBLIC LIBRARIES IN THE KNOWLEDGE SOCIETY

THE LIBRARIES IN A STATE OF FLUX

The municipal reform in 2007 had major consequences for the library service. The number of libraries decreased and the remaining libraries grew in size. The reform thus underlined and intensified various tendencies in library development over the past many years. The public library is in a state of flux. *Library service to children* from 2008 that chose as its point of reference the changes in children's use of the library. Thus this report had a strong focus on one target group and on how the library can develop new services to that group.

The present report also focuses on the target group, but slightly more on the institution–the public library. Based on a number of societal needs and new opportunitics thc rcport also considers how the library can be developed as an institution. The library offer is changing rapidly, but it continues to be much sought after. Two out of three Danes use the public library, and 29% of the adult population visit the library at least once a month. In 2008 the public libraries registered more than 34 mil. visits. This makes the library one of our most popular, public cultural offers, and this has been the case for many years. But the way we use the library is undergoing a change. On the one hand the loan of physical materials – books, CDs etc. – is falling.

In the period 2000-2008 the public libraries' loan of physical materials has thus fallen by 22%, from ca. 62 mil. to app. 48 mil. materials. On the other hand the use of digital offers is growing, an offer that spans from downloads of music and e-books to renewals of loans via the library's homepage. Bibliotekernes Netmusik, where as a library user you can via your municipality download music for free, experienced over 2,5 mil. downloads in 2008 – an increase of 48% compared with 2007.

One explanation of the change in borrowing patterns could be that the technology and media development has resulted in new media habits on behalf of the library users. At the same time the libraries' consistently high visiting figures show that they have succeeded in reorganizing and revitalizing themselves and continue to be attractive.

This happens by developing new library services, particularly digital services, but also by turning the library into something more than just a collection of materials, so that the physical library maintains its desirability.

Today the library is also a place for being and meeting, where one for example gets instruction, uses the Internet or gets help in the local citizen service centre. However, borrowing books remains the main reason why Danes visit the library.

The latest cultural habits survey from 2004 shows that 85% of adult library users visit the library to borrow books and journals. The same tendency becomes apparent in more recent studies.

In a Gallup poll conducted on behalf of the Danish Library Association, the Union of Danish Librarians and HK Kommunal (white collar workers' union (municipal) in 2009, "borrowing books" is the most frequent reason for visiting the library, followed by "borrowing electronic media", "taking the children to the library" and "watching events".

There is in fact also a growing interest in the library's non-users, as can be seen from the large number of new initiatives, which the libraries participate in at municipal level. In many cases these have a social aspect, and the library is here used as a partner in a targeted initiative towards certain target groups.

This effort is particularly relevant in the light of the challenges that globalization presents to less resourceful citizens. The focusing on non-users also has another angle, which is i.a. clearly expressed in former minister for culture, Carina Christensen's strategy Culture for everybody from 2009. Here the emphasis is on the value of participating in a cultural community and the individual citizen's benefit from cultural offers. The strategy suggests that all citizens should be able to take advantage of the cultural offers and consequently– that the cultural institutions focus more purposefully on non-users.

THE POLITICAL BASIS FOR THE COMMITTEE'S WORK

The appointment of the Committee on the Public Libraries in the Knowledge Society was decided by the minister for culture in connection with several consultations in Folketingets Kulturudvalg (parliamentary cultural committee), which took place in the wake of a large number of public library branches being closed down during the first year of the municipal reform. The discussion fuelled by this naturally included the media and technology development.

A suggestion for a more extensive, interdepartmental committee work was rejected by the minister, who referred to the work that had already been done by the Globalisation Council. The committee's work builds on the report *Future library service to children* from 2008. The report contains a number of recommendations as to how to make sure that a strong library offer continues to be available to all Danish children.

In 2008 the Danish Agency for Libraries and Media also published the report *The public libraries after the municipal reform*, which analysed the development within the public library area with particular focus on any consequences due to the municipal reform. The report concluded that the closure of the branches in 2006-2007 was a natural adaptation of the library service, and that at the same time it demonstrated a prioritisation in order to deliver a more up to date and value-enhancing library offer.

With the report from the Committee on the Public Libraries in the Knowledge Society we now have a number of recommendations as to how this prioritisation can be made so that the public libraries also in future will be able to meet the public's need for enlightenment, education and cultural activity. The committee presents its recommendations within an expenditure-neutral framework with the perspective that it may be both necessary and correct with local changes of priorities within the library field in order to support and strengthen the public library in the knowledge society.

THE COMMISSION'S ASSIGNMENT: MANDATE FOR THE COMMITTEE ON THE PUBLIC LIBRARIES IN THE KNOWLEDGE SOCIETY

The committee must focus on continuous development of the public libraries in Denmark. This includes the public libraries' interaction with other libraries and relevant institutions. Focus must be on the libraries as an easily accessible offer to everybody. The committee must build on the report *Future library service to children* and pay particular attention to service to youngsters and adults.

The committee must assess the public libraries' role in relation to the challenges facing the knowledge society, the globalisation strategy's focus on education, lifelong learning and societal cohesive force. The committee must assess to which extent there is basis for establishing new concepts for a library service that meets the public's needs in terms of enlightenment, education and cultural activity, and close to the citizens.

Likewise the committee must asses the possibilities for continuous development of traditional core services such as literature dissemination. In particular, the committee must asses the need for further development of the libraries' digital infrastructure and the interaction between digital and traditional services.

The committee must furthermore describe models for the mediation of digital cultural heritage and licensed digital media and models for various forms of learning and inspiration activities (*e.g.* in relation to citizens with poor reading and IT skills). The committee must likewise give examples of new partnerships, including inter-institutional cooperations and binding networking commitments.

Finally the committee must assess the need for competence development of library staff. On the basis of its analyses the committee must put forward recommendations and suggestions as to how the strategy's objectives can be realised within the present legislation and existing division of labour between state and municipalities. The committee's suggestions must be expenditure-neutral.

The committee is composed upon appointment, so that the minister for culture appoints three members, while Local Government (KL), Danish Library Association, Association of Library Directors, Danish Research Library Association, the Regional Libraries, Union of Danish Librarians and Børne-og Kulturchefforeningen each appoints a member. The Danish Agency for Library and Media's director general is chairman of the committee, and the Agency is the committee's secretariat. The committee must have completed its work primo 2010.

DIGITAL LIBRARIES AND SOCIETY

Digital libraries are large, organized collections of information objects. Whereas standard library automation systems provide a computerized version of the catalog—a gateway into the treasure-house of information stored in the library—digital libraries incorporate the treasure itself, namely the information objects that constitute the library's collection. Whereas standard libraries are, of necessity, ponderous and substantial institutions, with large buildings and significant funding requirements, even large digital libraries can be lightweight.

Whereas standard libraries, whose mandate includes preservation as well as access, are "conservative" by definition, with institutional infrastructure to match, digital libraries are nimble: they emphasize access and evolve rapidly.

The five stages in this part provide an excellent illustration of the huge variety of interesting issues in digital library research that impacts the Asia Pacific region. Unlike the New World, where most of the research on technological aspects of digital libraries originates, Asia has an exceptionally rich cultural heritage. This manifests itself in a huge legacy of documents, in various forms—from paper to palm leaves—and in various different conditions.

The need to preserve this legacy is particularly pressing in today's world, where political instability is rife and climate change is beginning to have an effect. As recent events have shown, disasters, both manmade and natural, can have a devastating effect on fragile cultural artifacts.

S.M. Shafi from the University of Kashmir, India, surveys the many issues involved with digital archiving of medieval manuscripts in Asia. Libraries are pillars of education, and it is natural to expect that digital libraries will provide new opportunities for innovative educational practices. These will be particularly relevant to the Asia Pacific region because of the huge disparities in access to education between the different communities there. Peer-to-peer learning has always been a crucial factor in personal development, although it is frequently ignored in educational studies.

Natalie Lee-San from Nanyang Technological University, Singapore, describes her studies of how digital libraries can provide an innovative, perhaps revolutionary, environment for peer-to-peer learning amongst youths. She touches on many practical issues: gender differences, different learning styles, different levels of media and computer literacy, and age-related differences.

Many economies in the Asia Pacific region are agricul-turally-based. Modern agriculture is a knowledge-based activity that can benefit greatly from digital libraries. Mila Ramos from the International Rice Research Institute in the Philippines describes a large-scale digital library system designed to support the growth, nurturing, harvesting, and distribution of that most Asian of staples, rice.

This digital library supports an institute whose goal is to improve the well-being of present and future generations of rice farmers and consumers, particularly those with low incomes. The institute's library houses the world's most comprehensive collection of technical literature on rice, and provides a widely-used international reference service.

As in many specialized libraries, digital library technology is seen to have special advantages in a world of shrinking library budgets. Intellectual property issues are a central driving force behind the market in information of which libraries are a part. And the questions become more complex as the nature of today's information shifts from a primarily book-based culture to one that embraces all types of multimedia objects, and large, carefully-curated, collections of such objects.

The stage on *"Multimedia digital library as intellectual property"* by Hideyasu Sasaki and Yasujshi Kiyoki at Keio University in Japan clarify the copyright situation as it affects multimedia collections and compilations. They go on to discuss the patentability of particular retrieval mechanisms, an essential component of digital libraries. The fifth stage in this part on how digital library research impacts the Asia Pacific region is the present one, on digital libraries in society. Most existing digital library projects, being research-oriented, are predicated on state-of-the-art equipment and interfaces, academic and research institutions, special collections. In contrast: digital library technology can and should be available to everyone, on all platforms, in all countries; and it can and should enable ordinary people to exercise their creative powers to conceive, assemble, build, and disseminate new information collections that are designed not just for western academics but for a wide diversity of different audiences throughout the world. Though less glamorous, this may, in the end, be a more important goal for society.

Digital libraries pose an inherent tension between the technologist's desire for advanced solutions that use the latest and greatest hardware and software, and the librarian's desire for wide, crossplatform availability and long-term preser-vation—as epitomized by the sustained success of paper as a delivery medium.

To achieve universal access for both information consumers and collection-builders is really a problem for HCI. We examine the social need for digital libraries, particularly in developing countries, by briefly sketching some trends in commercial publishing and contrasting them with a growing international perspective of information as a public good. We draw out the implications for the user interface, which is the principal bottleneck in allowing non-specialist people to make public information available in focused collections that are universally usable.

Then we introduce digital library technology and illustrate it with a particular example, the Greenstone digital library software, which is designed for a broad user base and is in widespread use in many corners of the world—from Uganda to the US, Kazakhstan to Canada, Nepal to New Zealand. Following that, we review a project that is applying digital library technology to the distribution of humanitarian information in the developing world, a context that is both innovative and socially motivated.

Next we discuss issues of universal access and illustrate them with reference to the Greenstone software. We include a brief demonstration of a prototype system that is intended to allow anyone to build and disseminate information collections, and illustrates some human interface challenges that arise when providing necessarily complex functionality to a non-computer-oriented user base.

We close with the hope that future digital libraries will find a new role to play in helping to reduce the social inequity that haunts today's world, both within our own countries and between nations.

BOOKS, LIBRARIES, AND THE SOCIALLY DISADVANTAGED

Today, the long-standing three-way tension between the commercial interests of publishers, the needs of society and information users, and the social mandate of public libraries, is being pulled and stretched as never before. First, the very notion of a "book" is evolving in many different directions: books become more interactive; publishers rent content; books are distributed under restrictive conditions that mechanically prohibit sharing.

While it would be premature to make specific predictions, it seems likely that these trends will further disadvantage the disadvantaged—particularly those in poorer countries who have yet to benefit from ready access to ordinary books. Second, a huge body of information is becoming freely available on the Internet. Much is of questionable quality, but some is very good indeed. In many cases the information is provided for the "public good" rather than for commercial profit, and the redistribution of such information is likely to be encouraged, rather than prohibited, by those who make it available.

Initiatives like UNESCO's "Information for all" programme and the upcoming World Summit on the Information Society highlight the importance of public information; they are founded on the belief that information literacy will help alleviate many of the problems confronting human societies.

Third, the implications for libraries are mixed. Whereas new controls by publishers over how the content they own may be used presents libraries with significant problems, the ready availability of "public good" information meshes well with library philosophy.

A new role is emerging for information professionals who can select material, index it, add appropriate metadata, and redistribute it in added-value form for the good of society. Suitable technological infrastructure is being provided by the open source movement, which is making available high-quality software for repackaging and distribution of information (and not just on computer networks).

Books

What future has the book in the digital world? The question is a complex one that is being widely aired. Authors and publishers ask how many copies of a work will be sold if networked digital libraries enable worldwide access to an electronic copy of it.

Their nightmare is that the answer is *one*: how many books will be published online if the entire market can be extinguished by the sale of one electronic copy to a public library? To counter this threat, the entertainment industry is promoting new *"digital rights management"* (DRM) schemes that permit a degree of control over what users can do that goes far beyond the traditional legal bounds of copyright.

Indeed, the acronym is more aptly expanded as "digital restrictions management" because it is concerned solely with content owners rights and not at all with user's rights. It is, in effect, a "private governance system in which computer systems regulate which acts users are and are not authorized to perform". Anticircumvention rules are sanctioned by the *Digital Millennium Copyright Act* (DMCA) in the US. The DMCA has been used, for example, to prosecute a Norwegian teenager for writing software to play a DVD that he had purchased on a computer for which no commercial playback systems exist.

Can DRM be applied to books? The motion picture industry can compel manufacturers to incorporate encryption into their products because it holds key patents on DVD players. Commercial book publishers are promoting e-book readers that, if adopted on a wide scale, would allow the same kind of control to be exerted over reading material.

Basic rights that we take for granted—such as the ability to lend a book to a friend, resell it on the second-hand market, keep it indefinitely, continue to use it when your e-book reader breaks down, donate it to charity, preserve it for your grandchildren, copy excerpts without resorting to a handwritten transcription—are in jeopardy.

DRM allows such rights to be controlled, monitored, and withdrawn instantly, and DMCA legislation makes it illegal for users to seek redress by taking matters into their own hands. Fortunately, perhaps, lack of standardization and compatibility issues are delaying consumer adoption of e-books.

In the realm of scholarly publishing, digital rights management is more advanced. Academic libraries license access to content in electronic form, often in tandem with purchase of print versions too. They have been able to negotiate reasonable conditions with publishers—probably because they represent the lion's share of the scholarly market.

However, the extent of libraries' power in the consumer book market is moot. One can envisage a scenario where publishers establish a system of commercial, pay-per-view, libraries for e-books and refuse public libraries access to books in a form that can be circulated. These new directions present our society with puzzling challenges, and it would be rash to predict what society's response will be. But one thing is certain: they will surely increase the degree of disenfranchisement of those who do not have access to the technology.

Public Information

In parallel with publishers' moves to reposition books as technological artifacts with refined and flexible control over how they can be used, an opposing trend has emerged: the ready availability of free information on the Internet. Of course, the world-wide web is an unreliable source of enlightenment, and undiscriminating use is dangerous—and widespread.

As early as 1996 complaints arose that the Web's contents are largely unattributed, undated, unannotated, unreliable; information about author and publisher is unavailable or incomplete; far too many resource catalogues are chasing far too few original or non-trivial documents—complaints that are very familiar today. But one thing has changed: search engines and other portals have enormously increased our ability to locate information that is at least ostensibly relevant to any given question.

Teachers complain bitterly that students view the Web as a replacement for the library, harvesting information indiscriminately to provide answers to assignments that are at best shallow and at worst incoherent and incorrect. One consolation is that the very same search facilities can be used to detect plagiarism. Nevertheless, the Web abounds with accessible, high-quality information. Many social groups, non-profit societies and charities make it their business to create sites and collect and organize information there. To take a single example at random, a Google search for *diabetes* returns three national diabetes associations in the top ten hits, and of course many more exist.

Each of these sites offers a cornucopia of valuable information on the disease, which is not commercial and provided for the public good. Widcspread use is strongly encouraged, and it seems likely that arrangements could be made for re-distribution of the material presented there, particularly it was intended as a not-for-profit service and appropriate acknowledgement was made.

One of the key problems with information distribution via the Web is that it disenfranchises developing countries. Although the Web does not extend into the homes of the socially disadvantaged in developed countries either, various national programmes are working to provide access.

But network access varies enormously across the world. Whereas in 1998 more than a quarter of the US population were surfing the Internet, the figures for Latin America and the Caribbean was 0.8%, for Sub-Saharan Africa 0.1%, and for South Asia 0.04%. Schools and hospitals in developing countries are poorly connected.

Even in South Africa, the bestconnected African country, many hospitals and 75% of schools have no telephone line. Universities are better equipped, but even there up to 1,000 people can depend on just one terminal. The Internet "is failing the developing world".

Prompted by this inequity, the importance of information, and particularly public information, is today being highlighted by prominent international bodies. For example, UNESCO's "Information for all" programme was established in 2001 to foster debate on the political, ethical and societal challenges of the emerging global knowledge society and to carry out projects promoting equitable access to information.

It reflects a growing awareness that information is playing an increasing role in generating wealth and human capital, and that participation in the "global knowledge society" is essential for social and individual development.

Information literacy is described as "a new frontier" by the Director of UNESCO's Information Society Division. The Inter-national Telecommunications Union has established a World Summit on the Information Society, held in Geneva in December 2003 and Tunis in 2005, to promote a global discussion of the fundamental changes that are being brought about in our lives by the transformation from an industrial to an information society, and to confront the extreme disparities of access to information between the industrialized countries and the developing world.

Libraries and their Role

What is the librarian to make of all this? The mandate of today's public libraries, in sharp contrast to that of publishers, is to facilitate the open distribution of knowledge. Librarians strive to enable the free flow of information. Their traditions are liberal, founded on the belief that libraries should serve democracy.

To help fulfil their mission as resource centers for citizens, public libraries maintain collections of records, policy statements, government documents, and so on. A recent promotional video from the American Librarian's Association exults that "the library is democracy's place of worship".

Clearly, the impending redefinition of the book as a digital artifact that is licensed rather than sold, tied to a particular replay device, with restrictions that are clearly laid out and mechanically enforced, is an innovation that goes right to the heart of libraries.

The changing nature of the book may make it hard, or even impossible, for libraries to fulfill their mandate by providing quality information to readers. And on the other hand, the emergence of a vast storehouse of information on the Internet poses a different kind of conundrum. Librarians, the traditional gatekeepers of knowledge, are in danger of being bypassed, their skills ignored, their advice unsought.

Search engines send users straight to the information they require—or so users think—without any need for an inter-mediary to classify, catalogue, cross-reference, advise on sources. The ready availability of information on the Internet, and its widespread use, really presents librarians with an opportunity, not a threat.

Savvy users realise they need help, which librarians can provide. A good example is Infomine, a cooperative project of the University of California and California State University.

Infomine contains descriptions and links to a wealth of scholarly and educational Internet resources, each of which has been selected and described by a professional academic librarian who is a specialist in the subject and in resource description generally.

Participating librarians see this as an important expenditure of effort for their users, a natural evolution of their traditional task of collecting and organizing information in print. What kind of technical infrastructure is needed to support and promote this kind of work?

Open source software is a powerful ally for librarians who wish to extend liberal traditions of information access. These systems make the source code freely available for others to view, modify, and adapt; and the very nature of the licensing agreement prevents the software from being appropriated by proprietary vendors. But the open-source movement is more than just a vehicle for librarians to use: its link with library traditions goes much deeper.

Public libraries and open source software both enshrine the same philosophy: to promote learning and understanding through the dissemination of knowledge. Both are pervaded by a sense of community, on the one hand the kind of inter-institutional cooperation exemplified by interlibrary loan and on the other teams of designers and programmers that frequently cross national boundaries.

New trends in information access present librarians in developed countries with difficult and conflicting challenges. Meanwhile, however, the situation in the developing world is dire. Here, traditional publishing and distribution mechanisms have failed tragically.

For example, whereas a US medical library subscribes to about 5,000 journals, the Nairobi University Medical School Library, long regarded as a flagship center in East Africa, last year received just 20 journals. In Brazzaville, Congo, the university has only 40 medical books and a dozen journals, all from before 1993, and the library in a large district hospital consisted of a single bookshelf filled mostly with novels.

Digital Libraries and the Challenge for HCI

Traditional libraries are substantial institutions that occupy physical space, present a physical appearance, and exhibit tangible physical organization. When standing on the threshold of a large bricks-and-mortar library you gain a sense of presence and permanence that reflects the care taken in building and maintaining the collection inside. Digital libraries, in contrast, are lightweight. But they provide potentially far greater accessibility, which means that they will have even greater social effects.

Once created, they can, without significant institutional support, continue to serve users. They can be distributed throughout most of the developed world over the Internet. In developing countries and remote corners of the developed world they can be circulated on removable media—CD-ROM, DVD, or 100 Gb disk units the size of videocassettes—and updated over radio. Issues of copyright pose difficult problems, but they are manageable.

For example, there is plenty of non-copyright material, or material whose owners are prepared to donate copyright for socially useful purposes, and trends towards more open access to academic and humanitarian information are visible. Not everyone sees digital rights management and the DMCA as the way forward, and in the longer term publishers, to remain viable, will have to investigate alternative revenue models for the information they own.

No wonder international organizations such as the United Nations, along with many smaller *non-government organizations* (NGOs), are keenly interested in digital library technology. Advances in digital library technology are radically lowering the bar for the design and production of richly-organized, coherent, focused collections of information.

Now, anyone with access to sufficient source material can use public-domain software to build large, fullysearchable, collections the size of traditional personal or institutional libraries—in minutes. Let the minutes stretch to hours and the collection can be polished, organized, branded, distributed. It can include fully-illustrated text, images, video, music.

It can present attractively-designed pages with consistent use of icons. Keywords, key phrases, even acronyms and their definitions, can be extracted—automatically—and used to underpin novel means of access. Let the hours stretch to days and metadata can be manually added that permits further levels of organization. Given access to programming skills, creative new facilities that stretch the imagination can be rapidly integrated into the system. All this, one might say, can be done with ordinary Web sites: there is no need for digital library technology.

However, bitter experience has shown that all but the most rudimentary sites do require significant institutional support—for organization and maintenance. The Web is littered with incomplete, unfinished, unmaintained, out-dated, inconsistently-organized, useless information collections.

Just as traditional library cataloging procedures integrate new works into existing collections with minimal overhead so that they immediately become first-class members of the collection, so digital libraries allow new documents to be added completely automatically.

In the case of traditional libraries this is done through the small but nonnegligible overhead of generating a new catalog entry. With ordinary Web sites it requires inserting links manually into index pages and the like, and may involve adding links not only into the new document but also into existing ones that ought to reference it—it's like rewriting the book, and maybe revising all other books in the library too!

In contrast, digital libraries bring access structures instantly and effortlessly up to date whenever new documents are added. The challenge for HCI is to design and build digital library systems that fulfill the potential of digital libraries as a "killer app" for computers in developing countries, which will bring concomitant benefits in almost every other sphere of application.

For the information consumer we need access to information that is guaranteed across space, time, and culture. We need flexible distribution mechanisms for documents, and for information objects of all types, that can be accessed on all computer platforms—including the lowliest. We need a choice of distribution over the Web or on removable media such as CD-ROM or DVD.

Digital libraries can incorporate flexible presentation that caters to individual differences, such as large-font displays or spoken output for the visually impaired. Libraries are places where information is preserved, not rendered obsolete, and digital libraries must instill confidence that information prepared today can be accessed next week, next decade, next century—regardless of technological changes.

An important aspect of digital libraries is their ability to work in local languages, promoting pluralism and reducing the risks of homogeneity. Because language is the vehicle of thought, communication, and cultural identity, this will encourage diversity and strengthen individual cultures. But there is a long way to go: even Unicode is woefully incomplete in certain areas, such as African languages.

Naturally, today's digital library systems focus principally on the reader: the consumer of the material stored in the library's treasure-house. But digital libraries make a more radical, and perhaps ultimately more important, contribution by empowering ordinary users to conceive, assemble, build, and disseminate new information collections themselves.

In principle, modest computing resources are quite sufficient to enable users to build new collections by gathering together material in local files or on the Web; augmenting it with appropriate metadata that supports convenient search and browsing operations; incorporating advanced features like key-phrase extraction, document summarization, and metadata extraction; designing an attractive and functional interface; and publishing the collection on a variety of different media that are suitable for the intended readership.

The HCI challenge is to realise this potential for users—such as most librarians—who have a strong understanding of information and its organization, but no more interest in computers than they have in papermaking technology, last millennium's vehicle for information dissemination.

WHAT ARE DIGITAL LIBRARIES

A digital library is an organized collection of information:

A focused collection of digital objects, including text, video, and audio, along with methods for access and retrieval, and for selection, organization, and maintenance of the collection. This definition deliberately accords equal weight to user and librarian. The latter functions are often overlooked by digital library proponents, who often work from a technology perspective rather than from the viewpoint of library or information science, but it is precisely these aspects that allow digital libraries to be used to democratize information dissemination.

As a concrete example, consider the Humanity Development Library, a collection of some 1200 authoritative books and periodicals, produced by many disparate organizations—UN agencies and other international organizations—on various areas of human development, from agricultural practice to economic policies, from water and sanitation to society and culture, from education to manufacturing, from disaster mitigation to micro-enterprises.

It contains 160,000 pages and 30,000 images, which if printed would weigh 340 kg, cost $20,000, and occupy a small library book stack. Instead, it takes the form of a digital library and is distributed on a CD-ROM throughout the developing world at essentially no cost.

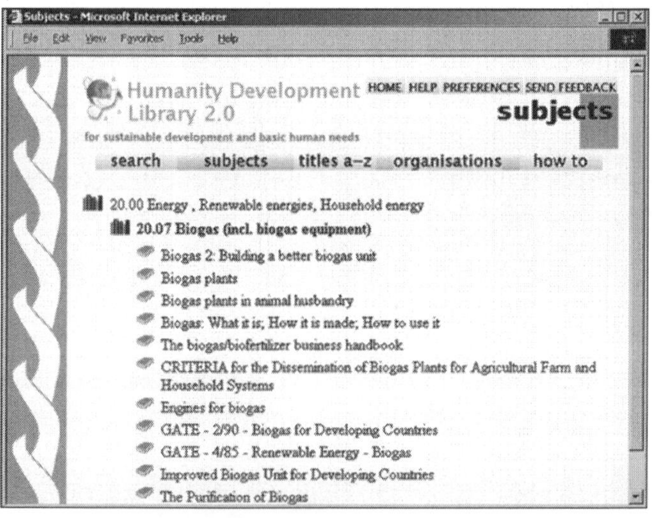

(a)

The Humanity Development Library is produced using the Greenstone software, a freelydistributed open-source project whose aim is to create novel digital library technologies and make them available for others to use. Greenstone digital libraries are arranged in *collections*. A collection comprises several documents, and a library may include several collections, each organized differently.

Collections built with Greenstone offer simple but effective searching and browsing facilities based on metadata and the full text of electronic documents. Each collection is individually designed to take advantage of whatever metadata is available.

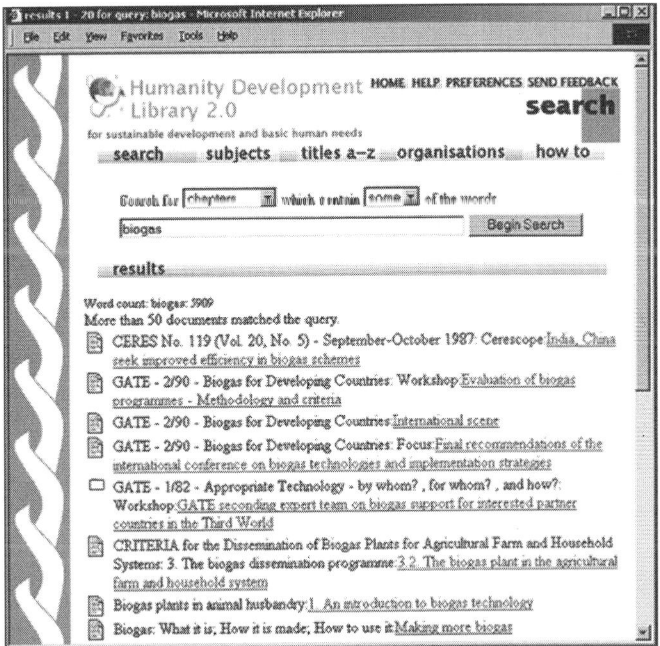

(b)

Fig. 1.1 (Contd.)

All collections support full-text searching and most provide several different browsing options, although they differ depending on the collection design and the metadata available. Typically you can search for particular words that appear in the text, or within a section of a document, or within a title or section heading. A variety of interfaces exist for browsing collections by *title*, *subject*, *date*, or any other metadata chosen by the collection designer.

Figure shows snapshots of the Humanity Development Library. In figure documents are being searched for stages containing the word *biogas*. In figure the collection is being browsed by subject: *Energy, Renewable energies, Household energy*. Pursuing an interest in energy from biogas, the user selects a book by clicking on its book icon. All the icons in the screenshots of figure are clickable.

The navigation bar beneath gives access to the searching and browsing facilities, which differ from one collection to another. This particular collection can be searched by book, chapter, or section, and browsed by subject, title, organization, and "how to" metadata as indicated by the navigation bar. Documents are presented as Web pages generated by Greenstone from the source material.

In figure, the book's cover is displayed as a graphic on the left, and an automatically constructed table of contents appears at the start of the document. The current focus, *Stirring the waste mixture*, is written in bold in the table of contents; its text starts further down the page.

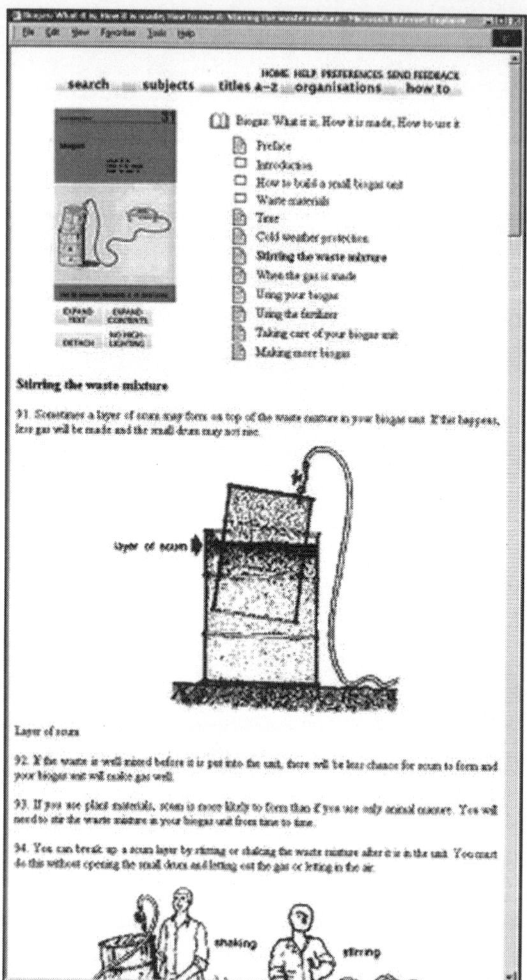

Fig 1.1. The Humanity Development Library: (a) Searching for *Biogas*; (b) Browsing by Subject; (c) Reading a Document.

Incidentally, the material in this collection on building household biogas plans is fascinating, though it is not directly relevant to this chapter. Greenstone collections present documents as automatically-generated Web pages.

This allows documents in different source formats to be presented in a consistent manner, and lets users view the entire collection with a standard Web browser—no special viewing applications are required. However, the collection maintainer may choose to present the original source document instead of, or as well as, the HTML version, and rely on the user's web browser to select a suitable application to display the document. In general, Greenstone deals well with documents and metadata in a wide variety of different formats.

USING DIGITAL LIBRARIES TO DISSEMINATE HUMANITARIAN INFORMATION

Digital libraries provide perhaps the first really compelling *raison d'être* for computing technology in the developing world. Priorities in these countries include health, agriculture, nutrition, hygiene, sanitation, and safe drinking water. Though computers *per se* are not a priority, simple, reliable access to practical information relevant to these basic needs certainly is.

In an article entitled "*The promise of digital libraries in developing countries*" Witten mention ten information collections, available on the Web and CD-ROM, from organizations ranging from UN agencies to small NGOs, in which Greenstone is being used to deliver humanitarian and related information in developing countries.

For example, the Humanity Development Library described is a compendium of practical information aimed at helping reduce poverty, increasing human potential, and giving a practical and useful education. We describe four new ones that have been created recently, and distributed in the same way.

Fig 1.2. A Selection of Recent Humanitarian Digital Library Collections on CD-ROM.

The Researching Education Development library is a project of the *Department for International Development* (DFID), a British government department responsible for promoting develop-ment. Its central focus is a commitment to an internationally agreed target of halving the proportion of people living in extreme poverty by 2015.

Associated targets include ensuring universal primary education, gender equality in schooling, and skills development. It works in partnership with other governments and multilateral institutions, with business and the private sector, with civil society and the research community. It has created a CD-ROM library containing many education research papers and other documents.

Each one represents a study or piece of commissioned research on some aspect of education and training in developing countries.

The Energy for Sustainable Development library was initiated as part of the outreach phase of the World Energy Assessment, which was initiated jointly by the *United Nations Development Programme* (UNDP), the *United Nations Department of Economic and Social Affairs* (UNDESA), and the *World Energy Council* (WEC), along with funding from the United Nations Foundation. This library contains a broad and valuable collection of 350 documents from UNDP, UNDESA, WEC and many other organizations.

It includes titles that all these organizations have published on the subjects of energy for sustainable development—technical guidelines, journals and newsletters, case studies, manuals, reports, and other training material. The documents are in English, Spanish and French, and one document has Arabic, Russian and Chinese translations as well.

The UNAIDS Library contains publications in the "Best Practice" collection which form a unique resource for those working in planning and practice. It is produced by the Joint United Nations Programme on HIV/AIDS, whose global mission is to lead, strengthen and support a response to the AIDS epidemic that will prevent the spread of HIV, provide care and support for those infected by the disease, reduce the vulnerability of individuals and communities to HIV/AIDS, and alleviate the socioeconomic and human impact of the epidemic.

The Health Library for Disasters is the result of a collaboration between the emergency and disaster programmes of the *World Health Organization* (WHO) and the *Pan American Health Organization* (PAHO), with the participation of many other organizations: the *United Nations High Commissioner for Refugees* (UNHCR), the *United Nations Children's Fund* (UNICEF), the International Strategy for Disaster Reduction (EIRD); the Red Cross Movement (ICRC and IFRC); the SPHERE Project; non-governmental organizations such as OXFAM; and national organizations such as the National Emergency Commission of Costa Rica.

It contains more that 300 technical and scientific documents on disaster reduction and public health issues related to emergencies and humanitarian assistance. A follow-up to the Spanish-language Biblioteca Virtual de Desastres discussed by Witten *et al.*, it includes technical guidelines, field guidelines, case studies, emergency kits, manuals, disaster reports, and other training materials.

UNIVERSAL ACCESS

Universal access to digital libraries presents huge challenges to software engineers and HCI practitioners. The Greenstone digital library software allows us to glimpse some of the issues, although it certainly does not yet effectively address them all.

Platforms and Distribution

Most digital libraries are accessed over the web, using any web browser. However, in many environments, particularly in developing countries, web access is insufficient and the system must run locally. And if people are to build and control their own libraries, a centralized solution is inadequate: the software must run on their own computers. Thus digital library systems intended for broad access should run on a wide variety of computer systems, particularly low-end ones. Developed under Linux, the Greenstone server runs on any Windows, Unix, or MacOS/X system. All versions of Windows are supported, from 3.1 up.

Supporting primitive platforms poses substantial challenges of a rather mundane nature: for example, Microsoft compilers no longer support Windows 3.1 and it is necessary to acquire obsolete versions. Under Windows, pre-built collections can be viewed on any system with at least 8 Mb RAM, but collections cannot be built under Windows 3.1/3.11—for this at least a Pentium processor is generally required, except for very small collections.

The fact that Greenstone does not run on early Macintosh systems is a serious drawback in certain environments. In an international cooperative effort established in August 2000 with UNESCO and the Belgium-based Human Info NGO, Greenstone is being distributed widely in developing countries with the aim of empowering users, particularly in universities, libraries, and other public service institutions, to build their own digital libraries.

UNESCO recognizes that digital libraries are radically reforming how information is acquired and disseminated in its partner communities and institutions in the fields of education, science and culture around the world, and particularly in developing countries. Their hope is that this software will encourage the effective deployment of digital libraries to share information and place it in the public domain.

The UNESCO distribution of Greenstone is a CD-ROM that contains the full source code and executable binaries for Windows and Linux, along with all necessary associated software. Full documentation and five demonstration collections are included.

The current CD-ROM is trilingual, with complete interfaces, instructions, and documentation in English, French and Spanish. For those with Web access, the same package is also available for download from the Greenstone Web site, often in a form that is slightly ahead of the CD-ROM version—for example, many other language interfaces are included and full documentation is available in Russian and Kazakh too.

Providing accessibility in different languages is more difficult than one might at first realise. As well as the manuals, installation instructions and installation prompts, the licensing agreement, and the readme files have to be translated too.

Access for Readers

Greenstone collections like the Humanity Development Library can be published as standalone collections on removable media such as CD-ROM, or presented on the Web. CD-ROM is a very practical format in developing countries.

Any Greenstone collection can be converted into a self-contained Windows CD-ROM that includes the Greenstone server software itself and an integrated installation package. The installation procedure has been thoroughly honed to ensure that only the most basic of computer skills are needed to install and run a collection under Windows.

Even standalone Greenstone users interact through a Web browser: Netscape is supplied on each CD-ROM for those who do not already have a browser. In standalone mode the software runs locally but incorporates a Web server so that if the system happens to be connected to a network—say a hospital or school intranet—information is available to other machines that may not possess CD drives.

This happens automatically: no special configuration is necessary. Another difficult engineering challenge is checking for the existence of a network. While installed network software is easily detected, it is hard to determine non-intrusively whether it is operational. Incorrectly installed or configured software is endemic in developing countries, because computers there are often cast-offs whose software is inappropriate to their present environment, yet system support to rectify the problems is unavailable.

It is essential for universal access that such problems are addressed properly and solved satisfactorily without involving the user, even though they are mundane and timeconsuming. Greenstone provides some support for the visually impaired by incorporating a "textual" mode of access that replaces all images by textual prompts. This output is suitable for users with speech synthesizers or other specialized access devices. However, the facility is not well advanced: in particular, we have not yet refined it through usability testing and interface improvement.

Building New Collections

Effective human development blossoms from empowerment rather than gifting. As the Chinese proverb says, "Give a man a fish and he will eat for a day; teach him to fish and he will eat for the rest of his days." Disseminating information originating in the developed world, like the Humanity Development Library, is a useful activity for developing countries.

But a more effective strategy for sustained long-term human development is to disseminate the capability of creating information collections, rather than the collections themselves. This will allow developing countries to participate actively in our information society, rather than observing it from outside.

It will stimulate the creation of new industry. And it will help ensure that intellectual property remains where it belongs, in the hands of those who produce it. Users whose skills resemble those of librarians rather than computer specialists should be able to build and distribute their own digital library collections. As an initial step in this direction, Greenstone includes an interface called the "Collector" that is intended to help people build their own library collections.

Collections may be built and served locally from the user's own web server, or remotely on a shared digital library host. End users can build new collections styled after existing ones from material on the Web or from their local files—or both, and collections can be updated and new ones brought on-line at any time.

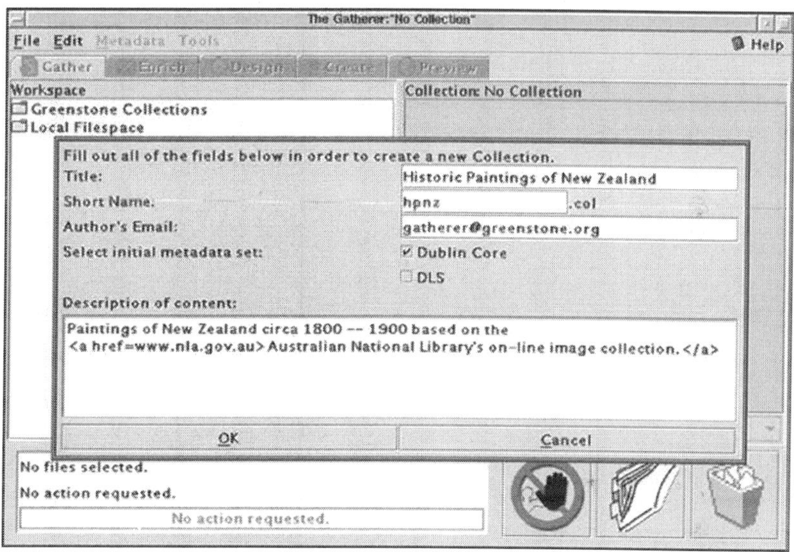

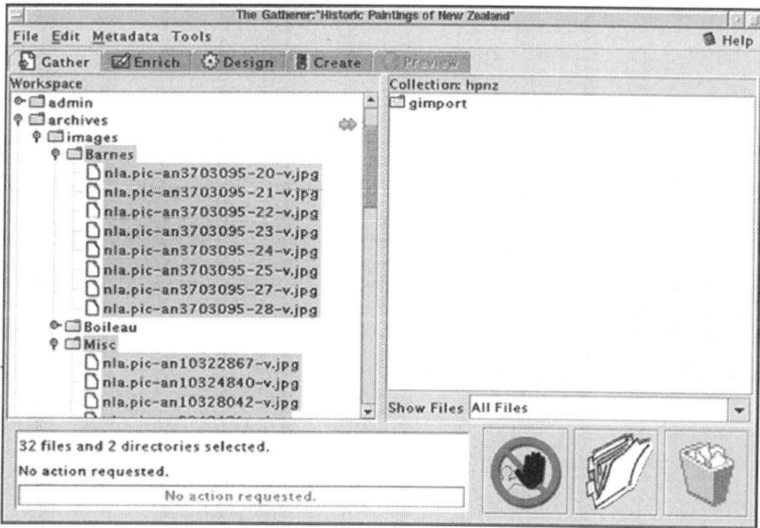

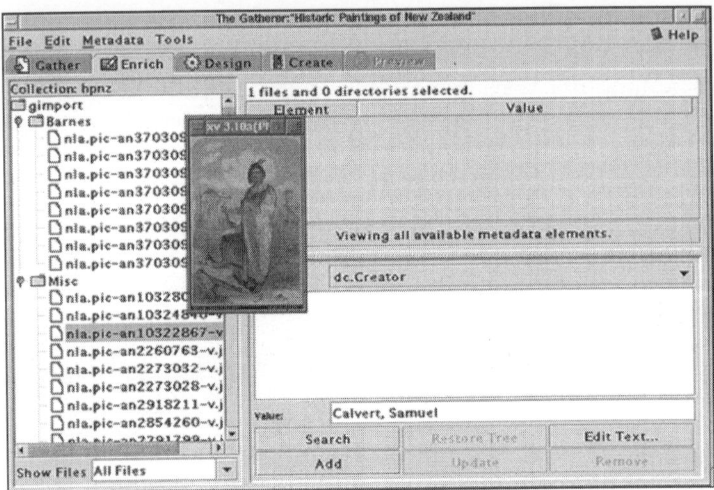

Fig. 1.3 (Contd.)

Fig 1.3. Building a Collection with the Gatherer.

The interface, which is intended for non-professional end users, is modeled after widely used commercial software installation packages, frequently called software "wizards"—a term we deprecate because of its appeal to mysticism and connotations of utter inexplicability. We chose this interaction style because it simplifies the choices and presents them very clearly.

Figure 1.3 shows a new Greenstone librarian interface, currently undergoing beta testing by UNESCO at sites in Argentina, India, Kazakhstan, Mexico, and South Africa, which builds on lessons learned from the Collector. It incorporates a great deal of additional functionality, particularly the ability for users to associate metadata with any item or group of items, and to reuse metadata elements without retyping them. In figure, it is being used to collate a selection of images for a digital library collection, augment these source documents with textual metadata and then build and view the collection. From here, it is a matter of a few further clicks to produce a self-installing CD-ROM version of the collection.

In this illustration the user is developing a digital library collection of historic paintings of New Zealand. The user creates a new collection using the file menu, and a resulting popup window prompts for some general information about the collection. Once the user has filled out this form the main window becomes active. A series of panels guide the user through the processes required to build the collection.

The left-hand pane of the *Gather* panel shows the file system and the right-hand one represents the contents of the collection, initially empty, which the user populates by dragging and dropping files. In figure, the user has moved to the *Enrich* panel and is adding textual metadata to the selected documents. The next two panels, *Design*, *Create*, help the user structure the collection, control its appearance, and build it.

On completion the result is viewed in the *Preview* panel. Figure shows a page from the newly built collection, in which source documents are alphabetically listed by artist. Shown alongside each thumbnail are the artist's name, its catalog number, image dimensions, and its download size.

The full-size image is shown by clicking on the thumbnail. The user may skip backwards and forwards through the panels using them to augment and enhance the collection, perhaps adding further source documents, editing metadata values, and altering the collection's appearance.

Customization

An important component of access is allowing people to control the appearance of the collections they create. Many who build digital libraries want to brand them to ensure that they with an appropriate personal, institutional, or corporate image, and some can only contemplate software solutions that allow them to do so.

Although Greenstone comes with the standard appearance shown in figure—a distinctive bar down the side of all pages except those that show documents in the library, a green access bar with yellow buttons, etc.—the interface is highly configurable. Greenstone creates all pages that appear on the screen on the fly: none are stored in advance. They are generated using macros, written in a simple language specially designed for the job, that perform textual replacement.

One reason is that Greenstone accommodates a large number of different interface languages and macros help cope with this. All text fragments are couched as macro definitions. To add a new language, just the macro contents need to be translated—no web pages need be reworked.

Every page displayed by the system is passed through a macro interpreter that expands all the macros on the page. The interpreter checks a language variable and uses the macro definitions pertaining to it, which loads the page in the appropriate language.

Macros can have parameters. In this case, the parameter is the language variable: it causes the appropriate text fragment to be used for the macro's expansion. If there is no Arabic version for a particular macro, the interpreter will automatically substitute the default version.

This lets system developers experiment with the interface without having to worry about translating every little bit of new text immediately. Defaulting to English is not ideal—it reflects an Anglo-centric mindset—but it seems better than displaying nothing. Macros are also used to deal with display variables. Whenever a web page contains information that is not known in advance—like the number of documents returned by a search, or the value of a particular metadata item, or the content of a document page—a macro name is used in the page description.

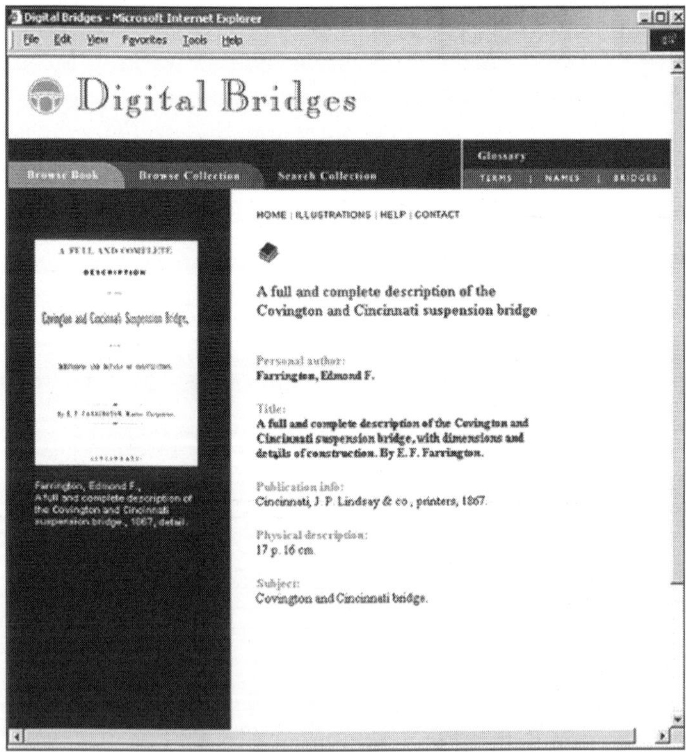

Fig 1.4. A Customised Interface to Greenstone.

Unlike language macros, these macros are *dynamic*: their content is not stored in advance but generated by the system in accordance with the value of the variable in question.

Users can completely alter the form of the user interface by rewriting the macro files—or even by writing their own web pages which embed the dynamic macros that generate bits of Greenstone output.

Figure 1.4 shows a Greenstone interface that has been heavily customised by Lehigh University Library, Pennsylvania. The standard Greenstone appearance has been completely obliterated in favour of an in-house style, yet all the Greenstone functionality is available. Figure shows a thumbnail of a book cover on the left, and full bibliographic information on the right. Entering a book displays facsimile images of its pages.

Internationalization

The international Unicode character set is used throughout Greenstone, and documents in any Unicode-supported language and character encoding can be imported. Collections of documents in Arabic, Chinese, Cyrillic, English, French, Spanish, German, Hindi, and Maori are publicly available.

The New Zealand Digital Library Web site hosts many of these, and the Greenstone Web site links to sites that contain further examples. It makes little sense to have a collection whose content is in Chinese or Russian, but whose supporting text—instructions, navigation buttons, labels, images, help text, and so on—are in English.

Consequently, the entire Greenstone interface has been translated into a range of languages, and the interface language can be changed by the user as they browse from the *Preferences* page.

All the language fragments in the interface are stored in macro files. These have been translated by Greenstone users in other parts of the world and contributed back to the project.

Figure 1.5 shows an example: a Russian collection. Currently, interfaces are available in Arabic, Czech, Chinese, Dutch, French, Galician, German, Hebrew, Indonesian, Italian, Kazakh, Maori, Portuguese, Russian, Spanish, Turkish, and English. Managing the organizational and software complexity of any comprehensive and evolving open source software system presents a significant challenge.

However, the challenge is greatly magnified when the interface is available in different languages, for enhancements to the software and changes to the interface must be faithfully reflected in each language version. No single person knows all interface languages; no single person knows about all modifications to the software—indeed there is likely no overlap at all between those who translate the interface and those who build the software.

Fig 1.5. A Russian Digital Library Collection.

Currently, Greenstone has about twenty interface languages and there are around 600 linguistic fragments in each interface, ranging from single words like *search*, through short phrases like *search for*, *which contain*, *of the words*, to sentences like *More than... documents matched the query*, to complete paragraphs like those in the on-line help text.

Maintaining the interface in many different languages is a logistic nightmare.

The solution adopted by Greenstone is to incorporate a language translation facility, which allows authorized people to update the interface in specified languages.

A standard version control system is used to manage software change, and from this the system automatically determines which language fragments need updating and presents them to the human translator.

GROWTH OF LIBRARIES IN INDIA

GROWTH AND DEVELOPMENT OF ORIENTAL LIBRARIES IN INDIA

Libraries have always had a pivotal role in the storage, processing, and dissemination of information. Some may serve general needs, but special libraries serve the needs of a particular community of users. Among special libraries, Oriental libraries hold an important place because they preserve the cultural heritage of a nation or a civilization.

Oriental Libraries

"Oriental Libraries" are those libraries that have literature pertaining to Oriental studies and languages. "Oriental" in this context refers to the ancient Near East, including India, Persia, and ancient Arabia, among other places, and the languages and literatures of those places and peoples.

Growth and Development

India is a vast repository of different cultures, both because it was invaded by a number of foreign countries and peoples, and because of its contacts with people from the East. The languages from those Eastern countries are part of Indian literature. The literature in those Eastern languages created India's Oriental libraries.

Their history can be traced back to the Vedic period, when the written literature was kept in Ashrams or Gurukuls. Gurukuls were mostly located peaceful forest environments. With the passage of time, Gurukuls were also established in cities.

Jain and Buddhist Era

Taxila was one of the famous educational centres where students came from different parts of the country. Varanasi also distinguished itself by having a large number of Gurukulas. During this period, the literature was preserved in the Sutra style of composition.

Buddhist and Jain Monastries acted as repositories of knowledge, for religious literature as well as other types. Monastic Oriental Libraries were also called Viharas. Over time, these Viharas developed into institutions of higher learning. A federation of Viharas constituted a Mahavihara, which was a larger educational institutional institution.

Nalanda Mahavihara is the best example. Fa-Hien, a Chinese traveller, also found a number of monastaries in India. Kanyakubja, Sravasti, Kusunagara, Vaisali, and Patliputra were centres of Oriental literature according to Fa-Hien. Hiuen-Tsang, another Chinese traveller, visited India during A.D. 629-645. He left a detailed account of his visit, which gives us significant information about Buddhist educational institutions possessing a rich variety of Eastern literature. Taxila was a center of learning in Ancient India and a large number of people from all over the world and the subcontinent itself visited this place to gain knowledge.

Literature related to medicine and archery enriched the library at Taxila. Rahula Sankrityayana, Angiris set up a seminary with a Granthakuti attached to it at Taxila, which later flourished in to an academy or university. Nalanda University is the best known of ancient India's universities. It has been called the treasure house of information by European archeologists. The information there helped locate Buddhist shrines in India.

It is believed that King Kumara Gupta built the first monastery at Nalanda to train Buddhist monks. Nalanda University was an expansion of this seminary. King Buddha Gupta, Jagatha Gupta, Baladitya, and Vijra made additions and expansions to the building.

There were three large libraries with vast amount of literature in Oriental languages on subjects such as science, medicine, astrology, fine arts, literature. The University of Valabhi was built by the Maitraka Kings during the years A.D 475-775. Its library had a variety of Eastern literature. This great university and its library lasted until the 12th century, when they were completely destroyed by Arab invaders.

Odantapuri University was founded by King Gopala and was a well-known center of learning. It had a library that was rich in Brahmanical and Buddhist works. Mohammad Bakhtiyar Khilji destroyed this monastic university along with its library. Somapuri also possessed a wealth of Oriental literature, but it was destroyed by fire in the middle of the 11th century.

Vikramasila monastery, built by King Dharmapala, had a variety of literature on metaphysics, tantras, grammar, ritualism, and logic. The library fulfilled the demands of outsiders, especially those from Tibet, by providing them copies of manuscripts in a most liberal way. Another University with a significant Oriental collection, especially in Tantric Buddhism, was Jagaddala, founded by King Ramapala.

Another monastery with a rich wealth on different aspects of Oriental literature was Kanheri University, built during the reign of Amoghavarsha. By the 10th century, the corpus of Jain literature had increased many times, and Jain monks had contributed substantially to nearly all branches of knowledge known at that time. The Jayendra monastery of Kashmir had a good library where the Chinese traveller Hiuen–Tsang spent two years copying manuscripts.

Similarly, he spent fourteen months at the Chinapati monastery. Several Hindu kings and their ministers, who flourished between 10th and 12th centuries AD, are credited with establishing libraries and supporting the library movement. Among them was King Bhoja of Dhara, who flourished in the 11th century, and was a distinguished scholar with a rich library. King Kumarapaladeva of the Chaulakyas is said to have established 21 Jain Libraries. He kept a copy of Kalpasutra written in golden ink in each one of them.

Mughal Empire

When the Muslims established their rule in India at the beginning of the 13th century, Muslim emperors paid special attention to libraries, taking care to establish libraries in educational institutions. They constructed no separate library buildings; rather, books were deposited and preserved in educational institutions, mosques, and Khangahs.

Many Muslim rulers were from the East, and they helped enrich libraries with Oriental literature. Paper began be used as a writing material in the 12th century, and this helped book production in this periods. Mughal sovereigns and their courtiers were educated and accomplished, and some maintained personal libraries.

The Muslim sovereigns collected and preserve the Vedas, the *Ramayana*, and other Hindu religious books. They also translated a variety of books in Hindi in to Persian and Arabic, and helped disseminate Hindu art and culture. After the establishment of Sultans of Delhi in 1202, a new period in the history of Oriental libraries came in to existence. These minor Muslim rulers and nobles encouraged Islamic learning and established *maktabs* (primary schools), *madrasas* (schools of higher learning), libraries, and mosques.

They encouraged Arabic and Persian literatures in all branches of learning, and enriched Oriental literature in the libraries. They gave shelter and protection to scholars, who brought literature from other parts of the world to India. The Library of Khwajah Nizam-ud-din Auliya was an important Oriental library.

It was the property of the *Waqf* (religious board) and was open to every man of letters. During the reign of the Khilji dynasty the number of Oriental libraries increased. Jala-ud-din Khiljee established the Imperial Library at Delhi and appointed Amir Khusru as its librarian.

The Tughluq Dynasty opened a new chapter in the history of Oriental libraries in India. Mohammad Tughluq built one thousand madrasas, each with a library with collections in Arabic and Persian. Humayun ascended the throne in 1530 and a library known as Khan-i-Tilism.

Humayun's library played a significant role in Mughal history. Akbar, the greatest of Mughal emperors maintained a very rich library. He added a sizable number of books, obtained from his conquest, from libraries in Gujarat, Jaunpur, Kashmir, Bihar, Bengal, and the Deccan.

His library was unique in its collection of rare books, among which was the Persian *Divan of Human Shah.* By the time of Akbar's grandson, Shah Jahan, the library was a complex organization with a large staff, and headed by Nazim, a noble of the court. In Kashmir, a picture of the first library is found in the Shrine of Hazrat Bulbul Shah, which was established by Muslims.

A magnificient monastery and mosque were constructed by the emperor of Kashmir, Sultan Sadruddin, for Hazrat Bulbul Shah. A library was attached to this mosque. Amir Kabir Syed Hamdani, a theologian and scholar had a well established personal library that contained Oriental literature. He established a number of libraries in Kashmir which added to the wealth of the Indian Oriental libraries.

The Sultans of Kashmir had given funds to establish madrasas and libraries. Each madrasa had a library. Sultan Zain-ul-Abedin-ul constructed a library which historians tell was one of the best in the world. Among the other libraries built by Budshah, Darul-ul-Uloom Nausherah was the best.

Another library, by the name of Madrasa-i-Sher, was built by Budshah near modern Islamabad. During the Chak Sultanate many libraries thrived and brought Oriental literature to the limelight. Akbar conquered Kashmir in 1587 and established many madrasas and libraries there. In Gujrat and Malwa, a number of libraries were introduced by Ahmad Shah I and Dilawar Khan.

Shah Jahan, like his predecessors, patronized learning and education and built a library with a rich collection of Arabic and Persian manuscripts. Dara Shikkoh, Aurangzeb, and Bahadur Shah Zafar also contributed to the development of Oriental libraries. Mughal rule was a period of literary excellence. Most of the emperors were themselves scholars, and also extended their patronage to scholarship and learning.

Other Kingdoms

There were kingdoms in other parts of India that also had libraries enriched by Oriental literature. The kingdoms of Bahmani and Deccan had independent kings who reigned for 340 years, and who were patrons of learning, as were the Bahmani kings, who continued their rule up to AD 1526 and had an empire that stretched from coast to coast.

They founded many colleges and libraries. Ahmad Shah built a magnificient college near Gulbarga. Muhammad Shah Bahmani II built another imposing college at Bidar that is one of the many beautiful remains of the grandeur of the Bahmanis. All these colleges had libraries that possessed an enormous amount of Oriental literature.

Arabian and Iranian literature brought by visitors and travellers were added to the libraries of Bahmanis. The Urdu language was at its zenith during the reign of Firoz Shah Bahmani, and a vast amount of Urdu literature enriched the Bahmani Libraries. The library of Gesudaraj was distinguished among the libraries of Deccan. Books on Sufism and religion were available in this library. The emperors of Qutub Shahi also established a good number of libraries during their reign, and a vast amount of literature in Persian was included. Tipu Sultan, son of Haider Ali and emperor of Mysore established a number of libraries.

"Zaimul-Umoor" was the great university of Seringa Patnam in his reign. He collected books from many countries including Europe. The library had a copy of the Holy Quran which was written by the hand of Aurangzeb Alamgir. It is estimated that the library had nearly 2,000 volumes of Persian, Arabic, and Hindi manuscripts from all branches of Islamic literature.

After the downfall of the Mughals, and with the invasion of Ahmad Shah Abdali, the literary wealth of the Indian libraries was looted away. In 1857, after the Sepoy mutiny, thousands of books were destroyed and thousands of important, valuable, and rare books were siphoned to England.

British and other Europeans

The growth and development of Oriental libraries was regenerated again during European and British rule. The interest shown by the British and European scholars in Oriental Learning and Indology, along with the social, cultural and religious movements spearheaded by eminent Indians, resulted in new Oriental libraries. These institutions established libraries for Oriental scholarship. The result of this renaissance is a number of special libraries devoted to Oriental and Indological collections in various parts of the country.

Rampur Raza Library, very rich in Indo-Islamic studies and arts, was created by Nawab Faizullah Khan in 1794, and has tremendous manuscript wealth. One can find manuscripts in Arabic, Persian, Urdu, Sanskrit, Sinhali, Tamil, Kannada, and other Oriental languages.

The Asiatic Society Library, Kolkata, a premier and leading oriental institutions of the country was established in 1784 by Sir William Jones. Colonel Mackenzie, an Englishman and an engineer by profession established an Oriental Library by the name of " *Government Oriental Manuscript Library* (GOML) " in Chennai.

Contemporary Libraries

Khuda Baksh Oriental Library was founded in 1842 by Maulvi Khuda Baksh Khan, who donated his entire personal collection. Since 1977 it has been issuing regularly a multi-lingual research quarterly *Khuda Baksh Library Journal.* The library has been recognized as a research center by seven Indian universities. The collection has a rich repository of Persian and Arabic manuscripts. Maulana Azad Library, Aligarh Muslim University was initially founded as "Anglo Oriental College (MAOC) at Aligarh in 1875 and raised to the status of a university in 1920.

The personal collection of Maulana Azad also enriches the library. The library has a total collection of over 1 million volumes and 14,571 manuscripts. The Maulana Azad Library has the largest collection of Urdu books in the Indian subcontinent, which is perhaps largest in the world as well.

The collection includes:

- Urdu
- Arabic
- Persian
- Sanskrit
- Hindi
- Sir Syed Collection
- Gandhian Collection
- Aligarh Collection
- Thesis Collection
- Archives
- Microfiche
- Manuscripts

Hakim Mohammad Syed Library, Jamia Hamdard, New Delhi is a leading university founded in 1906.

It has a well known Oriental library, which has a number of special collections:

- Nazaria Collection
- Abdul Sattar Siddiqui Collection
- Maulana Abdul Salam Niazi Collection
- Jaffri Collection
- Shafi Ahmad Collection
- Dr Tanveer Alvi Collection

The library has 4,500 rare manuscripts. Osmania University Library was established in 1918 and is considered seventh oldest in India, the third oldest in South India, and the first to be established in state of Hyderabad.

The library has a collection of rare books and manuscripts including Palm Leaf manuscripts. The National Library of India, which came in to existence in 1948, is the largest library in India. Previously it was known as the Imperial Library which was formed in 1891 by combining a number of Secretariat libraries.

It has a wide range of collections in a variety of national and international languages. A good number of Arabic and Persian documents are also available here. The Oriental library initiative that took place in ancient India reached its zenith in the period when the British and other Europeans came to India. The

Mughals also contributed a great deal to the development of Oriental libraries. Eventually, their extravagant ways caused the libraries to deteriorate, but social and political conditions eventually led to better libraries with larger collections.

ACADEMIC LIBRARIES IN INDIA: A HISTORICAL STUDY

Research in library history in India has remained largely neglected area which has resulted into availability of very limited and scanty literature. Commenting on the status of library history in India, Donald G. Davis, Jr. of the University of Texas at Austin, writes that "although a core literature on Indian library history exists, it has many imbalances and gaps. The scholars are very dispersed in their interests and their geographical location. With one person rarely contributing more than one work. There is little pattern to existing research efforts."

In this context, the role of historian happens to be much more crucial and significant to make an assessment of the growth and development of libraries in India, the factors responsible for their development and the impact of those factors on the library progress. Rajgopalan, in his 1987 presidential address to the Indian Library Association rightly said, "it is generally acknowledged that our libraries are underutilized in relation to investments being made in them.

Non-use and low-use of libraries amount to wastage of facilities being made available. Maybe the literacy rate, lack of reading habits, etc., are the causes for low use from the side of patrons... User education programmes must be organized by libraries in a way that libraries are fully utilized." He further remarked that, "if library historians would address the roots and trends of library issues, they would provide a valuable service to the profession and society."

The Father of Library and Information Science in India,Padmashri Dr. S.R. Ranganathan while giving a radio talk in April 1956 said: "an account of the libraries in the first four periods must necessarily depend upon the historical research. This has not yet been done. The library profession is too small in India to spare a person to fill up this antiquarian gap. Those trained in the scientific method of tracing history are too preoccupied with dynastic and political history to spare sufficient time for cultural history in general and library history in particular."

Thus, an historical study of the growth and development of academic libraries in India, is a desideratum, the fulfilment of which should go a long way in removing the imbalances and gaps. Such a study becomes significant not only in view of the tremendous activity concerning the growth and development of libraries in India, but also because their growth has been shaped in the first phase by the phenomena that have shaped the historical course of this period and, secondly, the rise of library as an important instrument in the advancement of knowledge and socio-economic transformation.

Source Material for Writing History of Libraries

For the purpose of scientific writing of history of libraries, an understanding of the nature of existing source material and knowing the art of using it is essential. The sources for writing the history are available in Pali, Sanskrit, Chinese, Arabic, Persian and European Languages and most of them have been translated into English. These exist in various formats, such as Manuscripts, inscriptions, copper plates etc.

They are either indigenous or foreign. The contribution of foreign travelogues such as Tibetan, Chinese, Muslim, Portuguese, English and other Europeans is highly useful. Some noteworthy foreign travelogues are Itsing, Fahien, Hieun Tsang, Alberuni, Ibn Batuta, Minhaj, Firishta, Badauni, Afif, bernier, mandelso, Manrique de Lara, Martin, Count Noer.

In addition to the contribution of the travelogues, the contribution of historians like Henry M. Eliot, John Dawson, Stanley Lane-Pool, Ishwari Prasad, R.C. Majumdar, Jadunath Sarkar, V.D. Mahajan, Mohammed Muhammed Zubair, J.S. Sarma and N.N. Law etc. is also significant.

Though scanty, yet there are articles written by the library professionals on history of libraries. A few efforts have also been made for conduct of research in the area of history of libraries and such like works have been consulted for the purpose of writing this paper.

University Libraries in Ancient India

In the Vedic age instructions were imparted "orally, without the medium of books." Taxila from 700 B.C. to AD 300 was considered to be the most respected seat of higher learning and education in India but still there is no evidence found so far in the archaeological excavations at Taxila that there had been a good library system in the Taxila University.

Fa-Hien noticed such libraries at Jetavana monastery at Sravasti. In A.D. 400, there came into being one of the biggest known universities, the Nalanda University, which by A.D 450. became a renowned seat of learning, its fame spreading beyond the boundaries of India. Nalanda near Patna grew to be the foremost Buddhist monastery and an educational centre. Most of what we know of the Nalanda University during the 6th and the 7th centuries A.D. is due to the accounts left by Hiuen-tsang, who lived in the institution for three years in the first half of the 7th century, and I-tsing who also stayed there for ten years towards the latter part of the same century.

Information on the Nalanda University Library is also found in the Tibetan accounts, from which we understand that the library was situated in a special area known by the poetical name the Dharmaganja, which comprised three huge buildings, called the Ratnasagara, the Ratnodadhi and the Ratnaranjaka of which the Ratnasagara was a ninestoried building and housed the collection of manuscripts and rare sacred works like Prajnaparamita Sutra etc. The library at Nalanda had a rich stock of manuscripts on philosophy and religion and contained texts relating to grammar, logic, literature, the Vedas, the Vedanta, and the Samkhya philosophy, the Dharmasastras, the Puranas, Astronomy, Astrology and Medicine. The University of Nalanda and its library flourished down to the 12th century A.D. until Bakhtiyar Khalji sacked it in A.D. 1197-1203. and set fire to the establish-ment of Nalanda.

The world famous universities, such as, the Vikramasila, the Vallabhi and the Kanchi were coming up in other parts of the country during the period from the 5th century A.D. to the 8th century A.D. All these universities possessed rich libraries and in the hall containing such books there used to be an image of the goddess Saraswati with a book in her hand.

The Nalanda and the Vikramshila universities were under the control of the king Dharmapala. He founded the Vikramshila monastery in the 8th century A.D. It had a rich collection of texts in the Sanskrit, the Prakrit and the Tibetan languages.

Regarding the library of the university, the *Tabaqat-i-Nasiri* informs us that there were great number of books on the religion of Hindus there; and when all these books came under the observation of the Mussalamans, they summoned, a number of Hindus that they might give them information regarding the import of these books; but the whole of the Hindu community was killed in the war.

Muslim vandalism caused the disappearance of the excellent collection at Vikramashila. The Jaggadal Vihara in Varendra-bhumi was also an important centre of learning with considerable collection of the reading material. It was established by the king Kampala, who ruled from A.D. 1084 to 1130.

The provision of facilities for reading, writing, editing and translating manuscripts shows that this library was in no way less than its contemporary libraries in importance. Though not as large as the library of Nalanda, it abounded in private collection of texts.

Likewise Mithila had been famous for its scholars since the days of Rajrishi Janaka and had a rich collection of various commentaries on the different branches of the Hindu *Shastras.* The library of its university played an important role in teaching and learning. A needle *(Shalaka)* was pierced through the manuscript on the subject of the student's specialization and he was expected to explain the last page pierced.

In this way the student's all-round mastery of the subject was tested. Mithila continued to enjoy its all India importance in the field of learning till the end of the 15th century AD. The university at Sompuri, like that of Vikramshila, occupied a significant position since the days of Dharampala. Like Nalanda, this university also had its own library. Atisa Dipankar, a noted scholar, lived there. He with the help of other scholars, translated into the Tibetan the *Madhyamkaratnapradipa* of Bhavaviveka. This university was destroyed by fire in the middle of the 11th century A.D. Efforts were made by the monk Vipulsrimitra to renovate the university but it could not regain its past glory.

At a time when Nalanda was famous for its *Mahayana* courses of study, the Maitrakakings provided their patronage to the Mahavihara of Vallabhi. This university was famous for its *Hinayana* studies. The fact that this university had a good library is supported by a reference in a grant of Guhasena, dated A.D. 559, wherein a provision was made out of the royal grant for the purchase of books for the library. This important seat of learning at Kanheri, on the West Coast, flourished during the reign of Amoghavarsha in the 9th century A.D. The library occupied a significant position within the establishment, and the donors provided money to buy books for the library.

The last of the famous seats of learning in Eastern India was Navadwipa in Bengal. It reached its height of glory from 1083 to A.D. 1106 as a centre of intellectual excellence as well as its rich library facilities, when Lakshman Sen, a king of Gauda, made it his capital. However, this library was also destroyed along with the centre by Bakhtiyar Khalji.

Situated in South India at Amaravati, on the banks of the Krishna, the Nagarjuna Vidyapeeth flourished in about 7th century A.D. Its library housed in the top floor of the five storyed building of the university had an enormous collection on the Buddhist philosophy, particularly of the *Mahayana* school that Nagarjuna had founded, science and medicine.

There is enough archaeological evidence that supports the existence of this 7th century university and its library. The enormity of the collection in this library is borne out by the fact that it not only had works on the Buddhist literature and the *Tripitakas,* but also works on several branches of scientific knowledge, such as, Botany, Geography, Mineralogy and Medicine. It was a great attraction for scholars from the different parts of India and from countries, like, China, Burma and Ceylon.

University Libraries in Medieval India

The existence of academic libraries during the medieval period of Indian history is not known, though the Muslim rulers did patronize libraries in their own palaces. A lone exception, however, was a library attached to a college at Bidar, having a collection of 3000 books on different subjects. Aurangzeb got this Library transferred to Delhi to merge it with his palace library. During the medieval period, due to Muslim invasions and political troubles, the powerful empires and kingdoms of Indian rulers fell one by one. This affected higher education and the development of academic libraries as well.

Libraries in Modern India

During the British rule in India, number of academic institutions were established by the East India Company, and by the Christan missionaries. Some of the worth mentioning events which led to the growth and development of higher education in India during this period were the establishment of the Calcutta College in 1781, Jonathan Duncan, then a British agent, founded the Benaras Sanskrit College in 1792. The Calcutta Fort William College was founded in 1800. All these colleges were having their own libraries.

The Charter Act of 1813, the foundation of Fort William and Serampore Colleges, Calcutta, Madras and Bombay universities and their libraries, Hunter, Raleigh and Calcutta University Commissions, library training programmes, the establishment of Inter University Board, Sargent Report and appointment of the University Grants Committee, the establishment of Madras University, University of Bombay, University of Calcutta and their libraries, the constitution of Inter-University Board, the appointment of Hartog Committee, the Montague-Chelmsford reforms of 1919, the Government of India Act of 1935, and the Sargent Committee Report etc. laid foundation for establishment of libraries in various parts of the country.

The Fort William College was founded in Calcutta on 18th August 1800 by the Marquis of Welleselay, the Governor-General of India during 1798-1805. Reverend David Brown, Provost of the college was instrumental in setting up the library which had a well rounded collection of Eastern manuscripts.

In the absence of adequate financial support, the library could not survive for long and in 1835 it was decided to close the library and its valuable collection was transferred to the Asiatic Society Library in Calcutta between 1835-39. The Charter Act of 1813 passed by the British Parliament gave the East India Company complete responsibility for educating Indians.

The establishment of C.M.S. College in Kottayam, Hindu College in Calcutta in 1816 and Raven Shaw College in Cuttack in 1816 was the immediate result of the Charter Act 1813. These and other colleges came into existence thereafter had their own libraries the day they were established. Serampore College during this period was founded by the Danes in 1818 and the King of Denmark in 1927 agreed to give this college an academic status by providing equivalence to the Danish Universities with power to confer degrees.

The library of this college too was established along with its foundation and at a later stage the college was given affiliation to the University of Burdwan for the purpose of conferring degrees. The 7th March 1835 decision of the British Indian Government to promote English literature and sciences in India was resulted into the spread of number of colleges in India and by 1839 there were over forty colleges with attached libraries in the British territory in India.

For their establishment, lots of money was made available by the Indians in the form of donations. In 1840 Presidency College was founded in Madras, followed by a medical college in Bombay in 1845. This progress in education was instrumental in establishing universities in India.

The Charles Wood dispatch of 1854 popularly known as the 'Magna Carta of English Education' in India also paved the way for the establishment of the universities in the presidency towns. Sir John Colville introduced the Bill to establish universities in India and it was passed by the Governor General of India Lord Dalhousie on 24th January 1857, paved the way for the foundation of three universities based on the London Universities Model in the Presidency towns of Calcutta, Madras and Bombay.

Indian Education Commission, popularly known as Hunter Commission was appointed by the British Indian Government in 1882 to study the progress of education under the new policy adopted in 1854 by the East India Company and transferred to the Crown and accepted by the Secretary of State in 1859. Sir William W. Hunter in his report had clearly stated that the conditions of the libraries was in a very poor state and declared them "hardly creditable." The Commission paid special attention to the colleges and their libraries and other facilities.

The direct result of the Commission was the establishment of Panjab University, Lahore and Allahabad University in 1882 and 1887 respectively but still the condition of the education and libraries remained in a poor state.

The Raleigh Commission 1902 appointed by Lord Curzon to investigate the conditions and prospects of the Indian universities and to recommend measures to improve their constitution and working and standards of teaching also paid special attention to the academic libraries and found that, "the library is little used by graduates and hardly at all by other students." Further, the Commission commented, "In a college where library is inadequate or ill arranged, the students have no opportunity of forming the habit of independent and intelligent reading."

Thus, the Commission specifically recommended that reference services must be made an integral part of all libraries in colleges and universities, and that one of the prerequisite conditions for the grant of university affiliation to a college be the accessibility of students to the library of the institution.

The recommendations of the Raleigh Commission were included in the Universities Act of 1904 and provided the power to all universities to require that all colleges applying for affiliation maintain proper libraries, equipment, library building, and lend books to all students but the situation and the status of libraries could not be improved much simply because the recommendations made by the Commission and the provisions made in the act could not be implemented properly. The Calcutta University Commission popularly known as Sadler Commission was appointed by the government in 1917 to study the situation and the status of education in the country and to make recommendations to solve the existing problems.

The Commission noticed that "one of the greatest weak-nesses of the existing system is the extraordinarily unimportant part which is played by the library" and found that "in some colleges the library is regarded not as an essential part of teaching equipment but merely as a more or less useless conventional accessory." The Commission made the recommendations regarding the libraries that college libraries be strengthened and that training should be given to the students and occasionally to the teachers about use of the library.

One of the immediate result of the Calcutta University Commission was the establishment of a few new teaching-cum-residential universities at Patna in 1917, Osmania in Hyderabad in 1918, Dacca, Aligarh, and Lucknow in 1921, Delhi in 1922 and Nagpur in 1923 and all of them were established along with the establishment of libraries as an integral part of the university system.

As stated earlier, the impact of the Commission could very well be seen in the establishment of several universities along with their libraries. This was the period when in the libraries scenario, a person appeared who at a later stage turned the entire scene and become the father of library science in India.

The man was none other than Dr. S.R. Ranganathan. The University of Madras appointed Dr. S.R. Ranganathan as its Librarian in 1924. He was trained at the University of London Library School before joining his duties at Madras. Things did change rapidly after his joining. For example, he introduced the lending and reference services at the Madras University Library and extended the library hours for the benefit of the readers.

Whereas the hours had previously been 7 a.m. to 4 p.m., they were changed to 7 a.m. to 6 p.m. He delivered a series of lectures to about two thousand teachers at the conference of the South Indian Teachers' Union in 1929 regarding the use and importance of the library services.

The Madras Library Association started a summer course in librarianship and the lectures for this course were mainly delivered by Dr. Ranganathan. The main objective of the course in its beginning was to spread the ideas of the value of good library services and modern library methods among potential users of the library. The budget of the university library of Madras had been very poor from the beginning and it was really a difficult task to manage, run and administer the library effectively within it.

Ranganathan brought this poor financial position to the notice of the then Chief Minister, Dr. P. Subbaroyan, when he delivered a speech during an educational conference held at Madras in 1926. In his speech, Ranganathan "gave a graphic account of the library network in Europe and the United States of America and compared it with the poor, appalling facilities existing in India....

added that paucity of funds prevented him developing his library." The Chief Minister was highly impressed by Ranganathan's speech and promised to give more State help to the University Library. Its immediate result was a grant of rupees 6,000 which was added to the annual grant from the State, and, in addition, rupees 100,000 in lump sum were sanctioned by the Madras State Government in the same year to buy books and periodicals in pure sciences, humanities, and social sciences.

Provision was also made for additional grants to the library, as and when new departments of study and research were established. In the words of Ranganathan, "This was the first time when such a forward financial step in the history of the university libraries in India was taken in the second quarter of the 20th century."

The University of Madras library made a good start under Ranganathan's effective leadership and administration. In 1930, the library had five well-trained reference librarians to help the readers, and they "carried the work to a high pitch of efficiency."

This was the first time in the history of Indian libraries that a special reference service was introduced in a university library. The library collection increased to 93,000 volumes in 1935 and on September 3, 1936, the library was shifted to its first new and permanent functional building. By 1944, when Ranganathan resigned from the position of the Librarian, to become the University Librarian at the *Banaras Hindu University* (BHU), the collection of the Madras University Library had augmented to 1,20,000 volumes.

The contribution of Dr. Ranganathan to the growth and development of libraries in general and the Madras University Library in particular is undoubtedly tremendous and unforgettable. It will not be wrong to say that the Library School of Madras and the Madras University Library were the laboratories of Ranganathan to propound his ideas in library science and to test them practically.

Some of the important and major ideas of Ranganathan were the Five Laws of Library Science which were enunciated by him in 1924, and their formulation and publication in 1929 and 1931 respectively. These laws are still considered a unifying theory for all library practices and services, and set of guidelines for the dynamic development and study of library science as a whole.

The University of Bombay Library received a special grant of rupees 50,000 from the Central Government in 1939 to strengthen its collection for graduate studies. During the period from 1931 to 1939, a few more special grants were given to the library for its collection development. A very special grant of rupees 10,000 was given by Kikabhai and Maniklal, sons of the late Premchand Roychand, in 1931 to replace the electric clock of the library tower. The collection, which stood at 4,504 volumes in 1900, rose to 70,000 in 1939 and

73,582 in 1947. Though higher education and academic libraries made some progress during the first quarter of the present century, yet their growth and development was not very well organized.

Academic institutions and their growth after 1916 created a few problems also and the general feeling was that the "quality of Education was being sacrificed for quantity." While such a situation prevailed, the Indian Statutory Commission, popularly known as the Simon Commission, was appointed by the Government in 1927 to study the conditions prevailing in India.

The Simon Commission appointed an Auxiliary Committee to look into the growth of education in India. Sir Philip Hartog, a former member of the Calcutta University Commission, and a former Vice-Chancellor of the University of Dacca, was appointed its Chairman.

In its report, submitted in 1929, the Committee stated that "the dispersal of resources for university teaching among a number of colleges had made it difficult to build up university libraries of the type required for advanced work both at the Honours and the research stage majority of the university libraries were inadequate and all needed great additions."

In addition to want of books, libraries also lacked good current periodicals in their collections. The Committee also made a special note of the low academic standards in many colleges and universities and the "unhealthy competition for candidates between neighbouring universities". This report, however, did not offer any comprehensive, detailed, and realistic solutions to the problems. In 1935, Ministry of Education was formed in each province, as per the provisions of the dyarchy in the Montague-Chelmsford Reforms of 1919, supplemented by those of the new Government of India Act of 1935.

The Ministry of Education in India requested the Central Advisory Board of Education in 1944 to survey the educational conditions in the country. The Board's report, known as the Sargeant Report, after its Chairman, Sir Sargeant, the Educational Advisor to the Government of India, came up with a master-plan for the development of education in the post-World War II India. Its terms of reference covered education at all levels-primary, secondary, and higher.

The Indian universities, as they existed then, despite many admirable features, did not fully satisfy the requirements of a national system of education. During the British rule, several committees and commissions set up periodically, paved way for the foundation of several colleges and the establishment of many universities and in many cases the libraries were also established along with them.

It is also true that as compared to the first two decades the development of university libraries after 1924 did make better progress but the college libraries were still neglected and were struggling to get their recognition. There were only 12 universities in India in 1924 and their number swelled to 18 by the time India got freedom in 1947. In fact, the academic libraries during the British rule had no significance in the academic life of the institutions of higher education and the pivotal role that can be played by the academic libraries in the life of the institutions could very well be seen in the policy statement of higher education of the free India and the fact was also proven when at the time of national reconstruction, the importance of libraries in teaching and research was recognized, and libraries received the early attention of the Government of India.

Academic Libraries in India after Independence

The actual process for the development of university libraries in India can be said to have been set in motion with the appointment of the University Education Commission presided over by Dr. S. Radhakrishnan and its recommendations, such as, annual grants, open access system, working hours, organization of the library, staff, steps to make students book conscious and the need to give grants to teachers to buy books.

The section on libraries of the report opens with a powerful statement on the importance of libraries in university education and states, "teaching is a cooperative enterprise. Teachers must have the necessary tools for teaching purposes in the shape of libraries and laboratories as also the right type of students."

The Commission in the course of its study of the academic libraries, found that "libraries were hopelessly inadequate to serve the curricular needs of a modern university. They were ill-housed, illstocked, and ill-staffed and were totally lacking in standard literary and scientific journals. Service was in the hands of personnel that had hardly any notion of the objectives of university education. The annual appropriation for book purchase seldom exceeded the ten thousand mark."

In addition, the annual grant for these libraries were not sufficient. Therefore, the Commission recommended that at least six per cent of the total budget of each academic institution should be set aside for the library. It added that if institutions were not willing to allocate six per cent of their budget to libraries, they should spend Rs. 40 per student enrolled. The Commission also suggested that greater attention should be paid to improve the reference services in the university libraries. Documentation and biblio-graphical services must be developed in order to promote research among the faculty and students, make libraries proper centres for research activities, and to raise the standards of services.

As far as the library staff is concerned, the Commission was of the view that it is very important to have well-qualified staff, including the Director, in order to provide excellent service in any library. The Director's qualifications must include Ph.D. in Library Science and he must have the rank and salary of a professor, capabilities of organization and management, and should have full powers of an administrator to run the library effectively.

University Education Commission. There is no doubt that the recommendations of the Commission "were based on the needs of the modern library services in universities for the promotion of research and creative learning." It was for the first time that such detailed attention was paid to the library matters by a commission on university education in India.

Ranganathan Committee (1957)

The most comprehensive and significant document on the university and college libraries is the Report of the UGC library committee, chaired by Ranganathan. The Report was published by the University Grants Commission in 1959 entitled 'University and College Libraries.' It was perhaps the first attempt by any Library Committee in India to systematically survey the academic libraries on a national basis, and it was also the first time that the government of India had decided to seek advice from a professional librarian regarding academic libraries. The committee was to advice the UGC on the standards of libraries, building, pay scales, and library training.

After the survey the library committee invited all academic librarians to a seminar on "Work flow in university and college libraries," at Delhi from March 4 to 7, 1959 to keep them informed about the progress the committee had made surveying the academic libraries. It wanted to discuss its recommendations with them. Some of the recommendations of the Committee included the provision that the UGC and the State Government should help the college and the university libraries in the collection development of both books and periodicals.

The formula suggested by the committee was that funds be given "at the rate of Rs. 15 per enrolled student and Rs. 200 per teacher and research fellow. There should also be special initial library grants in the case of a new university and of a new department in an existing university, a similar scale should be followed for the college libraries. In order to promote co-operation among libraries, a Union Catalogue of books and a Union List of periodicals to be prepared.

The Committee strongly recommended that an open access system be introduced in every academic library. Committee also stressed "that reference service is the essential human process of establishing contact between the right reader and the right book by personal service. Reference service is vital in promotion of reading habit in student each library should provide an adequate number of reference librarians to function as library hosts and human converters."

Other recommendations included building up a microfilm collection, copying facilities for microfilms and book material, appointment of a committee to look into the standards of teaching, examination and research in the library schools, and appointment of full-time teaching faculty members rather than asking librarians to teach part time in the library schools.

The Committee added that "the status and the salary of the library staff should be the same as that of the teaching and research staff', *i.e.*, Professor, Reader, and Lecturer etc." The recommendations of the committee had a farreaching effect on the development of the university libraries later.

They had not only provided a framework to the UGC to implement its grants-in-aid programmes but also given to the university authorities important guidelines. Particular mention, in this connection, may be made of the recommendations concerning the library finances which had helped libraries to secure enough finances by way of annual grants from the universities themselves and of development grants from the UGC.

The recommendations on the library personnel and staff strength have given to the library staff status and salaries equivalent to the academic staff and ensure provision for adequate staff for various library operations. The Committee submitted its report to the UGC with the hope that it will provide a blueprint for the systematic development of university libraries in the country.

Hence, inspite of many hurdles like education being a state subject in the Indian Constitution, considerable development in the university libraries has taken place and as such the condition of these libraries in 1953 was much better than in the 1940's and even the early 1950's.

Kothari Commission

The Education Commission under the chairmanship of Dr. D. S. Kothari marked another important stage in the history of university libraries in India.

The Commission devoted considerable attention to the development of the university libraries and made suitable recommendations on the following points:

- Norms for financial support;
- Long range planning for library development;
- The need for the establishment of a well equipped library before the starting of a university, college, or department;
- Suitable phasing over of the library grants;
- Encouraging the students in the use of books;
- Interdisciplinary communication; and
- Documentation service in libraries etc.

The Education Commission had also addressed itself to the role of libraries in adult education and recommended establish-ment of a network of public libraries. It wanted the school libraries to be integrated with public libraries for purposes of the adult education programmes. The Report, submitted by Dr. D. S. Kothari, on June 29, 1966, emphatically pointed out that "nothing can be more damaging than to ignore its library and to give it a low priority. No new college, university or department should be opened unless adequate number of books in the library are provided."

The Commission was shocked to note that the recommen-dations of the Radhakrishnan Commission had not been fully implemented, for only four universities in India has spent five per cent or more of their budget on books and periodicals acquisitions, though the 1948's Commission has suggested that six per cent of the total budget be spent on libraries. Other universities had spent less than five per cent of their budget on libraries, "Surprisingly enough there are five universities which spent even less than one per cent of the total budget on the libraries."

It was clear proof that the university libraries in India were not functioning properly to fulfil the needs of higher education. The Kothari Commission recommended that a long range plan for library development should be drawn up for each academic institution taking into consideration anticipated increase in enrollment, introduction of new subjects and research needs etc., and documentation service be encouraged in libraries, and documentation experts be appointed to help researchers and do indexing and abstracting. It was further recommended that "the book selection should be oriented towards supporting instruction and research." The library should "provide resources necessary for research in fields of special interest to the university; provide library facilities and services necessary for the success of all formal programmes of instruction."

Monetary guidelines were also suggested by the Commission. "As a norm, a university should spend each year about Rs. 25 per student registered and Rs. 300 per teacher depending on the stage of development of each university library." It was also suggested that "the foreign exchange needed for university and college libraries should be allowed separately to the UGC."

The Wheat Loan Programme

During the 1950's and early 1960's the Indian academic libraries received huge grants from the UGC amounting up to Rs. 100,000 for books, buildings, equipment and even for additional staff. At the same time many libraries got additional grants from a special US fund called the 'Wheat Loan Programme.' The American Congress passed a special Act, in 1951 known as the 'Public Law 480' to loan India $ 19,000,000 to buy much needed wheat from the US. Under the agreement of the loan, India had to buy American books, periodicals and scientific equipment worth $ 50,000 to be used for research purposes in the Indian libraries.

This, money India had to pay as interest on the loan. Part of the money was to be spent on the exchange of scholars, including librarians, between the two countries. The United States authorities bought some educational material and equipment from India for research purposes and higher education in the American Universities.

During 1951-1961 Indian libraries spent US $ 1,400,000 of the purchase of American books, US dollar 160,000 on libraries, US $ 40,000 on the travel and study grants for thirty three Indian librarians to visit the United States and US $ 75,000 on the travel and study grants of the five Americans.

College Libraries

The College libraries in India have a significant role to play in higher education. Majority of the undergraduate students, *i.e.*, 88.5 per cent and graduate students, *i.e.*, 53 per cent, attend these colleges. When India attained Independence many among the 533 affiliated colleges did not have their own libraries, but at present, every college in the country has a library.

Majority of the college libraries do not have proper facilities to meet the needs of their users. Their collections are not up-to-date, budgets are their very inadequate and limited, and a large number of them are single libraries. In many colleges, there is neither a library hall nor a sufficient big room, not to think of a separate building for the library.

Any unused room, quite often somewhere out of sight, would be considered adequate to house a few shelves of books. And in most college libraries there is complete darkness even during the day time, as the windows are closed out of a fear that the books may be stolen.. Different studies, conducted by scholars and Srivastva have explicitly established that the condition of the college libraries in India are far from satisfactory.

The college libraries are open only six to eight hours a day. Many do not have any qualified librarian on their staff and have closed stacks only. The several commissions and committees, like the Radhakrishnan Commission of 1948, did not stress the importance of the college libraries in their reports. However, the University Grants Commission gives more importance to the college libraries.

As the quality of higher education and research, especially at the graduate level, depends upon, among other things, the standard of the college libraries and their services. Therefore, the UGC has played a significant role in the growth and development of college libraries since 1953 by giving grants for books, equipment, staff and library buildings and has done a remarkable job in salary improvement of the college librarians.

The UGC's contribution to the college libraries is at the rate of Rs. 15 per student with a maximum of Rs. 10,000 with some additional and special grants for text books, when a new subject is introduced in the Curriculum.

On the other hand, the colleges and the state governments have failed to provide their equal share. The total Expenditure on the college libraries according to the recommendation of the Education Commission should be 6.25 per cent of the total budgets of the colleges, but in most cases it has remained between 1.5 per cent and 2.3 per cent.

Sardana Collection development of the college libraries are done without taking into consideration the actual needs of the faculty and the students of the colleges as sixty per cent of them consist of text books and 20 per cent cover fiction.

Even this small inadequate collection, in depth and content, is not used effectively due to the closed stacks system and lack of staff and facilities for instruction concerning their use. The net result is that the utility factor of the college libraries comes practically to nothing.

In most college libraries, books are neither properly classified nor catalogued. In several libraries no systematic classification is followed for collection arrangements. The only service the college library renders to its clientele is book-lending. There are colleges where students are not even allowed inside the library.

The UGC is aware of the slow progress of the college libraries. In addition to providing financial help for development, it has also from time to time organized seminars to keep the college librarians aware of the new developments in the field. But these seminars have made only a limited effect on the progress of the college libraries. The condition of the college libraries in the country should be a cause for alarm among the academic community.

In the interests of the development of higher education in the country along proper lines, it is important to make a detailed study of the style of functioning of the college libraries and of the utilization of the library resources and facilities by the students and teachers. This will help in the preparation of more realistic and operational policies and programmes for ensuring the proper functioning, utilization and development of the college libraries. The college library has to be made the intellectual hub of the institution, serving equally, both the students and teachers.

This is all the more necessary because about 90 per cent of the students in higher education in India pursue their studies in colleges and they have only very small and substandard college library resources to fall back upon. Although, owing to various efforts of the UGC as well as other forces, the traditional concept that the college library is a custodian of books has changed, yet there is evidence enough to show that the condition of the college libraries is generally poor, their development is rather slow and that the position of the college libraries and their librarians in India, with a few exceptions, is pitiable.

University Libraries

University libraries all over the world have their own place of importance in the scheme of higher learning. Libraries are not only repositories of knowledge but also dispensers of such knowledge. There is no doubt that where libraries of universities and institutions of higher learning are ignored or not given due recognition, the country as a whole suffers because the standards of study, teaching and research very heavily depend upon the qualitative and quantitative service rendered by the university libraries.

The Radhakrishnan Commission expressed that "the library is the heart of all the university's work, directly so, as regards its research work and indirectly as regards its educational work, which derives its life from research. Scientific research needs the library as well as its laboratories while for humanistic research the library is both library and the laboratory in one. Both for humanistic and scientific studies, a first class library is essential in a university."

The growth of university libraries since Independence can be seen in respect of the initiatives taken by the Central Government considering the vital importance of higher education and role of libraries in the educational development, commitment to fulfill the demand of higher education, and the foundation of the UGC in 1953 by an Act of Parliament. The Radhakrishnan Commission recognized the value and importance of a well equipped and organized library system and its role in higher education.

It had found many drawbacks and pitfalls in the university libraries and had made many recommendations for the improvement of library facilities. The Ranganathan Committee, appointed by the UGC in 1957, made some outstanding recommendations, which included standards for library building, collection development, staff and services and furniture etc. These recommendations were accepted by the UGC and forwarded for implementation.

The Kothari Commission also made valuable recommen-dations for this purpose, but the role of the University Grants Commission deserves special mention, because it has played a vital role by "regularly providing appropriate grants and funds to all universities for development of libraries, to purchase books and journals. . . ., construction of new library buildings and for library equipment and furniture."

Dr. D. S. Kothari, the Chairman of University Grants Commission, said, "Libraries play a vital role in the development of institutions of higher learning. The University Grants Commission attaches great importance to the strengthening of library facilities in the universities and colleges and their efficient administration. The commission has also been giving grants to institutions for books and journals construction of library building and appointment of library staff."

One of the most remarkable and identifiable development in the history of higher education and libraries was the foundation of the INFLIBNET in 1991. Information and Library Network Centre is an autonomous Inter-University Centre of the UGC of India. It is a major National Programme initiated by the UGC in 1991 with its Head Quarters at Gujarat University Campus, Ahmedabad. Initially started as a project under the IUCAA, it became an independent Inter-University Centre in 1966.

Its objectives are:

- To promote and establish communication facilities to improve capability in information transfer and access, that provides support to scholarship, learning, research and academic pursuit through cooperation and involvement of agencies concerned.
- *To establish Inflibnet*: Information and Library Network a computer communication network for linking libraries and information centres in universities, deemed to be universities, colleges, UGC information centres, institutions of national importance and R&D institutions, etc. avoiding duplication of efforts.

Inflibnet performs following major activities:

- Provides grants to universities to automate the libraries, establishing the network facilities and create an information technology environment.
- Developed and distributed Software for University Libraries (Soul) which is an integrated userfriendly library management software. The latest version of the software is 2.0 which is competent to operate with the latest technologies and international standards such as MARC21, Unicode based and NCIP 2.0 based protocols for electronic surveillance and control.
- Indian Catalogue of University Libraries in India (IndCat) is Online Library Catalogue of books, theses and journals available in major university libraries in India which provides bibliographic description, location of the material in all subjects available in more than 112 university libraries. Thus, IndCat has over 10 million bibliographical records of books from more than 113 universities. In addition, the database of theses, expert databases, project databases and Sewakoffline database access facilities are also extended to the libraries of higher learning institutions.
- To enhance the skills of university library staff for implementation of Inflibnet programme, it conducts training programme for library staff,

onsite training for member library staff, training on SOUL software, holding Caliber convention every year and workshops for senior level staff of the university libraries are conducted.

- It has brought out a document entitled 'Inflibnet Standards and Guideline for Data Capturing' prepared by a task force of experts based on Common Communication Format (CCF).

Another very important and significant landmark in the history of higher education and development of libraries in India is the establishment of "Ugcinfonet Digial Library Consortium" by the UGC on the concluding day of its Golden jubilee celebrations by his Excellency the then President of India, Dr. A.P.J Abdul Kalam at Vigyan Bhawan on 28th December 2003.

UGC-Infonet is an innovative project launched by UGC to facilitate scholarly e-resources to Indian academies through joint partnership of UGC, Inflibnet and Ernet.

This includes interlinking of universities and colleges in the country electronically with a view to achieve maximum efficiency through Internet enabled teaching, learning and governance. The UGC-Infonet is overlaid on Ernet infrastructure in a manner so as to provide assured quality of service and optimum utilization of bandwidth resources. The network will be run and managed by Ernet India.

The project is funded by UGC with 100 per cent capital investment and up to 90 per cent of recurring costs. UGC and Ernet India have signed the necessary MoU for this purpose. A joint technical and tariff committee, has been setup to guide and monitor the design, implementation and operations of Ugcinfonet. Information for Library Network (Inflibnet) an autonomous Inter-University Centre of UGC, is the nodal agency for coordination and facilitation of the linkage between Ernet and the Universities.

Under this programme, information and communication technologies (ICT) and internet will be used to transform learning environment from a monodimensional one to a multidimensional one. This was created to help and benefit more than 310 universities and about 14,000 colleges affiliated with these universities and approximately 10 million students with the e-journals, thus, is a boon to higher education system in many ways.

The UGC-Infonet digital Library consortium has the following objectives: Bhatt,

- To subscribe electronic resources for the members of the consortium at highly discounted rates of subscription and with the best terms and conditions.
- Promote the rational use of funds.
- Guarantee local storage of the information acquired for continuous use by present and future users.

- To impart training to the users, librarians, research scholars and faculty members of the institutions on the electronic resources with an aim to optimize the usage of the electronic resources.
- To have more interaction amongst the member libraries.
- To increase the research productivity of the institutions in terms of quality and quantity of publications
- Strategic alliance with institutions that have common interests resulting reduced information cost and improved resource sharing.

National Knowledge Commission

The National Knowledge Commission was set up by the Government of India on 13th June 2005 with a time-frame of three years, from 2nd October 2005 to 2nd October 2008.

As a high-level advisory body to the Prime Minister of India, the National Knowledge Commission was given a mandate to guide policy and direct reforms, focusing on certain key areas such as education, science and technology, agriculture, industry, e-governance etc. Easy access to knowledge, creation and preservation of knowledge systems, dissemination of knowledge and better knowledge services are core concerns of the Commission.

The Commission envisaged the future road map for the growth and development of academic libraries by imbibing core issues such as, set up a national commission on libraries, prepare a national census of all libraries, revamp LIS education, training and research facilities, re-assess staffing of libraries, set up a central library fund, modernize library management, encourage greater community participation in library management, promote information communication technology applications in all libraries, facilitate donation and maintenance of private collections, and encourage public private partnerships in LIS development, etc.

SARASWATHI MAHAL LIBRARY

Saraswathi Mahal Library is located in Thanjavur, Tamil Nadu, India. It is one of the oldest libraries in Asia, and has on display a rare collection of Palm leaf manuscripts and paper written in Tamil, Hindi, English, Telugu, Marathi, and a few other languages indigenous to India.

The collection comprises well over 60,000 volumes, though only a tiny fraction of these are on display. The library has a complete catalogue of holdings, which is being made available online. Some rare holdings can be viewed on site by prior arrangement.

HISTORY

The Saraswathi Mahal library started as a Royal Library for the private pleasure of the Nayak Kings of Thanjavur who ruled AD 1535-1675. The Maratha rulers who captured Thanjavur in 1675 patronised local culture and further developed the Royal Palace Library until 1855. Most notable among the Maratha Kings was Serfoji II, who was an eminent scholar in many branches of learning and the arts.

In his early age Serfoji studied under the influence of the Dutch Reverend Schwartz, and learned many languages including English, French, Italian and Latin. He enthusiastically took special interest in the enrichment of the Library, employing many Pandits to collect, buy and copy a vast number of works from all renowned Centres of Sanskrit learning in Northern India and other far-flung areas. Since 1918 the Saraswathi Mahal Library has been a possession of the state of Tamil Nadu. Its official name of the Library was changed to "The Thanjavur Maharaja Serfoji's Sarasvati Mahal Library" in honour of the great royal Marathan patron.

EFFORTS

The library is open to the public; it also supports efforts to publish rare manuscripts from the collection, as well as ensuring all volumes are preserved on microfilm. The Library has installed computers in 1998 for the Computerisation of Library activities. As a first phase, the Library catalogues are being stored in the Computer for easy information retrieval. It is also proposed to digitalise the manuscripts of this Library shortly.

THE COLLECTION

The bulk of the manuscripts (39,300) are in Sanskrit, written in scripts such as Grantha, Devanagari, Nandinagari, Telugu. Tamil manuscripts number over 3500, comprising titles in literature, music and medicine. The Library has a collection of 3076 Marathi manuscripts from the South Indian Maharastrian of the 17th, 18th, and 19th centuries; this includes the hierarchy of the Saints of Maharashtra belonging to Sri Ramadasi and Dattatreya Mutts. The Marathi manuscripts are mostly on paper but a few were written in Telugu script on palm-leaf. There are 846 Telugu manuscripts in the holdings, mostly on palm leaf. There are 22 Persian and Urdu manuscripts mostly of 19th century also within the collection.

Apart from these manuscripts there are 1342 bundles of Maratha Raj records available at the Library. The Raj records were written in the Modi script of the Marathi language. These records encompass the information of the political, cultural and social administration of the Maratha kings of Thanjavur.

SOME OF THE RARE BOOKS AND MANUSCRIPTS

- Dr. Samuel Johnson's dictionary published in 1784
- The pictorial Bible printed in Amsterdam in the year 1791
- The Madras Alamnac printed in 1807

- Lavoisier's *Traité Élémentaire de Chimie* ("Elements of Chemistry")
- The notes of Bishop Heber on Raja Serfoji II
- The correspondence letters of William Torin of London who purchased a lot of books for Raja Serfoji II and the Saraswathi Mahal Library
- The Globe used by the raja.
- Ancient maps of the world
- Town planning documents of Thanjavur including the underground drainage system, the fresh water supply ducting system
- Pictorial charts of the theory of evolution of man as evinced by Charles Le Brun

LIBRARY MUSEUM

A Museum is located in the Library building to reveal the importance of the Library to the Public. This Museum is small but organised into sections highlighting ancient Manuscripts, Illustrated Manuscripts, Printed copies of the Original Drawings, Atlases, Thanjavur-style Paper Paintings, Canvass Paintings, Wooden Paintings, Glass paintings, Portraits of the Thanjavur Maratha kings, and the Physiognomy charts of Charles Le-Brun. These materials give an idea of the total variety in the vast collection within the Library.

The Saraswati Library is situated within the campus of the Thanjavur Palace. Visitors can have a glimpse of preserved books and can sit and read in the library premises. Better preservation of books and facilities like air-conditioning with dehumidifiers, redesigning of space for comfortable reading, online catalogue facility should be taken up to preserve this internationally renowned treasure trove of books and palm-leaf manuscripts !

Efforts were made to microfilm and catalogue the contents way back in 1965 when Indira Gandhi was Information and Broadcasting Minister, Government of India who sanctioned the fund for the library's development. Since then no efforts were made to scan the documents and computerise the same using present day technology. It is also a designated 'Manuscript Conservation Centre' (MCC) under the National Mission for Manuscripts established in 2003.

KHUDA BAKHSH ORIENTAL LIBRARY

Khuda Bakhsh Oriental Library is one of the national libraries of India. It was opened to public in October, 1891 by Khan Bahadur Khuda Bakhsh with 4,000 manuscripts, of which he inherited 1,400 from his father Maulvi Mohammed Bakhsh.

It is an autonomous organization under Ministry of Culture, Government of India, and is governed by a Board with the Governor of Bihar as its ex-officio Chairman. known for its rare collection of Persian and Arabic manuscripts. It also hosts paintings made during the Rajput and Mughal eras of India. It is also a designated 'Manuscript Conservation Centre' (MCC) under the National Mission for Manuscripts.

HISTORY

The library finds its origin in private collection of a bibliophile Mohammad Bakhsh and expanded by his son Khuda Bakhsh, who inherited 1,400 manuscripts and continued to add to the collection and eventually converted it into a private library by 1880. The library was opened to public upon its inauguration by Sir Charles Elliot, Governor of Bengal on 5th October, 1891.

In 1969 through a Federal Legislation, an Act of Parliament, namely 'Khuda Bakhsḥ Oriental Public Library Act (1969), the Government of India declared Khuda Bakhsh Oriental Public Library a centre of national importance and government took over the funding, maintenance and development of the library. Today it continues to attract scholars from all over the world.

Past directors of the library have been Dr. Abid Reza Bedar, who after remaining with the Raza Library, came as Director to the institution in 1972, and did some important work towards reviving the library along with his successor Habibur Rehman Chighani, at present the Director of the library is the Dr. Imtiaz Ahmad, since February, 2004.

COLLECTION

Some of the notable manuscripts are *Timur Nama* (*Khandan—Timuria*), *Shah Nama*, *Padshah Nama*, *Diwan-e-Hafiz* and *Safinatul Auliya*, carrying the autograph of Mughal Emperors and princes and the book of Military Accounts of Maharaja Ranjit Singh. Apart of it the library also has specimens of Mughal paintings, calligraphy and book decoration and Arabic and Urdu manu-scripts, including a page of Quran written on deer skin.

BHANDARKAR ORIENTAL RESEARCH INSTITUTE

The Bhandarkar Oriental Research Institute (BORI) is located in Pune, Maharashtra, India. It was founded on July 6, 1917 to honour the life and work of Dr. Ramakrishna Gopal Bhandarkar (1837–1925), long regarded as the founder of Indology (Orientalism) in India. The institute is well known for its collection of old Sanskrit and Prakrit manuscripts.

THE INSTITUTE

This institute is of a public trust registered under Act XXI of 1860. Initially, the institute received an annual grant of 3000 Rupees from the Government of Bombay. Presently, it is partially supported by annual grants from the Government of Maharashtra. The Institute also receives grants from the Government of India and the University Grants Commission for specific research projects. The institute has one of the largest collections of rare books and manuscripts in South Asia, consisting of over 1,25,000 books and 29,510 manuscripts. The institute publishes a journal, *Annals of the Bhandarkar Oriental Research Institute* four times a year. The Institute also hosts the Manuscripts Resource and Conservation Centre under the auspices of the National Mission for Manuscripts, a project of the Ministry of Culture, Government of India. In 2007, the Rigveda manuscripts preserved at the Institute were included in UNESCO's Memory of the World Register.

THE MANUSCRIPT COLLECTION

The Government of Bombay, in 1866, started a pan Indian Manuscript Collection project. Noted scholars like George Bühler, F. Kielhorn, Peter Peterson, Ramkrishna Gopal Bhandarkar, S. R. Bhandarkar, Kathavate and Ghate collected more than 17,000 important manuscripts under this project. This collection was first deposited at Elphinstone College in Bombay.

Then it was transferred to Deccan College (Pune) for better preservation. After the Bhandarkar Oriental Research Institute was founded in 1917, the BORI founders proposed to offer even better preservation and research. Hence Lord Willingdon, the then Governor of the Bombay Presidency and the first president of BORI, transferred the valuable Government collection of manuscripts to the BORI on April 1, 1918. The first curator, P.K. Gode took active initiatives to enhance this collection. Presently, the Institute has over 29,000 manuscripts.

The largest part of the collection (17,877 Manuscripts) is part of the "Government Manuscript Library", while there is an additional collection of 11,633 manuscripts also. The most prized collections include a paper manuscript of the Cikitsâsâra-sangraha dated 1320 and a palmleaf manuscript of the Upamiti-bhavapra-pañcakathâ dated 906. Among the several scholars referring to the works at BORI, the most well-known person arguably is the Bharat Ratna awardee, Pt. Pandurang Vaman Kane.

THE CRITICAL EDITION OF THE MAHABHARATA

A long term project under the auspices of BORI, started on April 1, 1919, was the preparation of a Critical Edition of the Mahabharata. V.S. Sukhtankar was appointed general editor of the project on August 1, 1925 and he continued until his death on January 21, 1943.

After his death, S.K. Belvalkar was appointed general editor on April 1, 1943. On April 1, 1961 P. L. Vaidya appointed as General Editor of the project on the retirement of S. K. Belvalkar. R. N. Dandekar appointed as the joint general editor on July 6, 1957. To widespread acclaim, the completion for publication was announced on September 22, 1966, by Dr. Sarvapalli Radhakrishnan, then President of India, at a special function held at the institute.

The Critical Edition was collated from 1,259 manuscripts. This edition in 19 volumes (more than 15000 demi-quarto size pages) comprised the critically constituted text of the 18 *Parvas* of the Mahabharata consisting of more than 89000 verses, an elaborate Critical Apparatus and a Prolegomena on the material and methodology. Further work since the initial publication has produced a Critical Edition of the Harivamsa, a Pratika Index, a Bibliography of ancillary materials, and a Cultural Index. The project of preparing a critical edition of the Harivamsa was inaugurated by the President of India, Rajendra Prasad on November 19, 1954. The publication was completed in November, 1971.

The critical edition in two volumes consists the 4 *Parvan*s of the Harivamsa. The Pratika Index in 6 volumes consists 360000 verse quarters with appendices. Two volumes of the Cultural Index have been published so far. The constituted text of the critical edition has also been made available on the CD-ROM.

VANDALISM IN 2003

The institute was vandalized in December 2003 by a mob made up of members of an extremist self styled Maratha youth squad, calling themselves the Sambhaji Brigade, named after Shivaji's elder son. They claimed to be angered by the help provided by the institute's staff (in translating manuscripts) to a Western writer, Dr. James Laine, who discussed the telling and retelling of stories about Shivaji's parentage and life in his book on narrations of the Shivaji story.

The mob also damaged thousands of manuscripts and attacked Shrikant Bahulkar, a Sanskrit scholar who had only explained some Sanskrit references to Laine. The incident provoked widespread reaction and historian Gajanan Mehendale to destroy parts of his in-progress biography of Shivaji.

The vandalism and a ban on the book were denounced by historians who put their signatures to the statement include R.S. Sharma, R.C. Thakran, Suraj Bhan, Irfan Habib, D.N. Jha, Shireen Moosvi and K. M. Shrimali. Oxford University Press-publisher of James Laine's, 'Shivaji: Hindu king in Islamic India', withdrew the book after protests from Ninad Bedekar and other right-wing politicians as it contained allegedly objectionable statements about Shivaji.

ASIATIC SOCIETY LIBRARY

At present, the library of the Asiatic Society has a collection of about 1,17,000 books and 79,000 journals printed in almost all the major languages of the world. It has also a collection of 293 maps, microfische of 48,000 works, microfilm of 387,003 pages, 182 paintings, 2500 pamphlets and 2150 photographs.

The earliest printed book preserved in this library is Juli Firmici's *Astronomicorum Libri* published in 1499. It has in its possession a large number of books printed in India in the late 18th and early 19th centuries. The library also possesses many rare and scarcely available books. The library has a rich collection of about 47,000 manuscripts in 26 scripts. The most notable amongst them are an illustrated manuscript of the *Qur'an*, a manuscript of the *Gulistan* text, and a manuscript of *Padshah Nama* bearing the signature of Emperor Shahjahan. The number of journals in thepossession of the library is about 80,000 at present.

The early collection of this library was enriched by the contributions it received from its members. On March 25, 1784 the library received seven Persian manuscripts from Henri Richardson.

The next contribution came from William Marsden, who donated his book, *History of Island of Sumatra* (1783) on November 10, 1784. Robert Home, the first Library-in-Charge (1804) donated his small but valuable collection of works on art.

The first accession of importance was a gift from the Seringapatam Committee on February 3, 1808 consisting of a collection from the Palace Library of Tipu Sultan. The library received the Surveyor-General Colonel Mackenzie's collection of manuscripts and drawings in December 1822.

MANUSCRIPT COLLECTION

Manuscript Collection of the society is varied and rich, and covers most of the Indian languages and scripts and even several Asian ones, *e.g.*, Assamese, Bengali, Gujarati, Gurumukhi, Kanarese, Urdu, Marathi, Modi, Nagari, Newari, Oriya, Rajasthani, Sarada, Armenian, Sinhalese, Arabic, Persian, Pushto, Javanese, Turki, Burmese, Chinese, Siamese, Tibetan etc. The materials used for the manuscripts are also varied: palm and palmyra leaves, barks of different trees, papers of various grades.

Sanskritic Manuscripts

The manuscripts cover the period from 7th c. A.D. down to the 19th century. These are useful source materials to illustrate the development of the Indian scripts (especially Bengali, Nagari etc.). The colophons and post-colophons contain information relating to socio-economic conditions of the people.

Besides, they help us to fix the chronology of the Royal dynasties of India. Where the inscriptions fail to ascertain dates and chronology, the manuscripts may throw some light, provided a thorough critical study of these and their colophons and postcolophons were made.

Some of the rare Sanskrit manuscripts may be mentioned here:

- Brihati,
- Amrita Vindu,

- Kiranavali,
- Charucharya,
- Nartaka Nirnaya,
- Parasika-prakasa,
- Sanskrita-ratnakara,
- Lalitavistara,
- Horoscope of a Muslim of the Mughal Court (A.D. 1640) A Deed of Mortgage (1639),
- Ramayana (Bengali) of Ramananda Yati,
- Vajrayana text (11th c.),
- A text on Buddhist Nyaya,
- Rigveda Padapatha,
- Laghu-Kalachakra-tika,
- Kalachakravetara,
- Kuttanimatam,
- Vajravalinama mannadalopayika,
- Ramacharita of Sandhyakar Nandi,
- Bhattikavyatika of Srinivasa, and
- Paragali Mahabharata.

The manuscript of Kubjikamatam is of the 7th Century A.D. The manuscript of Rigveda Padapatha, copied in A.D. 1362, is perhaps "the oldest manuscript of the Rigveda."

Islamic Section

Of the many Islamic Manuscripts there are some which are extremely rare and unique.

Of these only a few may be mentioned:

- Tahdhib Sharh As-Sab' at Mullaqat (early 12th c. Arabic),
- Qalaid al-Iquian wa Mahasin al-Ayan (12th c.),
- Kharidat al-Qasr (12th c.),
- Al-Jam Baynas as-Sahihin abridged version with autograph, (13th c.),
- A-Madkhul(13th c.),
- Tafsir-i-Quran (Persian, 13th c., important also for calligraphy),
- Tuhfat al-Ahbar fi usul at Hadith wa'l Akhbar (15th c.),
- Kitab al-I'lan (18th c.),
- Saha' if-i-Shara' if or Durarал Mansur (Persian, 19th c., an autographed copy), and
- Adab-i-Alamgiri (18th c.).

There are large numbers of illuminated and illustrated manu-scripts of different schools, many of which are unique for their calligraphy, delicacy of their lines, and elegance of composition and charming colour schemes. These miniatures still afford glimpses of India's past achievements, of these unique manuscripts (earliest belonging to the 10th Century A.D.) mention may be made of a few:

- Astasahasrika Prajnaparamita,
- Aparimitayurnama Mahayana sutra,
- Pancharaksha,
- Paramarthanama Sangati,
- Devimahatmya,
- Viveka Panchamrita,
- Bhagavatgita,
- Shahnama,
- Kullayat-i-Saadi,
- Suwaru'l aqalim,
- Farang-i-Aurang Shahi,
- Ain-i-Akbari,
- Diwan-i-Makhfi,
- Qissa-i-Nush-Afarin,
- Jamiut-Twarikh,
- Amir nama Tutinama,
- Iyar-i-Danesh,
- Bihar-i-Danesh,
- Tarjuma Mahabharata,
- Tafribul-Imarah (by Silchand, dedicated to J. H. Lushington), and
- Imaratut-Akbar (by Chitarmal for James Duncan).

Many scholars are using the collection for editing their texts and for translation in modern languages.

English Manuscripts

In the Library there are preserved a large number of old letters some of which date back to1784, just after the Society was founded. These letters were received by the Society from persons belonging to different walks of life, requesting information on such subjects as old and rare manuscripts, ancient monuments, coins etc.

Some among the writers of these letters were persons well known for their literary, scientific and other cultural accomp-lishments. These old files constitute important documents relating to the history of the Society, as also of many other scientific and humanistic organisations that were established in India either in the 19th or in the 20th century.

Urdu Manuscripts

The Society has a fine collection of about 234 Urdu manu-scripts many of which were received as a gift from the Fort William College.

Sino-Tibetan and Burmese Manuscripts

The Society has a complete set of Kanjur and Tanjur texts of the Buddhist scriptures and some extra-canonical works. These were collected by B. H. Hodgson and A. Csoma de koros. A section of the collection has been catalogued. There are over one hundred titles of Chinese books, some of which are rare and valuable for Chinese studies.

These cover almost all the subjects relating to Chinese Culture, Civilization and Science and Buddhism. Subjects covered include Classical Literature, Language. History, Geography, Topography, Philosophy, Religion, manners and customs, biography of scholars, sciences (Botanical, Astronimical, Zoological).

The Society has a valuable collection of about 162 Burmese manuscript written on parabaikes and palm leaf. The manuscripts deal with Buddhistic texts, Religion, History of the world and also of Burmja and Arakan, works on Gramour (including that of kaccayana) and Rhetoric, Buddhist cosmography, Astrology, Medicine etc.

Bengali Manuscripts

Other than Sanskrit, a few Bengali manuscripts have been found written by Bengali Brahmins residing in Varanasi. Parageli Mahabharat, Chuti Khan's Asvamedha Parva, and many other important manuscripts were purchased. Mss. donated by Justice Ramaprosad Mukherjee and Sri A Roy enriched the collection. The society has 703 Bengali and 12 Assamese manuscripts in the collection. It comprises Asiatic Society's own collection, Government collection, Indian Museum collection and donors' collection.

At present, the collection of Bengali manuscripts in the possession of Asiatic Society is rich in respect of number and rarity. The Society has manuscripts on Ramayana, Mahabharata, Srimadbhagavat, Mangala Kavyas, treatises on Vaisnava faith and its allied subjects. Folk literature, erotic verses and Vaisnaba Sahajiya Cult etc.

Rajasthani Manuscripts

The Society possesses very rare, valuable and important Rajasthani Manuscripts which date the pre-middle and middle years. The Society prepared and brought out a descriptive catalogue of Rajasthani manuscripts comprising 636 manuscripts.

RARE BOOK DIVISION

In 1978 the Council decided to open a Rare Book Division. The preliminarhy screening of the collection has since been started.

Among the earliest printed books mention may be made of the following:

- Julii Firmici Astronomicorum libri octo integri (Venice 1499),
- Kitabal-Qanum (Arabic/Romae 1595),
- Kripar Sstrer Arthabhed (Bengali in Roman Character, Kisbon 1743);
- S. Purchas's Purchas: His Pilgrimage (London, 1 61 4),
- N. Halhed's Grammar of the Bengal Language, (Hooghly, 1778),
- Malabar and English Dictionary, (Madras, 1779),
- Rasamanjari (Sanskrit, Banaras, 1791),
- Ram Ram Bose's Lipimala (Bengali, Serampore, 1802),
- The Ramayana 3 vols, (Bengali, Serampore, 1803),
- Hitopadesa (Sanskrit, Serampore, 1804),
- Colebrooke's Grammar of the Sanskrit language vol. 1 (Serampore, 1805).

2

Dr. S.R. Ranganathan

BIRTH AND PARENTAGE

Ranganathan was born in Shiyali in Tanjavoor District of Tamil Nadu (then part of Madras Presidency) in his maternal grandfather's house in North Rampart Street, (Vadakku Madavilaga Theruvu) around 9.30 A.M. on 9th August 1892. It was a Gayathri Japam day in the month of *Adi* of the year *Nandana.* On that day and at that time, South Indian Brahmins recite Manthram to Gayathri to redeem them from the sins committed by them thus far.

His Janmanakshatra was *Danishta* and Lagna *Kanya.* He was the first child of his parents and the first grandchild of the grandparents both paternal and maternal. His father, Ramamrita Ayyar, belonged to the village of Ubhayavedanthapuram in the Nannilam Taluk at Tanjavoor District.

He was a landlord holding a medium-sized property of wet land, growing paddy, the principal food crop of the Cauvery delta. He was a learned and cultured man, used to giving *Ramayana Pravachanam* to small audiences was influential and was held in high esteem by the people of the neighbourhood and by visiting officials. The parents had three sons and a daughter—one of the sons died in its early age and the daughter was born a posthumous child.

Ramamrita Ayyar died (on 13 January 1898) rather suddenly after a bout of illness at the age of 30, when Ranganathan was only six years old. Ranganathan's mother survived this loss for nearly 55 years and died at Delhi due to a fire accident at the home in January 1953. Ranganathan's another brother Nateshan died in 1964 at Madras and his sister is alive.

FAMILY LIFE

Ranganathan married when he was fifteen years old in 1907. Rukmini was his wife's name. She was very devoted to Ranganathan and an able house keeper. But she died in an accident on 13 November 1928 at the Parthasarathy Koil Tank, Triplicane, Madras where she had gone for a bath. The couple had no children. Ranganathan married again in 1929 to Sarada in December 1929; she was also devoted to Ranganathan and helped him to work ceaselessly for the cause of the library profession.

She even persuaded him to donate large sums of money for the Chair of Library Science in Madras University and to the Endowment. She died at the age of 78 years on 30 July 1985 in Bangalore. Ranganathan was blessed with only one son, Shri R. Yogeswar, born in 1932.

He is an Engineer by profession and is an international consultant on machine tool design and development. He has two sons and a daughter. All of them are living in Luxembourg. Ranganathan had a simple taste for food. He would not unnecessarily waste money and energy. He was sympathetic to good people; encouraged intelligent students and guided them towards better goal and achievements.

EDUCATION

Ranganathan's education was initiated on Vijayadasami day in October, 1897 with *Aksharabyasam* at Ubhayavedan-thapuram near Shiyali. After this, Ranganathan was admitted to a school in Shiyali, and was handed to the care of Subba Ayyar, a brother of his maternal grandfather and a primary school teacher.

During his school days, Ranganathan came under the influence of two of his teachers who shaped his mind - R. Antharama Ayyar and Thiruvenkatachariar, the Sanskrit teacher. From them Ranganathan learnt about the life teachings of nayanars (*Shaivaite Bhaktas*) and *Alwars* (*Vaishnavaite Bhaktas*).

Depth of scholarship and essence of life were ingrained in Ranganathan which kept in good stead in his later life to make decisions at crucial junctures. Ranganathan attended the S.M. Hindu High School at Shiyali and passed Matriculation examination in 1908/1909.

Ranganathan passed the examination in First Class, in spite of sickness such as anaemia, piles, and stammering. In his high school career he came under the influence of P.A. Subramanya Ayyar, a scholar on Sri Aurobindo. Ranganathan joined the junior intermediate class at the Madras Christian College in March 1909. Even in those days, there were paucity of college seats. Ranganathan was picked up for his excellent marks in all the subjects and the principal.

Prof. Skinner spotted him in a crowd of students and admitted him into the course. Ranganathan passed B.A. with a first class in March/April 1913. In June, same year, he joined the M.A. class in Mathematics with Professor Edward B. Ross as his teacher. Being a favourite student of Prof. Ross, Ranganathan had an excellent Guru-Shishya relationship. More than class room discussions, corridor and staircase discussions were taken recourse to. Ranganathan ingrained this trait into his own discipline later on. Ranganathan did his Master's degree in 1916 and he wanted to be a teacher in Mathematics. He also took a course in teaching technique and gained L T degree from a teachers' college.

During his college days, Ranganathan cultivated intimacy with his teachers, Professors Moffat and J.P. Manickam of Physics, Prof. Sabhesan of Botany, Prof. Chinnathambi Pillai and L.N. Subramanyam of Mathematics. But Prof. Ross remained his favourite Guru throughout his life.

TEACHING CAREER

In 1917 Ranganathan was appointed to the Subordinate Education Service and worked as Assistant Lecturer in the Government College in Mangalore and Coimbatore between 1917 and 1921. In July 1921, he joined the Presidency College, Madras as Assistant Professor of Mathematics.

At Mangalore and Coimbatore, Ranganathan taught Physics and Mathematics and at the Presidency College, he taught Algebra, Trigonometry and Statistics. He was a follower of the individual method of teaching putting discussion method into active use. The classes used to be lively, learning-active, and teaching-purposive. Ranganathan earned an epithet *born teacher.* He would interpose his teaching with many anecdotes and examples from life which would keep his students engaged and attentive.

Each hour of his class used to be punctuated by applauses. He also adopted the technique of assigning students with new topics, to gather data from books, and learning from discussions among themselves and amidst teachers. He organised several seminars and colloquia for students. He continued the same methods with greater vigour while teaching Library Science to students. Ranganathan was also active in extracurricular activities. From 1921 to 1923, he was Secretary of the Mathematics and Science Section of the Madras Teacher's Guild. He roused public awareness by lectures.

He introduced some uniformity and standardization in compiling the question papers for various examinations. He obtained pension facilities for private school teachers through his writings in papers and association journals. He augmented the finances of the Indian Mathematical Society.

He was a popular figure in the mathematical circles and was regarded as an efficient organiser of meetings. His friends have quoted Ranganathan's attitude to work, thus: Our right is only to do the work falling to our share, never to the fruits of our work. Flirt not with fruits.

TOWARDS LIBRARIANSHIP

Ranganathan left Presidency College in January 1924 to take appointment as the first librarian of Madras University. It was natural for Ranganathan-who was a lively teacher and had thrilling intellectual experiences with students and faculties of the Presidency College-not to opt for the post of librarian, even though it carried a handsome salary.

Ranganathan quite often narrated to us that he never wished to be a librarian. He said that Providence had made him one, for which he never regretted in his later life. In spite of his diffidence and lack of interest, his colleagues and supervisors being keen on using his innate abilities—saw to his appointment as the Librarian of the Madras University in 1924.

He took charge of the University Library at 4.00 P.M. on Thursday, 4th January 1924. But Ranganathan was back within a week at Presidency College to plead with the Principal, *I have come with a specific request. I can't bear the solitary imprisonment day-after-day. No human being, except the staff. How different from the life in the college.*

The principal, Mr. Duncan, had to pacify him by saying: "If you feel bored even after you return from England, I shall certainly take you. I shall see that your place in the college is not permanently filled up till you come back from your travel and training abroad." Ranganathan left for England in September 1924 and returned in July 1925, after 9 months of study-cum-observation tour. In England, Ranganathan came in close contact with W.C. Berwick Sayers, Chief Librarian of Croydon Public Library and a lecturer in the University School of Librarianship, London. Under his guidance, Ranganathan visited a large number of libraries. He witnessed how the libraries there had become community reading centres. He also found how the libraries rendered service to various strata of the society: to children, to the working class and to women, besides other groups. This made a lasting impression on his mind; it considerably changed his outlook and he discovered a social mission in his mind; thus he discovered a social mission for the library profession and for himself.

The impact of these experiences was expressively stated in 1931 by Sir P.S. Sivaswamy Aiyar, one of the enlightened statesmen of Madras Presidency at that time: He has brought to his task extensive knowledge of literature on the subject of libraries, personal acquaintance with methods of management of libraries in Britain, trained analytical intellect and a fervid but enlightened enthusiasm for the library movement. He has been the pioneer of the library movement in the Madras Presidency and has been carrying on an energetic propaganda to spread it. He knows how to rouse and sustain the interest of the reader.

ACTIVITIES AT MADRAS

After returning to Madras, Ranganathan began a mission for librarianship. He began to reorganise the University Library. His first concern was to attract more readers to the library and provide facilities for them. He took it upon himself to educate the public on the benefits of reading to one's society and to oneself. He charged the library with a mission of self-education for every one. He used mass media to make the library hub of activity. The University Library soon acquired a niche in the world of the enlightened public of Madras. The Government of Madras took a keen interest in this and offered a handsome annual grant on a statutory basis. Within the library, Ranganathan initiated behind the scene work in several aspects of ab initio.

Here emerged the Five Laws of Library Science, the Colon Classification, the Classified Catalogue Code. and the Principles of Library Management. Active reference service began to blossom. He introduced open shelved system and provided open access. This gave impetus for readers to come quite often. The atmosphere throbbed with human activity and intellectual atmosphere. Ranganathan designed a functional library building near Madras Beach.

All these changes did not happen in a piecemeal but were developed in a holistic manner, inspired by his Five Laws of Library Science:

- Books are for use;
- Every reader, his book-,
- Every book, its reader,
- Save the time of the reader; and
- A library is a growing organism.

Outside the library, Ranganathan, launched an endless and eternal mission. He gathered the enlightened persons of the area and formed the Madras Library Association, which became the living symbol of the library movement. Ranganathan worked as the Founder Secretary from 1928 until he left Madras in 1945.

He pushed the library movement to all the comers of the Madras Presidency, which at that time covered almost two-thirds of South India. Looking at his efforts today, after nearly 60 years, we see that the public library network is quite widespread in South India.

The seed sown by Ranganathan has been cultivated for nearly 60 years, and it is currently yielding fruits. A school of library science was also initiated by Ranganathan in 1929, first under the auspices of the Madras Library Association and later taken over by Madras University.

Ranganathan was the director of the school for nearly 15 years. Later in 1957, during centenary celebrations of the University, he donated his life's savings of one lakh rupees to the University to endow a chair known as Sarada Ranganathan Professorship in Library Science. The students of this school have taken leading parts at all levels of activity-local, national, and international.

ACTIVITIES AT BANARAS

Having performed active library service for 21 years, Ranganathan sought voluntary retirement in 1945 and wanted to engage himself in active research.

But he received an invitation to develop the library system of the Banaras Hindu University, by the then Vice-Chancellor Sir. S. Radhakrishnan. At Banaras, Ranganathan found the library in a chaotic condition. He reorganized the entire collection single-handedly, classified and catalogued about 100,000 books with a missionary zeal during 1945-47. He also conducted the Diploma Course in Library Science during the same period.

ACTIVITIES AT DELHI

Ranganathan moved over to Delhi University in 1947 on an invitation from Sir. Maurice Gwyer. He did not take the responsibility of organising the library. He confined himself to teaching and research in library science. Prof. S. Das Gupta, one of Ranganathan's brilliant students, became the librarian of Delhi University.

Delhi began courses in Bachelor of Library Science and Master of Library Science between 1947 and 1950. It was probably for the first time in the whole of the Commonwealth, Study Circle and Research Circle meetings were organized.

The Research Circle met every Sunday at his residence. Many new ideas and innovations began to emerge. Team research began to develop. Ranganathan was also elected the President of the Indian Library Association (ILA) and Shri S. Das Gupta was elected as its Secretary. The Association was activated and as part of its programme a confluence of three journals, *viz..* Annals, Bulletin, and Granthalaya were founded.

An acronym ABGILA was given to this composite, three-in-one periodical. The Annals contained research papers of the Delhi Research Circle and soon gained international acclaim. While Ranganathan was in Delhi, his international contacts began to grow. He had a close liaison with Donker-Duyvis, the then dynamic Secretary-General of FID.

Ranganathan was the Chairman of the Classification Research Group of the International Federation for Documentation (FID) between 1950-62, when he produced 12 research reports for FID and from 1962 he was the Honourary Chairman of FID/CR till his death in 1972. While he was in Delhi, Ranganathan drafted a comprehensive 30 year plan for the development of library system for India as a whole.

He was intimately involved in the founding of the Documentation Committee of the Indian Standards Institution of which he was the Chairman till 1967. In 1950, the Indian National Scientific Documentation Centre (INSDOC, Delhi) was founded. During this period, he also promoted the Madras Public Library Act. He also initiated the Classification Research Group at London. He visited USA in 1950 under Rockfeller Foundation and wrote the book *Classification and Communication.*

TOWARDS ZURICH

In order to gain first hand knowledge of Industrial documentation and to meet his international commitments Ranganathan moved over to Zurich. He wrote the second edition *of Prolegomena to Library Classification* (Published by the Library Association, London). He also regularly contributed to the Annals of Library Science published by the INSDOC.

ACTIVITIES AT BANGALORE

In 1957, Ranganathan moved over to Bangalore. He did not plan for any institutional organization of documentation activities. But it happened that Bangalore began to be industrialized and was in its ascendancy towards metropolis.

Ranganathan was helping as an adviser, the INSDOC, the Planning Commission, and the University Grants Commission. However, soon Ranganathan's solitude ended. Many young librarians of Bangalore began to gather around him. Informal discussions and research investigations were carried out to publish books and other research papers.

The crowning point of Ranganathan's activity was in the founding of *the Documentation Research and Training Centre, Bangalore* under the auspices of the Indian Statistical Institute in 1962. The main functions of this Centre are centred around research and teaching activities in library and information science. Ranganathan was the Honourary Professor of this Centre during 1962-72. He directe" the institutional activities with great efficiency and created an atmosphere of academic excellence and simplicity. It was like a Gurukula.

Around Ranganathan were his young students eager to learn from him and Ranganathan was equally eager to get the new ideas from them. In 1965, Ranganathan was recognised by the Government of India and made him the National Research Professor in Library Science.

This was also an honour to library science and librarianship. At that time, only four other National Research Professors were there. They were Dr. C.V. Raman (Physics), S.N. Bose (Physics), P.V. Kane (Law), S.K. Chatterjee (Literature and Linguistics). Ranganathan was honoured by Delhi University and Pittsburgh University by awarding Doctor of Letters degrees in 1948 and 1964. Ranganathan received these awards and honours in simple and humble stride and advised his students to do hard work saying that reward would come in appropriate time.

He used to say "God has chosen me as an instrument, the honour done to me should act as an incentive to the younger generation to devote their lives wholeheartedly to library science and service." Most of his salary as National Research Professor and the royalties on his books were donated to the Sarada Ranganathan Endowment for Library Science (1961). During the last five years, Ranganathan abstained from travelling and did deep thinking and intensive writing. He wrote many books and articles. He postulated *Absolute Syntax* for indexing language. He kept on working on Colon Classification and proved that the design and development a scheme for classification is a life time activity.

Until the end of his life, to the very last day, Ranganathan kept on working. He died on 27 September 1972 after a fruitful 80 years of his life. While he himself contributed to the field of library service, science and profession, he catalysed a human movement whose manifestation is witnessed even today. He wrote sixty books and 2000 articles. His life was a symbol of immortality.

The integral nature of Ranganathan's theory emerged from occasional intuition; and his intellect strove to make it more explicit to the rational mind of the scientific worker. His contributions sometimes bordered on a poetic beauty and sometimes on uncouth prose-but his life and work in the field of library science modelled an ever-enquiring mind, well-entrenched in the philosophy of *Bhagavad Gita* (Chapter 18, Verse 20).

3

Impact of Outsourcing and Privatisation

INTRODUCTION

For many years libraries have contracted with outside agencies to perform tasks and functions that are necessary to library operations, but not necessarily part of the library's core services. Examples of such routinely-accepted "contracting out" include not only such obvious non-library functions as janitorial services and photocopying services, but also services more characteristically associated with libraries, like binding services.

Even functions commonly regarded as "core" to library operations, such as cataloging, have long been procured through contractual arrangements with outside service providers.

As early as 1901 the Library of Congress began mass-producing catalogue cards and providing them to other libraries, in the process becoming perhaps the first vendor of cataloging services. Over the years, libraries have contracted out not only cataloging services, but other functions as well, including the development of automated systems and the acquisition of materials.

These practices were not generally labeled as outsourcing when first adopted, and they are common practice today. Several events in the mid 1990s led to growing concerns within the library profession about increasing outsourcing of library functions, to the point that some librarians were concerned about the complete privatisation of publicly funded libraries. These concerns led the American Library Association to establish in the fall of 1997 and Outsourcing Task Force (OTF).

The charge to the OTF was to:

- Advise the association on issues related to outsourcing, subcontracting and privatisation of library services;
- Gather data, examine the literature on outsourcing and evaluate the impact of outsourcing on library services and operations;
- Examine past ALA positions and determine how these issues relate to the ALA Code of Ethics and other association policies;

- Provide ALA Council with a comprehensive report with recommendations at the 1999 Midwinter Meeting.

The OTF reviewed the literature, examined ALA policies, held hearings at Midwinter 1998 and Annual Conference 1998 and prepared a report to the Executive Board with recommendations which were presented as motions to the ALA Council at the 1999 Midwinter Meeting. Among the recommendations of the OTF was that ALA should commission a formal study on the impact of outsourcing and privatisation on library services and management.

The recommendation was adopted by the ALA Council. ALA issued a Request For Proposals and this study was funded and carried out in response to that RFP. As part of its normal curriculum, the School of Library and Information Studies at Texas Woman's University regularly offers a Doctoral level seminar in Trends and Issues in Library Management. Subsequent to receiving the grant from ALA to carry out the study on outsourcing and privatisation, the Project Director, Dr. Robert S. Martin, the instructor for the course in the Spring 200 semester, established outsourcing and privatisation as the major focus of the course. The majority of the readings and discussion for the course were on the topic of outsourcing and privatisation, and the required class project was to carry out the study. We used part of the funding provided by the contract to underwrite tuition and fee waivers for all students registered for the course.

This served as an inducement to assist in recruiting experienced practitioners to the project team, and provided compensation for all of the participants (except the Project Director) for their contributions to the work of the project. To ensure equity, tuition and fee waivers were provided to current students and special students alike. Registration in the course was limited to fifteen students; consent of instructor ensured all who enroll were qualified to participate in the project. An assertive public information campaign was focused on the public, academic, and school libraries in the Dallas-Ft. Worth area, advertising the opportunity to participate in this important study by enrolling in the course. Fifteen students were admitted to the course.

Four were students already enrolled in the doctoral programme at TWU SLIS. Of these, two are pursuing doctoral studies full-time and two remain employed as librarians full-time while they pursue their studies on a part-time basis. One advanced student in the TWU SLIS master's programme also enrolled.

The remaining ten students–two-thirds of the class–were special non-degree students drawn from the professional community in the Dallas-Ft. Worth metropolitan area, recruited specifically to participate in the research project. The resulting research team was made up of experienced librarians, representing in aggregate more than 250 years of varied library experience.

WORK PLAN AND METHODOLOGY

As the ALA Outsourcing Task Force's report noted, there is nothing new about outsourcing. The proximate cause for the work of the Task Force, however, stems from major outsourcing and privatisation initiatives, in Hawaii and California, dating from 1996 and 1997. We therefore limited the scope of the study to assessing impact of these recent major outsourcing and privatisation efforts, focusing on events in 1997 and later.

We limited the scope of our literature review to the decade of the 1990s. Upon notification of award of contract on November 5, the Project Director immediately finalised the syllabus for the course, incorporating the study as the core element of the course.

Together with TWU Libraries staff, and assisted by a graduate assistant provided by the SLIS, we compiled a comprehensive citation list of publications on the topics of outsourcing and privatisation, and prepared copies of relevant articles and other materials to distribute to the research team.

We anticipated that to fully understand outsourcing and assess its impact on some aspects of library services it was necessary to conduct field visits to actual outsourcing sites. The Project Director identified and contacted selected library organisations in which outsourcing has been initiated and secured cooperation for the project. These included the Riverside County Library System, the National Aeronautics and Space Administration and Fort Worth Public Library System.

The project team met for the first time on Wednesday, January 19, 2000, and met weekly thereafter through May 10. At the first class meeting on January 19, the Project Director established project work teams, with separate teams for outsourcing of cataloging, selection, and management. Literature to be reviewed was divided topically and assigned to relevant teams.

All members of the research team reviewed the report of the ALA Outsourcing Task Force, as well as other relevant literature on outsourcing and privatisation, not only from the field of librarianship, but also from the literatures of management and public administration. The literature review was completed by February 9.

The project teams proceeded to develop definitions for the key concepts, terms and variables to be assessed. This was one of the most important and difficult steps in carrying out the project. For purposes of consistency and continuity, we tried not to deviate from commonly accepted definitions whenever possible. We had intended, therefore, to accept the definitions of outsourcing and privatisation as written in the Outsourcing Task Force's report.

These definitions were as follows.

- Outsourcing is the contracting to external companies or organisations, functions that would otherwise be performed by library employees.

- Privatisation is the shifting of policy making and management of library services or the responsibility for the performance of core library services in their entirety, from the public to the private sector.
- Core services are those professional activities that define the profession of librarianship. These include collection development and organisation; gathering and providing information; making the collection accessible to all library users; providing assistance in the use of the collection; and providing oversight and management of these activities.

We found the Task Force's definition of *outsourcing* to be similar to many in the literature and agreed to accept it. We found, however, the definitions of *privatisation* and core services to be unworkable in the research context and completely unamenable to the development of operational definitions.

First, from the literature, there appears to be a complete lack of consensus about what constitutes a "core service"–what is core in one institutional context may well be considered to be peripheral in another. Even if there were agreement about the definition of "core services," there would still be difficulties with "privatisation." For example, would the shifting of one "core service" to the private sector be sufficient to constitute privatisation? Our team thought not. Given what the literature review revealed about the probable extent of outsourcing in American libraries, it seemed to us misleading and unhelpful to label the majority of American libraries as "privatised." What then was an adequate extent of outsourcing of "core services" to constitute "privatisation"?

We were not surprised to find that the Task Force itself found its definitions inadequate:

- It is acknowledged that the distinctions between the terms "outsourcing" and "privatisation" are not exact and are subject to arbitrary interpretations. Within the context of this report, the Task Force has utilised the term "outsourcing" for contracting for specific services; and the term "privatisation" when the responsibility for day-to-day management of a library or for establishing or altering policies that affect the delivery of service, is delegated to an external commercial agency.

In other words, in spite of its own definitions, the Task Force recognised that a library could in fact contract out "core services" such as selection or cataloging, and still not be considered as "privatised." Only if the library contracted out for day-to-day management of operations, or relinquished control over policy to a contractor could it be considered "privatise." From at least one perspective, however, "day-to-day management of a library" might be construed as a "specific service" to be contracted out, and from that perspective, a library that contracted out its day-to-day management but retained control over policy could not be construed as "privatised." We determined that the only consistent factor that seemed to enter into a definition of privatisation was control over policy. We established, then, the following operational definition of privatisation:

- Privatisation is contracting out for services in a way that shifts control over policies for library collections and services from the public to the private sector.

This definition renders moot the debate over the definition of "core services." Operational definitions of the other elements to be studied were difficult to develop, and occupied considerable time in the project schedule. We determined that different operational definitions to were needed to assess different aspects of the outsourcing landscape. Each work group developed its own definitions to assess the factors in its milieu, and then established the specific qualitative and/or quantitative data needed for assessment were established.

Given the time constraints for the project, these data were limited to what might reasonably be collected and analysed. For example, the work group studying the Riverside County Library System determined to use quality of library services as an indicator of the success of outsourcing, and established an operational definitions based on hours of service, measured by reported hours, and user satisfaction, measured by survey of library users. The project teams then identified sources for the needed data, and constructed the survey and interview instruments needed.

Data collection commenced in late February. As the project developed, the teams were further subdivided to focus on specific aspects of their topic. For example, the management outsourcing team was divided into two teams, one focusing on NASA and one on Riverside County. The Riverside team visited Riverside, California, during early March to carry out on-site evaluation. This team conducted on-site interviews with library managers, professional and support staff, library users, and elected officials. Other project teams will conduct site visits in the Dallas-Ft. Worth metro area. During March the project teams began to process incoming data and survey returns. Follow-up contacts were required to ensure adequate data returns on surveys and other data collection procedures.

Follow-up letters and phone calls were carried out through March and into April. In April the work teams completed data analysis and begin drafting the report. Follow-up contacts with respondents to clarify information were made by members of the work teams. Analysis of quantitative data was carried out utilising standard statistical software packages available at TWU. The initial draft of the report, with the final input from the work team members, was completed by May 10. This report constituted the final examination for the course. The Project Director completed the report for submission to ALA. The Project Director will attend ALA Annual Conference to make a presentation on the projects results to ALA Executive Board and/or Council, and to respond to questions.

LITERATURE EXAMINATION

Definitions of "outsourcing" vary widely, ranging from the simple–getting someone else to do your work for you–to the complex–the acquisition of services from external service providers. Basically defined, outsourcing is the transfer of an internal service or function to an outside vendor. Outsourcing is a new name for the old practice of "contracting out" for services that organisations chose not to provide internally with their own staff. Whatever the definition, outsourcing has become a standard practice in both the corporate and the not-for-profit worlds. A 1995 survey indicates 40 per cent of Fortune 500 Companies outsourced some department or service.

In thc corporate sector, outsourcing became popular in the 1980s primarily as a way to reduce costs and increase profitability. The automotive industry led the way in outsourcing by contracting with companies specialising in a particular aspect of the manufacturing process. Both Ford and Chrysler significantly reduced inventories by outsourcing component manufacturing for their cars.

Their profits remained steady, while General Motors, which chose to remain a wholly in-house operation, saw profits plummet. This scenario lent credibility to outsourcing as a positive and strong cost cutting measure. First a cost cutting measure, outsourcing exploded in the 1990s and became identified as a method of spinning off unnecessary work in order to focus the organisation on its primary goals. Processes and functions identified as not central to the enterprise are contracted out to other firms that specialise in providing those products or services, in theory enabling the contracting organisation to concentrate its resources on the core business.

Retail credit, marketing, information technology systems, and human resources management are examples of functions that are increasing procured through contracting with outside service providers. In the 1990s outsourcing thus was transformed from a simple efficiency tactic to an innovative management strategy focused on streamlining the company. Following this transformation, interest in outsourcing significantly increased. The literature reflects this change. A 1980s survey of the business periodical literature reveals an average of three articles per year about outsourcing. This number increases dramatically in the 1990s to more than six hundred articles annually.

Libraries have followed the general business trend. Routine non-library services, like janitorial services and photocopying, have long been procured through contracts with outside vendors. In the early part of the 20th century, the Library of Congress began mass-producing catalogue cards and providing them to other libraries, in the process becoming perhaps the first vendor of cataloging services. Over the years, libraries have contracted out not only cataloging services, but other functions as well, including the development of automated systems and the acquisition of materials. These practices were not generally labeled as outsourcing when first adopted, and they are common practice today. Outsourcing is a topic of interest to most librarians in all types of libraries.

The library literature reflects a continuing discussion of outsourcing of such routine library operations as collection development, materials selection, materials processing, cataloging, and management. A search using Library Lit and ERIC databases yielded 103 articles related to outsourcing published during the 1990s. This literature consists almost exclusively of either opinion pieces commenting on the pros and cons of outsourcing, or else "how we did it good" reports of specific outsourcing projects.

There is almost no quantitative research concerning the impact of outsourcing on library operations or on the quality of library services. Opinion articles range from those that present outsourcing as a wonderful strategy for improving both efficiency and effectiveness, to those that posit a more moderate wait-and-see attitude, to vehement denunciations of the practice as inimical to the values of the profession. Ronald A. Dubberly, retired director of the Atlanta–Fulton Public library, states that only the outsourced will survive in lean economic times. Leaving no question concerning his attitude, Dubberly titles his article in *Library Journal*, "Why Outsourcing is our Friend." Dubberly argues that libraries caught in the economic crunch of having to provide more services with reduced revenue can do so only by utilising outsourcing. Also, Dubberly predicts government will merge tax-supported service oriented departments, including libraries.

Those public libraries that fail to adapt will cease to operate. Librarians must consider outsourcing as a tool to provide better service using less money and to insure continuing library service to their communities. Clara Dunkle, "Outsourcing the Catalogue department: A Mediation Inspired by the business and Library Literature," notes a variety of businesses effectively use outsourcing to become more effective and reduce costs.

While not a good idea to totally outsource cataloging functions, Dunkle suggests cataloging by vendors may provide greater accuracy and consistency of cataloging records. Kevin Miles provides a law librarian's perspective on outsourcing in his 1996 survey. With a relatively small sample of respondents, he concludes that law firms–regardless of size–are "aggressively outsourcing parts of their libraries". "A Tempest in a Teapot." describes outsourcing according to Anne Woodsworth, Dean of Palmer School of Library and Information Science, Long Island University.

Library managers use outsourcing as a tool when they implement blanket and standing orders to vendors. Vendors assume the role of acquisitions staff and bibliographers. John N. Berry's February, 1998, *Library Journal* editorial questions the wisdom of outsourcing, saying that no systems for measuring outsourcing's impact are in place. Cost cutting and efficiency are not the only issues in a service-oriented venue such as a library. The most important measure of any change is in the quality of library service offered to all users and potential users. Michael Gorman is one of the most outspoken critics of outsourcing, especially outsourcing of cataloging and technical services. He state with some asperity that the outsourced catalogue is "corruption of the bedrock of library competence".

More recently he wrote that library managers who decide to contract with outside vendors for cataloging, selection or acquisition services "are saying, in effect, that professional library skills and experience can be replaced by distant vendors who probably lack the former and certainly lack the latter." He opposes outsourcing because in his view it leads to an "inevitable debasement of service," and because it undermines "the very foundations of our profession". Pat Schuman, a past president of ALA, is perhaps even more vehement in her opposition to outsourcing. In Schuman's view, outsourcing and privatisation–which considers merely different faces of the same phenomenon–"threaten the profession's very core–perhaps its very 'soul' as a public service."

She examines and attempts to refute three assumptions that she believes underlie all outsourcing decisions:

- The private sector can–and will–do it better and cheaper;
- Private sector accountability tot he marketplace is more effective than government bureaucracy; and
- Libraries have always outsourced, and managers should be free to employ this useful tool.

She concludes with a plea for librarians to articulate a clear, passionate, and convincing case for America's premier democratic institutions–out libraries". There is very little in the library literature in the way of empirical research on outsourcing in libraries and its effects on service. Our survey revealed only two articles published during the 1990s. Katherine Libby and Dana Caudle conducted a survey on outsourcing of cataloging in academic libraries to determine the extent and success of such ventures. The study reveals that out of the 117 libraries responding to the survey, thirty-three were outsourcing cataloging functions and sixteen libraries were considering the practice. Of the thirty-three libraries outsourcing their cataloging, most appeared to be pleased with the results. Each indicated that they would continue outsourcing the cataloging function. Karen Wilson, Assistant Director at the J. Hugh Jackson Library, at Stanford University, provides some data in her case study detailing the outsourcing of copy cataloging and processing at her library.

Blackwell North America, Inc. and Blackwell Ltd. provided J. Hugh Jackson Library staff with catalogue records for 86 per cent and 57 per cent respectively for the monographs purchased from them. During the period in which Blackwell North America and Blackwell, Ltd. provided records, library staff accepted 69 per cent and 61 per cent respectively without making changes. Staff edited another 25 per cent of the records slightly to reflect local concerns. Less than 2 per cent of the records contained errors. This project demonstrated that outsourcing reduced costs and reduced the time it takes to process materials, but had no discernable detrimental effect on the quality of cataloging records. Wilson hails the outsourcing at J. Hugh Jackson as a new paradigm for the future of technical services operations in academic libraries. Outsourcing in libraries remains controversial. In the business world, functions that are not central to the organisation's perceived core business are those most likely to be outsourced, while core competencies or functions that are essential to the company are kept in-house.

The central issue then becomes: what constitutes a core competency or function? Libraries operate in a constantly evolving environment. What they do, what services they provide, and how they organise their resources to provide those services, are all subject to a changing paradigm. That changing paradigm is reflected in the literature.

OUTSOURCING CATALOGING DEPARTMENT FUNCTIONS

Outsourcing of cataloging functions in libraries is the area that has seen the most activity and has also provided the largest number of contributions to the literature during the decade of the 1990s. The pattern of publication reflects a swelling of interest in the topic during the middle of the decade, followed by a rapid decline.

There were no articles on outsourcing cataloging in the first two years of the decade, followed by a rapid growth to more than forty articles in 1996 and 1997. Following Libby and Caudle's comprehensive review in 1997, there was a steady decline in the number of articles. Fewer than ten appeared in 1998 and only two in 1999.

This pattern appears to represent a rapid and visible growth in the practice of outsourcing cataloging functions, a brief period of concern and controversy, followed by a recognition that this phenomenon was now "business as usual." The overwhelming body of literature on outsourcing cataloging functions is focused on the academic community. Since 1995, there have been two articles from public libraries, two from special libraries, and only one from school libraries. In addition to Libby and Caudle's comprehensive survey there are number of excellent overviews on the topic. *Outsourcing Library Technical*

Services Operations published by the American Library Association provides sixteen case studies, eleven featuring examples from academic libraries, three are from public libraries and two from special libraries. A more recent survey by the Urban Libraries Council, however, provides data from 72 member libraries, showing that 51 per cent of those libraries responding are outsourcing almost half of their cataloging and 68 per cent are outsourcing at least 40 per cent of their materials processing.

These same libraries have been outsourcing cataloging for an average of ten years and materials processing for an average of six years. Ruschoff supplies a historical context for outsourcing in technical services operations, reporting and evaluating "the warnings, suggestions, enquiries, and findings" which appeared in the literature. He does this from the perspective of addressing the "forces" shaping libraries; funding, desire of libraries to do more, satisfying the customer's informational needs, and the Internet.

Wilson also provides an historical perspective on outsourcing cataloging and physical processing and documents, beginning as far back as 150 years ago. She also notes that "virtually no literature on library outsourcing of cataloging and physical processing existed in 1991". Outsourcing was such significant issue in the mid-1990s that in 1996 ALCTS devoted a Preconference to the subject. Themes arising in the proceedings of the Preconference included: every outsourcing situation is different, librarians have always adapted and embraced new technology and change, importance of knowing your internal costs, guidelines are needed for evaluating outsourcing services, reorganisation can be done in a team-like atmosphere, know what type of service that you want to outsource, importance of collaboration with, and the partnership that exists, between vendors and librarians.

Dunkle provides with a different slant to the topic as she highlights the difficulties of outsourcing a cataloging department by contrasting outsourcing in business and in libraries.

She begins first with the decision "not whether to outsource–but how much to outsource." The points out that the work of highly trained, highly skilled cataloging staff can distance them from other professionals in the organisation, yet, their work is vital to the success of the organisation.

Dunkle disputes many of the assumptions of outsourcing. She focuses on the "real" costs, the potential for more flexibility on the part of the staff, the belief that a vendor will provide a high-quality product with little guidance, and the human resources issues. The author outlines the necessary steps to implementing a successful outsourcing project, and, in summary, states that "outsourcing is not a substitute for management's accountability and responsibilities." Dunkle examines the most prevalent reasons for outsourcing cataloging in detail.

The first, which always elicits emotional reactions, is that cataloging "performs a process which is not critical to the organisation's mission"–or that it is not a "core" department. The second is that administrators lack the knowledge and understanding of this department's function, and as a result may feel they cannot communicate effectively with the workforce. And, finally, the department may indeed be inefficient, wasting money and resources and lacking the power or will to adapt to the changing environment of its own free will. The most comprehensive treatment of outsourcing cataloging in libraries is without question the Hirshon and Winters work *Outsourcing Library Technical Services*, published in 1996. It was specifically designed as a step-by-step guide to walk librarians through the steps of reengineering, outsourcing, and the procurement process.

In its preface, the authors stress that

- ...outsourcing is not an objective, but a tool. Simply put, a library should not set out to outsource. Rather, the library should look for ways to improve its internal processes and to become as efficient and as effective as possible. Before a library engages the services of an outside vendor, it is essential to first undergo process reengineering to ensure that outsourcing is indeed the best course of action.

Perhaps the best and most recent introductory article related to outsourcing technical services is by Barry Baker in 1998. He gives a brief overview and history of reengineering and outsourcing. The most frequent rationale for outsourcing is its "potential to reduce costs, increase customer satisfaction, and provide effective and efficient improvements." He points out that "the success of the outsourcing project depends on how well the library plans and does its homework before entering into an agreement with a provider.

A good contract and a good relationship with the vendor will help the library monitor performance, quality, and maintain control of the operation." Other good general treatments of outsourcing technical services is Joyce Ogburn, which gives an excellent overview, and Gary Shirk, who provides the vendor's perspective, encouraging both vendors and librarians alike to proceed with outsourcing, but with caution.

Discussion of outsourcing of cataloging took place not only in the published professional literature, but also provided a major topic of discussion in the online discussion lists. An excellent example on the AUTOCAT discussion list was a posting by Lowell Ashley, listing thirty-six points to be considered before making a decision to outsource.

Opinion Pieces

Opinions abound on the pros and cons of outsourcing cataloging functions. Many writers, concerned with the ramifications of outsourcing, successfully raised some thought-provoking considerations that should be addressed by administrators who are contemplating outsourcing as *the* solution for their libraries. Holt tells us that, like automation, "outsourcing does not solve cataloging problems. Instead, it creates a different set of cataloging problems, many of which are quality-control issues that can only be handled by a manager".

Holt also challenges libraries to thoroughly evaluate the costs of in-house cataloging to be able to make responsible decisions. Within that context, one must also examine the level and expenses related to customisation of cataloging records and determine whether a library can really afford to continue that process.

Harmon equates providing quality library service to applying the highest possible standards to bibliographic records that are contributed to the national databases, and thus providing thorough access to resources. In his concluding statement he reminds us all that "it is well to keep in mind that we collect and catalogue for the future as well as for the present". In 1993 Sheila Intner highlighted the pitfalls of removing cataloging activities from libraries altogether and simultaneously challenging catalogers to share their expertise, as it relates to the topic of outsourcing, and for administrators to ask and listen to their advice.

Since that time, she continues to preach caution, reminds us of the critical role that cataloging plays in the delivery of quality library service, and takes the stand that we still need cataloging expertise to organise information and informational materials for access. Perhaps most eloquently and visibly, Michael Gorman makes a strong case for preserving cataloging within libraries as a core function, allowing libraries to carry out their mission of selecting, acquiring, providing access to, and preserving records. Most of those who have come out in support of outsourcing cataloging functions are quick to remind us that the decision and process is not "flawless."

From a school library perspective, Eisenberg and Repman put it simply:

- we have a finite amount of energy and resources. Of course we should fight for those things that are truly central to our mission and to our professional identity. But we must consider when the reality of change suggests that we spend our energy and resources on battles that we can and should win.

Fast explains why he believes that libraries can't respond adequately to the demands of increased productivity in technical services departments and how vendors can and do save money for libraries. Basically, it's the "culture" of the library verses that of business–the library is devoted to providing quality customer service while business's goal is to do whatever it takes to make a profit. The challenge of libraries, as he sees it, is to control costs without loosing its mission. Libraries must also continue to work with vendors in outlining our needs and the services we want them to provide. Waite has been one of the most out-spoken advocates of outsourcing cataloging. Waite argues that the decision to reengineer technical services departments is a reaction to stagnant administration of those aspects of library administration.

It is also a reaction to the changing information needs of library users, and "to rigid professional standards that no longer meet the needs of our patrons". Rather than downsising and doing away with the cataloging department, her goal is to use the cataloging staff to organise bibliographic files more effectively, develop web pages and resource guides, and to restructure the files of uniform titles to local settings. Varner provides a thought-provoking article on outsourcing from the perspective of managing technical services in libraries.

It is her premise that outsourcing presents "an opportunity for leadership...and that the possibilities for structural change will greatly affect technical services personnel." Careful analysis is needed to identify the most productive process to use in changing the subculture and that only then can "a new shared vision and mental model" be possible. She contends that staff development is the key to the entire process towards success. Rider also focuses on the cataloging staff and the new roles that they must assume in the outsourcing process.

She reaffirms the importance of paraprofessionals in the cataloging process and encourages libraries to assist them in redefining their roles on the basis of "education, knowledge, and skill levels required to perform certain tasks," not on the actual performance of those tasks. Janis Johnston and Richard Block both view outsourcing as just another "tool" to use. Both see it as a project-oriented, strategically implemented process, rather than a vehicle for reengineering or downsising an entire department. Johnston sees outsourcing as attractive because it is an effective way to deal collectively with a range of issues, among them the labour intensive–and thus expensive–character of cataloging and processing activities; the continuing increase is personnel costs; and the enormous increase in the number and variety of services libraries are now expected to provide.

Block provides a good overview as to what libraries should understand about outsourcing and general considerations to focus on prior to the decision-making process. Among those he lists are: knowing what the goals of outsourcing are; understanding what the future might hold in the way of new formats, technologies, etc., that will impact cataloging staff; the implications of loosing local control over bibliographic records; lingering cataloging projects; realistic in-house costs of cataloging; implications of outsourcing on the entire technical services workflow; user impact; and staffing and staff skills assessment. Walker points out that "the areas of concern with outsourcing can be grouped into two general categories: the "can" and the "should"... One should not talk about outsourcing without also addressing issues like cataloging quality, database integrity, costs, and professional declination." With that he also suggests that a good starting point into outsourcing for libraries might be to tack on "value-added services" to already existing contracts and/or price agreements.

Bordeianu and Benaud present the real issues of outsourcing cataloging functions in a concise and straightforward manner. They point out that "two reactions are guaranteed when the topic comes up; librarians always have an opinion about it, and everybody has an outsourcing story to tell". They provide us with the perspective that outsourcing has evolved "from an impersonal relationship between two companies, to a closer collaboration leading towards a fuller partnership between supplier and buyer." They also surmise that determining what constitutes a core library service is at the very heart of the profession's controversy on the topic.

Briefly, they outline why libraries outsource, what kinds of tasks can be, the pros and cons to outsourcing, and outlines trends in various types of libraries today.

They conclude by stating that there is no foolproof method of evaluating the success/failure of outsourcing as it is

- ...neither good nor bad. It is only a tool that libraries can use to improve their operations. The library's specific circumstances, and the manner in which outsourcing is implemented are the main factors that will determine success or failure.

The most recent overview of the decision-making process related to outsourcing cataloging Janet Swan Hill's. After walking the reader through a very concise history of what has been outsourced in the past, she turns to such tasks as original cataloging, database maintenance, and administrative functions–setting priorities, workflow, and general oversight into the day-today operations.

Outsourcing Projects

Numerous articles outlining "project" outsourcing in libraries appear regularly in the literature. These include reports on outsourcing of cataloging for a specific type and or collection of materials – AV, foreign language, government document collections, and pre-order titles. Case studies on the use of PromptCat and TechPro from OCLC abound as well–most recently, Duke, Leiding, Rider, and Somers.

The general consensus appears to be that this service may not be right for everyone, implementing it requires a period of adjustment and problem solving, but where it is being utilised the libraries are generally pleased with it. Tsui and Hinders describe the authority control work underway at the University of Dayton Libraries, Dayton, Ohio. This collaborative effort involves the library, its automated online system, and an authority service vendor to provide ongoing authority control in an efficient and cost-effective manner. While recognising that their vendor services are not flawless, they cite the end result of their efforts as accurate, standardised headings, which ultimately enhance the effectiveness of online searching and retrieval by the library's online users. Wilson and Colver cite four successful examples of outsourcing authority work– Emory University Libraries; Houston Public Library, William Henry Smith Memorial Library; Project Muse for the John Hopkins University Press; and the University of California, Santa Barbara Library.

They also provide us with several cases of successfully outsourcing the physical processing of materials. Libraries included are: Albuquerque/Bernalillo County Public Library; Chubb Law and Business Library, Warren, New Jersey; Florida Atlantic University Libraries in Boca Raton; Fort Worth Public Library; Houston Public Library; University of Alberta Library; University of Arizona Library; University of Manitoba Libraries; and the William Henry Smith Memorial Library.

As noted earlier, Wilson provides an historical overview of physical processing in libraries as well as documenting Stanford's successful "pilot project" of the mid-90s. Wilson concluded outsourcing of copy cataloging and physical processing was feasible, it did not have a detrimental effect on the quality of cataloging and processing received by the library, and it did save money. Secondarily, it enabled cost reductions in staffing – through attrition as well as reassignment into public service areas. Easton briefly describes two academic models as she summarises the ALA Annual Conference in 1996. The University of Akron began receiving all of their approval plan materials fully processed.

The two primary motivations for this action were improved productivity for staff and the increased number of 9xx fields made available by the vendor in the MARC record.

The need for on-going communication between the vendor and library staff received special emphasis. In edition, a cautionary note not to get "hung up on the dollar cost, but instead to consider the amount of staff time that will be freed by shifting this work," as well the importance of paying attention to personnel issues and morale. Easton also reports on Louisiana State University's shift of some processing responsibilities to a vendor "as part of a larger reorganisation of technical services".

They reworked processing based on "the assumption that outsourcing was a positive opportunity, that teamwork among technical services units was important, and that cross-training of staff was essential in adjusting to the demands placed on technical services." The acquisitions staff now performs copy cataloging on approximately 90 per cent of their new materials. Very little authority work was done and what was done was treated as a "post-cataloging process of record improvement." Somers goes into greater depth in describing

LSU's experience with the use of PromptCat and shelf-ready materials. The fact that cost-efficient, vendor-supplied cataloging and shelf-ready services currently exist for libraries is the focus of the article by Giambi.

In addition to allowing libraries to relieve cataloging departments from handling newly received items altogether; outsourcing also gives libraries the opportunity to review local practices, eliminating some outdated and, essentially, unnecessary procedures. The vendor's perspective is represented in several articles. Bush, Sasse and Smith provide the results of a survey relating to the capabilities of vendors for cataloging and other technical services functions and Shirk provided us with a general rationale approach to outsourcing of technical services. Gordon and Moore outline the steps involved in establishing a division of Information Systems Management in Winnipeg, Canada to provide technical services to libraries.

In their view, cooperation between vendor and library staff in implementing a project is critical to the success of outsourcing.

- With the implementation of such projects comes inevitably an intermeshing of the internal procedures of each operation. With cooperation on both sides, it is possible to develop procedures that enhance the efficiency of each party's workplace.

If the "partnership" between libraries and vendors is truly to be seen as critical in the ongoing process, then as suggested, need to hear more from the vendor's perspective, regularly. Such dialogue is crucial in order to keep librarians current on trends and issues – from the vendor's perspective - and remind us constantly that only we, as professionals, can affect the changes necessary to enhance and improve existing services.

OUTSOURCING COLLECTION DEVELOPMENT FUNCTIONS

Outsourcing in collection development occurs less frequently than in other library functions, but libraries have increasingly responded to financial and staff constraints by handing over responsibility for selection to private companies. The provision of collection development services by outside vendors can be seen as a further development in a growing trend that started with centralised selection, the preparation of opening day collections by vendors, and subscriptions to provide first copies of bestsellers. Although the privatisation of selection has evolved gradually, the library world remains in controversy over both the efficiency and the ethics of such an activity.

The decision to contract out always involves complex issues, but perhaps no other outsourced activity inspires as much contention as collection development because many librarians identify it as one of their core professional roles. Attitudes about outsourcing, whether positive or negative, often depend on perceptions rather than hard data. Library management often decides to outsource based on "the appearance of fiscal economies", rather than measurable standards of cost effectiveness. Crisis situations requiring immediate action often prevent in-depth assessment of the advantages of outsourcing over in-house labour.

The Ft. Worth Public Library experienced just such a situation in the early 1990s when it was faced with budget cuts and a moratorium on staff hiring. Initially, Ft. Worth chose to outsource several library functions, including the selection of adult bestsellers and children's books. Upon discovering that the volume of bestsellers purchased did not make contracting out efficient or fiscally desirable, the FPL returned responsibility for this task to on site staff. Children's selection remains an outsourced activity, although there exists little to no data in this particular situation with which to compare the merits of vendor collection development to in-house work.

The outsourcing of collection development attracts controversy in library circles, both in Fort Worth and elsewhere throughout the United States. Perhaps no single outsourcing situation has generated such rancor as the Hawaii State Library's outsourcing of all selection functions to Baker and Taylor in 1997. Facing major budget cuts, then-state librarian Bart Kane conceived of the plan to contract out collection development in all of Hawaii's public libraries in order to avoid firing employees and to divert all existing staff into public service positions.

Kane envisioned the outsourcing programme as both a solution to the state library system's immediate budget difficulties and a model for the future of libraries. However, problems with Baker and Taylor's performance arose almost immediately, adding fuel to a fire of discontent among Hawaii's public librarians. Library staff complained about Baker and Taylor's flat rate on all books and about their purchases of duplicates and materials that were unsuitable for Hawaiian collections. For example, Baker and Taylor provided books on sheep herding–a common activity in New Zealand, but not in Hawaii. Eventually, due to public outcry and Baker and Taylor's inability to meet the agreed upon terms, Hawaii dissolved the contract and the legislature passed a bill prohibiting any further outsourcing programme that did not provide for local librarians' input into book selection.

The disaster in Hawaii spurred debate about the nature of public library collections: did they possess similar characteristics that could be sustained and developed by off-site vendors or did they have unique qualities that could only be addressed by the guiding hand of local librarians? The controversy over outsourcing selection remains a pervasive theme among library scholars and professionals. Critics of collection development outsourcing make the argument that librarian's involvement in the selection process is an important part of maintaining the familiarity with the collection necessary to perform reader's advisory.

Also, those opposed to contracting out selection claim that surrendering a skill that requires both formal and on-the-job training to outside vendors will devalue the profession and forge a path that will lead to even lower salaries and benefits. Yet, proponents of outsourcing say that patrons do not "know or care how books get on the shelf" and point to outsourcing as a means of economising in "a political climate where taxpayers refuse to pay more for government services".

The only solutions to the questions and concerns that surround collection development outsourcing lie in further research. Yet, an extensive evaluation of the literature, employing several databases including Library Lit, ERIC, and Academic Abstracts, reveals only opinion pieces and narratives about the experiences of individual libraries. Unfortunately, as long as there is a lack of reliable research, contention over the merits of collection development outsourcing will continue to reign.

OUTSOURCING MANAGEMENT FUNCTIONS

The literature of outsourcing management functions focuses on how best to utilise outsourcing as a strategy, rather than debating the merits of outsourcing. The library literature appears to reflect outsourcing as a common practice. How can outsourcing provide better service to patrons? As Ronald Baker points out, complete outsourcing of library management is not the norm. Baker traces the events leading to the decision to completely outsource public library service in Riverside County, California, to a private company.

Financial woes led to serious deterioration of library services to Riverside County residents. In March 1997, Riverside County issued requests for proposals for library service providers. LSSI was granted the contract and has managed the library system since. Baker describes the situation as a model for the future that resembles nothing so much as pre-World War II library operation. He does not believe great numbers of public libraries will enter into total management contracts like Riverside County, California.

The question for library directors and managers centers on why and how outsourcing is utilised. As in the business world, outsourcing started as a cost-cutting measure, then emerged as a management strategy for transforming the organisation in order to meet future challenges. Outsourcing to gain partnerships, create alliances, and use existing resources to full advantage reflect the positive aspects.

However, alliances must be entered cautiously and selectively to assure their appropriateness. "Exploring Outsourcing: Case Studies of Corporate Libraries" is intended to provide information to assist corporate managers to decide if outsourcing will help achieve a more efficient organisation. Seven companies representing vastly different business interests were extensively interviewed concerning outsourcing their corporate library functions. Two firms had already outsourced library services, others outsourced selectively. A key finding of the survey was managers cited four main reasons for outsourcing library service. Cost reduction, centralising services, control of access to information, and a renewed emphasis on business information. Also, no company interviewed had any means of evaluating the benefits of the outsourcing currently being done. Managers do not want to lose control over the organisation.

Library managers must consider the implications of losing local control. Once a vendor starts providing a traditionally in-house service, it is difficult to change vendors. Also, once the service is no longer provided on-site, historical continuity may be lost and the ability to provide the service no longer exists. Simply stated, the organisation has lost the ability to provide the service in a locally unique fashion.

The patron loses the personalised approach to local service. The library staff loses the opportunity to practice an important job skill. To maintain control, and keep service standards high, library managers must develop methods of dealing with outsourcing.

Three distinct phases are present in an outsourcing project, planning, implementation, and managing. The planning phase takes the most time. The library examines costs and workflow, going through painstaking data gathering. Once the decision has been made to outsource, the bidding process begins and a vendor or service provider is selected. Then the implementation phase begins, leading to the third phase, the management process.

During the planning phase, basic questions should be addressed. What will be the significance to the library as an organisation? Will outsourcing provide better patron service? Will this service be at a lower cost? Will outsourcing allow a renewed focus on core competencies or will core competencies be actually outsourced? What control will be gained or lost? Will outsourcing best serve the patron's needs? Any decision to turn over library functions to a vendor requires extensive questioning and analysis.

A good partnership with the service provider is extremely important in the implementation phase. Libraries have a long tradition of contracting with vendors and jobbers in technical service and selection areas. Understanding the service provider's capabilities is paramount to a successful outsourcing project. Greater opportunities exist for managers now to explore outsourcing acquisitions, cataloging, and collection development. Libraries need to become full partners in the development of contract services.

To do this library managers must understand the risks, costs, and capabilities of contracting with outside service providers. Herbert S. White concurs in his article, "Why Outsourcing Happens and What to do About it." There are valid reasons to outsource library operations. Cost effectiveness is often achieved by hiring a firm that already has the skills, equipment, and staff to do the job. They can perform the job better and at a lower cost, without effecting quality. Often, a backlog of work can be eliminated through outsourcing. This is especially true of technical service functions. Then personnel previously assigned to this area can be reassigned to public service functions. However, White warns, the cost savings are not worth much if libraries lose quality of service. "No contractor could possibly match the quality of understanding, caring, interest and proactivity you contribute to the organisation." What services lend themselves to outsourcing? Much of the controversy stems from outsourcing library core competencies.

How do librarians define core competencies? Cataloging, acquisitions, and collection development functions are the agreed upon core competencies cited in the literature. Michael Gorman strongly opposes outsourcing cataloging functions. He maintains cataloging and a library's bibliographic records form the institution's core. Bibliographic records prepared outside the organisation constitute a misuse of the public trust and an eroding of librarianship as a profession. Clara Dunkle takes a softer approach, stressing that outsourcing cataloging may be a more efficient and economic way of addressing that function. She also suggests cataloging vendors may be able to achieve greater accuracy and consistency in cataloging than in-house staff. However, Dunkle discourages total cataloging outsourcing.

There are still some items and areas better cataloged at the local level and by outsourcing the main cataloging functions, local catalogers are better able to concentrate on the unique local items. Michael Eisenberg agrees that an understanding of cataloging principles and processes is important, but in the real world most librarians do not put these principles into practice. They do not have time or the inclination to create original cataloging. Eisenberg also asks if this cataloging model could also apply to the selection process. He suggests an outsourced baseline collection while using available discretionary funds for local purchases. Outsourcing as an effective management tool is greatly misunderstood according to Richard Abel, outsourcing pioneer consultant.

Library management's slowness to accept the concept is misguided. Libraries must position themselves strategically to maintain a long-term level of functionality. "Core -collection" building is one of the collection development easiest outsourced. After basic core collection, outsourcing collection development is only prudent when the selection criteria can be well defined. Abel warns against giving total control to vendors because the selection function is to closely related to the singular requirements of a particular library. Outsourcing has become a common management tool in both the private and public sector. As long as budgets and staffs shrink, managers are forced to creatively seek ways to stretch resources. Outsourcing emerged as one of those ways.

OUTSOURCING OF CATALOGING

Describing the collection of a library and making it accessible to patrons is an old and honoured core competency of the library profession. This process is cataloging, and it has weathered the change from manual hand written cataloging filed in wooden card cabinets to electronically transmitted machine readable cataloging transmitted via the Internet and accessed through an integrated library management system. Throughout the developments in cataloging, codes have been developed to aid the professional cataloger, and the MARC format has been established as the primary vehicle for sharing cataloging data. Subject analysis and description of materials are accomplished through standards agreed upon with regional variations throughout the world. Cataloging has gone from a backroom operation with shelves of backlog to streamlined operations with tremendous productivity aided by computerisation and communications with extremely large databases of shared records.

With the rapid advances in library technology and the competition for funding, libraries have adapted operations to remain competitive in their environment. Spine labels and catalogue cards have been purchased for decades to aid in making materials available for use. Cataloging is considered a core library service along with materials selection, reference and library management. Cataloging has seen changes in the library personnel performing this core service through the years.

The professional cataloger has gone from being the sole source of cataloging, to using services like the Library of Congress cards, to the services of the OCLC Union Catalogue database. In addition, as libraries struggled for scarce funding available to them, the professional cataloger enlisted and trained highly skilled assistants. This resulted in increased productivity and reduced personnel costs for professional catalogers. With the advent of the shared databases of OCLC, RLG, RLIN and other sources, the rise of copy cataloging overtook the original cataloging performed by the professional cataloger.

As more and more external sources for cataloging became readily available, the library began to look for means to reduce costs, reallocate personnel, and improve productivity. Outsourcing of the core service of cataloging began based on sound management study and decisions. Outsourcing is the contracting to external companies or organisations, the functions of cataloging that would otherwise be performed by library employees. Outsourcing is a management tool that allows the opportunity to direct or redirect staff to other core functions of the library while through monitoring and analysis maintaining the quality of the cataloging being provided by the external vendor.

Libraries practice sound management in choosing the external cataloging organisation through negotiation of an agreement including a detailed schedule of practices that are followed to make the cataloging received acceptable. The recent activities in this area are simply an out growth of many functions that were contracted out piecemeal in the past. With the decision by Wright State University to outsource its entire cataloging function in 1993, this process has received much attention.

Many libraries of all types have outsourced cataloging in one form or another. For example, most libraries outsourced retrospective conversion of records when developing an online library information system.

Many companies exist today to provide individually specified cataloging as well as processing of materials ready for shelving. The outsourcing of cataloging is a common occurrence. Outsourcing is used as a means to reduce backlogs, increase productivity, and allow for shifts in staff. Outsourcing is also used to gain expertise in foreign languages that is not available from the local staff. Publishers, book jobbers and companies offering outsourcing of cataloging functions have come on the scene recently. The outsourcing of cataloging has been described and surveyed in the literature.

The future of outsourcing appears to be growing in all types of libraries. The Urban Libraries Council surveyed 127 member libraries in 1998. Seventy-two libraries responded, for a response rate of 56.7 per cent. The libraries reported that half anticipated outsourcing more functions in the future and 47 per cent would anticipate the same amount of outsourcing. No library anticipated decreasing the functions outsourced. Cataloging was reported outsourced by 61 per cent of the respondent libraries. No respondent library reported that more over half of the cataloging was outsourced. In comparison, binding was outsourced by 82 per cent of the respondents and 97 per cent of the binding was outsourced. Commercial vendors were the source of outsourced cataloging 71 per cent among those reporting outsourcing.

Other sources were:

- Government agencies (15%),
- Library consortia (5%),
- Other non-profit agencies (5%) and
- Other libraries (3%)

The respondent libraries reported outsourcing is an established practice with all but two of the functions queried having been outsourced an average of five years or more. Outsourcing of Internet service provision, and web page design and maintenance are recent technological innovations and not highly outsourced among libraries responding to this survey. Over half of the outsourced functions have been outsourced ten or more years. Among the Urban Library Council libraries responding, outsourcing was not significantly driven by government mandates.

Those who outsource mandated only three functions: cataloging, payroll and other personnel functions. Outsourcing of cataloging was mandated for 31 per cent of those outsourcing this function. The most important reasons for outsourcing were better use of staff, followed by increased efficiency and better customer service considered at least moderately important. Cost savings were sited as a slightly to moderately important reason. In 1997 a survey on outsourcing was sent to 109 members of the Association of Research Libraries (ARL) and to 110 medium-sized non-ARL academic libraries. Sixty-nine ARL and seventy non-ARL libraries returned surveys, for a response rate of around 63 per cent. Eighty-eight (63 per cent) libraries report outsourcing cataloging functions, with more ARL libraries doing so.

Main vendors listed were:

- Marcive (44 per cent),
- TECHPRO (25 per cent), and
- PromptCat (18 per cent).

Forty-five per cent of the libraries reported acquiring U.S., federal document records, followed by unique collections, unique languages and LC records.

Twenty-seven per cent were also buying valueadded services like:

- Labeling (17 per cent)
- Table of contents (12 per cent)
- Security taping (15 per cent).

Twenty nine per cent indicated they had no plans to outsource in this area - 40 per cent for non-ARL libraries–while 28 per cent indicated that they did have outsourcing plans. Sixty per cent indicated they did or had outsourced retrospective conversion. OCLC has been a major participant in outsourcing throughout its history. In data from the OCLC TechPro Service, PromptCat and Retrospective Conversions, hundreds of libraries have outsourced portions of the cataloging activities. Retrospective conversion projects have been outsourced by 937 libraries through the services of OCLC. OCLC has performed this service for 391 academic libraries, 85 public, 65 corporate and 164 international libraries among the 937 participating libraries. No total of titles converted was given during a phone conversation. Statistics presented by the OCLC TechPro Service, revised December 1999, report that 461 libraries have used this service.

Academic libraries total 213, corporate and special libraries 73, federal libraries 62, public libraries 43, medical and pharmaceutical 37, art and museum libraries 18, and state libraries 15. The number of titles processed was 1,293,141 through December 1999, of which 776,237 were for academic libraries. The greatest portion of the cataloging provided is copy cataloging 976,234 titles (75 per cent), original cataloging 262,511 titles (20 per cent) and other cataloging 54, 396 titles (4 per cent). The largest TechPro project is for Wright State University with 78,406 titles reported in an ongoing project.

TechPro reports that all formats, General and Medical using LC, NLM and MeSH in the specifications listed. Most of the projects are less than 15,000 titles with only 9 academic, 2 corporate, 2 Federal and one public library from Sweden reported with more titles. The average size of the projects would be 3,022 titles with a range of 0 to 78,406. The OCLC PromptCat Service reports use by 123 libraries and 15 participating vendors. PromptCat delivers and average of 31,989 records each month with 383,686 delivered in FY 1998/99. Label files are created for 53 libraries with 153,336 labels delivered in FY1998/1999.

Similar statistics have not been gathered from other vendors, although the survey of academic libraries indicates that many vendors are being used for outsourcing all or parts of cataloging. Vendors for outsourcing of cataloging request specific individual library specifications for the cataloging and processing they perform. Vendors are doing functions that could be performed by the staff of the cataloging and processing units of a library. Wright State and other libraries have prepared detailed instructions for the services of the vendor. This is truly outsourcing of cataloging services, not privatisation. Privatisation involves the shifting of policy making and the management of the library services or the responsibility of core library services entirely from the library to another agent. With the library providing individual specifications for its acceptable cataloging, the policy making remains within the library. Even in outsourced or privatised library operations as Riverside County or NASA, there are standards, specifications and operational requirements for cataloging.

There are undeniably drawbacks to outsourcing cataloging, negative consequences for both the profession and the individual library. There are also advantages to using outsourcing as a management tool. Whether or not to outsource is a decision that can be seen either positively or negatively, depending on the perspective of the beholder. The professional cataloger may see outsourcing as denigrating his/her importance to the organisation. The library manager may see outsourcing as a means to control costs of cataloging and to shift the responsibilities of professional librarians. Selectively outsourcing of cataloging can unquestionably provide expertise not otherwise resident in a cataloging unit.

Outsourcing foreign language and other specialised cataloging are cases in point. Copy cataloging is an area were the benefits of outsourcing are especially apparent. Easy access to bibliographic data coupled with the growing expertise of cataloging service vendors has reduced much copy cataloging to the level of rote work. Wright State University and Florida Gulf Coast University are examples of a trend in academic libraries to outsource such cataloging, and there appears to be a surge to use such services to provide shelf ready materials in libraries of all types. Total outsourcing of cataloging means that some other agency outside the library will provide all the bibliographic data needed to describe all additions to the collection. Few libraries outsource cataloging to this extent because most libraries recognise that there is a continuing need for some level of local cataloging.

The cataloging staff may be much reduced, however, and those remaining may have very different duties and responsibilities. In addition to addressing the residual local cataloging needs, remaining cataloging staff will probably focus on managing the flow of outsourced cataloging and ensuring quality control. There are many criticisms of outsourcing of the "core service of cataloging". Although outsourcing in one form or another stems from the LC catalogue card service introduced in 1901 and the advent of OCLC in 1967, many objections can be made to outsourcing. The cataloger sees outsourcing as a threat to his/her value to the organisation.

The analytical skills of the cataloger are seen as no longer valued and given to the vendor, a faceless entity. The benefits of individualised cataloging for a library are removed to some degree by the use of a record seen as acceptable to many, but not tailored to the individual library. Cataloger's duties change from the creation of a bibliographic record to alteration of the record to aid in the use of the record by individual library patrons. Much more care and feeding of an automated library information system and its tables of parameters are required instead of cataloging the individual item. In a library where outsourcing of cataloging is the norm, the cataloger becomes more of a technician dealing with a system. The focus shifts to helping the patron find material rather than to creating an intellectual record for an item in the collection.

The application of cataloging skills in this manner is, from management's point of view, very valuable to the mission of the library. Bu it is different from the traditional idea of the cataloger uninvolved with the patron except in unusual circumstances. There is a clear need for more research on outsourcing of cataloging.

The impact of the shift of the cataloging function outside the library organisation, the difficulty in maintaining quality control, and possibility of shifts in materials selection due to lack of locally available cataloging expertise are all areas that should be studied.

Change in the place of cataloging in the Library and Information Science curriculum is another potentially fruitful area of study. Any change in the bibliographic network, the result of the shared expertise of many catalogers, from the rare book cataloger to the copy cataloger, should be studied for any effects in the outsourcing of cataloging.

The reasons for outsourcing cataloging have been discussed extensively. Since Wright State University became the first academic library to outsource its cataloging, more and more attention has been paid to this area. This growth in outsourcing can be attributed to budgetary shortages, technological advances, and maybe the lack of visibility of the cataloger in a library. Most libraries do not get continuous substantial fund increases to deal with inflation and to provide additional services demanded by the patron. Managers have looked at the high cataloging costs associated with books and serials making cataloging operations a quick target for budget cuts.

Technology and the invisibility of the cataloging operation to the library's public have also contributed to making cataloging a target for cuts. The need for additional reference service and instruction in online searching and the rise of the Internet have brought pressure for additional staff in these areas. Managers have begun redirect their technical services staff, primarily catalogers, to the public services areas as they outsource cataloging functions. The increase in vendors of cataloging services and the technology to deliver the bibliographic data via telecommunications have provided less costly alternatives to the maintenance of the cataloging unit.

Managers have outsourced cataloging to bring greater efficiency by using a vendor's catalogers, whose primary duties are to catalogue rather that participation in the other meetings and other non-productive activities associated with in-house staff.

Higher productivity is realised in many cases, as the vendor often integrates the activities of the jobber with that of cataloging and processing. Outsourcing saves on staff dollars and ties the cost of cataloging to a per item cost. Overhead costs are eliminated by the library and replaced with predictable costs depending on the units of materials acquired.

The staff dollars associated with cataloging are shifted to areas where needed. The vendor operates on economies of scale, providing cataloging for mainstream publication many times based on one effort to produce the records. In the instances where original cataloging is required, the vendor charges a premium for this service, but the library still reaps savings in staff dollars. Value added services as tables of contents and other record enhancements again come under the economies of scale and are available to many library customers on the basis of one action. The shifting of professional librarians from cataloging duties to tasks that involve direct interaction with patrons provides libraries the means to move limited resources to other areas. Staff are often retained within the library, but moved to different duties. Each reason library management use for outsourcing the cataloging operation has drawbacks. Greater efficiency, as evidenced by reduced backlogs, means greater availability of materials, but does not automatically mean higher quality of bibliographic records.

The ability to maintain quality assurance of records is not automatic with outsourcing of cataloging. Attention to this area must be retained or re-allocated as a part of the outsourcing process. The shift of catalogers to public service duty does not mean that each staff member reassigned will provide excellent service immediately. The skills that are need in public service become skill-building opportunities for the cataloging staff and have associated costs. The impact on the library operations can be more than just closing or reducing the size of the cataloging unit. Cataloging staff is shifted to the point that a skeleton cataloging unit is left responsible of very different task that performed by a fully staffed unit.

Emphasis changes from cataloging to managing the outsourcing operation and bibliographic record management. The remaining staff manages the cataloging contract, oversee the downloading of records, manage the authority control procedures, and concentrate on record maintenance of volume and copy numbers. Deletion of records as materials are lost or withdrawn and location changes are done.

The remaining staff is responsible for rush items, and handling local information that needs to appear as gift recognition. Outsourcing of cataloging must provide for successful operations at the local level. If the basic capabilities are not retained, there will be a detrimental effect due to the outsourcing of cataloging. This is an opportunity for study, and the responsibility of management of the library. A pre and post outsourcing research project could be devised to study the effect on the local catalogue and access to materials.

OUTSOURCING OF MATERIALS SELECTION

Selection of Library materials is certainly viewed by most librarians as one of the fundamental tasks of the professional librarian. Although specific instances of contracting out this core function have been infrequently reported in the literature, in many libraries much of the selection function is in fact contracted out by means of vendor approval plans. This approach to building library collections is commonplace in academic libraries, and is not uncommon in many public libraries.

Approval plans are generally established with care by expert selectors, monitored carefully during their operation, and reviewed and revised regularly by the contracting library's collection development staff. Aside from approval plans, there is very little outsourcing of selection reported in the library literature. The most visible and controversial case in recent years was undoubtedly the Hawaii Public Library System's contract with Baker and Taylor to provide materials selection services.

The case was widely reported in the public press and the library literature. Concerns arising from the Hawaii situation led directly to the Council of the American Library Association's action establishing a Task Force to study outsourcing and privatisation. It seemed important, therefore, for this study to review the facts of the Hawaii outsourcing effort. Although few similar contracts have been the focus of much public attention, it appears very likely that many libraries contract all or part of their selection functions to vendors. One such instance that merited our inspection was the outsourcing of selection of children's materials by the Fort Worth Public Library.

THE HAWAII PUBLIC LIBRARY SYSTEM CASE

Bartholomew A. Kane, Hawaii State Librarian since May 1, 1982, assembled a Reengineering Committee in August 1995 to examine library structure, determine core services and make recommendations for redesigning the 49-library system of the state. On August 1, 1995, Hawaii's Governor announced budget cuts requiring the reduction of 1294 state employees throughout the state. The library system budget was reduced 25 percent, resulting in a projected elimination of 120 and redeployment of 80 employees. Rather than impose massive layoffs and close at least 20 branches Kane, through the Reengineering Committee, proposed outsourcing all book selection for the system to Baker and Taylor, a book vendor from Charlotte, North Carolina. The proposal, a contract for $11.2 million over five years, was approved by the Board of Education after seven minutes of discussion.

The contract, which covered selection, acquisition, cataloging, processing and distributing books, spoken word audio, video and multimedia titles became effective March 28, 1996. At the same time Kane decided to convert the library system's automation vendor from Data Research Associates, Inc. (DRA) to Ameritech's Dynix system and add Information Access Company's online serials database. Therefore, rather than begin providing books to branches within two weeks of awarding the contract, Baker and Taylor's shipments were delayed several months and duplicates were supplied. CARL Corporation of Colorado contested the contract with Ameritech, delaying the transition further.

In order to supply materials of local interest Baker and Taylor signed a partnership agreement with Booklines Hawaii, Ltd. to supply Hawaiiana and other titles relevant to Asia and the Pacific to the statewide library system. As early as October 1996, complaints began to mount against Baker and Taylor. Specific charges were: unrequested duplication of titles; inappropriate titles, such as *A Practical Guide to Lambs and Lambing Care* and 61 copies of Newt Gingrich's novel, *1945*; cheap books not worth the flat $20.94 per item assessed in the contract; too few reference materials; disregard for profiles provided by branch librarians; and inability to return unwanted titles. Library staff and patrons became increasingly vociferous in their complaints. Baker and Taylor presented a list of Performance Targets to the Board of Education Committee on Public Libraries.

Specific points of selection, acquisition reporting, cataloging, technical processing and distribution were addressed. For example, 90 percent of items purchased will circulate at least once during the first twelve months. Representatives from the Library Association of Hawaii testified before the

State Senate Committee on Government Operations and Housing on January 11, 1997 requesting that an immediate audit be performed on the library system paying particular attention to the Baker and Taylor and Dynix contracts. On January 16, 1997 Baker and Taylor presented to the Board of Education's Library Services Committee a detailed action plan stressing better communication with librarians. Concern over the situation in Hawaii began to mount within the library profession.

Early in January, 1997, the Alternatives in Print Task Force of the American Library Association's Social Responsibilities Roundtable created a Hawaii Working Group to study the performance of the Baker and Taylor outsourcing project. Patricia Wallace, a graduate student at Texas Woman's University's School of Library and Information Studies, was appointed to head the Working Group. On February 2, 1997, Senator Marshall Ige introduced Senate Bill 1370, which would prevent the board of education or the state librarian from entering into contractual agreements allowing outside firms to select books and other resources for the public library system. The Board of Education announced in a news conference on February 11, 1997, that it was establishing a Blue Ribbon Committee of library, business and government people to review and make recommendations on Baker and Taylor's performance through June 30, 1997.

At the same time Kane sent a letter to Arnie Wight of Baker and Taylor, itemising nine areas of concern: Standing orders, Hawaiiana, reference books, Library for Blind and Physically Handicapped materials, bestsellers, children's selections, award books, and response to library community profiles. At a news conference on June 6 the Committee recommended that Baker and Taylor's contract be terminated June 30, 1997 due to poor performance. The Attorney General's office would be consulted. On February 13, 1997 Senators Mike McCartney and Les Ihara introduced Senate Bill 538 requiring materials selection throughout the library system be performed by public service librarians exclusively.

After revision to remove the restriction against the State Librarian authorising outside book selection, adding a recommendation that book selection be handled by state employees, and removing the cancellation of current book selection contracts, the Committee on Ways and Means recommended passage of Senate Bill 538. On June 10, 1997, the Hawaii Government Employees Association filed a class action lawsuit against the Board of Education, the State Librarian, and Baker and Taylor, Inc. claiming unlawful privatisation of public services.

Specific consequences were itemised in the suit. On June 19, 1997, the Board of Education voted unanimously to terminate Baker and Taylor's 5-½ year, $11.2 million dollar contract.

The Attorney General would determine the specific timeframe and procedure. Kane sent a formal letter of cancellation on July 11, 1997. A ten-day extension was granted in which Baker and Taylor must supply 60,000 materials. On July 21, 1997 Kane sent a final letter of cancellation with a notice of non-acceptance of any subsequent materials shipped. On July 24, 1997 Arnie Wight from Baker and Taylor stated in a press release that they were victims of wrongful termination. He claimed that the alleged failures were a direct result of decisions made by the HSPLS staff. A formal suit was filed on November 10, 1997. At the same time, the Coalition for Improved Libraries issued a call for removal of Kane and assignment of new leadership, citing an 82 percent vote of "no confidence" in the current State Librarian. The State Board of Education voted 11 to 2 in favour of retaining Kane for six months at its July 25, 1997 meeting.

He was tasked with settling all remaining issues concerning the termination of Baker and Taylor's contract and developing a plan to address selection procedures in the future. In January 1998 the Hawaii state auditor issued a report stating concerns over the management of the library system. Redeployment of technical service personnel to public service did not improve customer service and assigning Baker and Taylor to book selection did not save money.

On February 20, 1998 the Board of Education voted seven to six to remove Bart Kane as State Librarian. On May 18, 1998 Kane announced that he was suing the Board of Education for wrongful termination. June 30, 1998 was Kane's last day as State Librarian. On July 23, 1999 the state of Hawaii settled their lawsuit with Baker and Taylor agreeing that $75,000 worth of books be selected by the library system.

The initial suit charged that $700,000 was sent to Baker and Taylor with no books received in return. On September 7, 1999 the Hawaii Government Employees Association won its suit over the privatisation of the state library system's book buying services.

Since book selection was customarily and historically provided by civil service employees, it is forbidden to be privatised. Baker and Taylor agreed to pay some of HGEA's legal fees. Outsourcing of book selection for the Hawaii State Public Library System was a daring experiment that failed due to a combination of circumstances.

It appears that Bart Kane did not seek sufficient input from library staff before making the outsourcing decision. Major changes already underway in the library system undoubtedly complicated the situation. Baker and Taylor apparently were not sufficiently prepared for the complexity of the task. From the enviable perspective of today, it appears that several improvements in planning could have lead to better results for the project. However, the resentment and skepticism resulting from the failed experiment render it extremely unlikely that the Hawaii Library System will attempt anything similar in the future.

THE FORT WORTH PUBLIC LIBRARY SYSTEM CASE

Historical Background

Since Fort Worth Public Library's inception in 1901, unit librarians have been responsible for materials selection. This changed in 1989 when an in-house task force on selection and ordering recommended adopting a centralised materials selection process as a means to free staff time for other duties and as a quality control measure. A collection development unit was created consisting of an Adult Materials Coordinator, a Children's Materials Coordinator, and three support staff.

The unit's title became the Materials Collection Development Unit (MCDU). Collection development staff selected new books from primary review journals for the systems then eleven agencies based on unit profiles. Despite centralisation, unit librarians remained responsible for selecting audio-visual materials, new materials not covered in primary review sources, foreign language materials, and duplicate/replacement titles. The changes made in selection in 1989 were not made with the intention of eventually going to outsourcing, but it did position the library to take that step when confronted with a fiscal crisis.

In the 1992/93 fiscal year massive budget cuts throughout the City of Fort Worth resulted in the reduction of library hours, staff and materials budget. The majority of branches went from three to two librarians, leaving only the Branch Manager and the Assistant Branch Manager/Children's Librarian. Taking on the responsibilities of Assistant Branch Manager, the Children's Librarians had little time to spend on materials selection. At this same time the Children's Materials Coordinator position was eliminated along with the MCDU's Clerk/Typist. Cutting support services staff was another method library administrators economised. The Catalogue Unit was cut from six positions to two. The Processing Unit went from nine staff members to five. Additionally, the Support Services Coordinator retired and that position was eliminated. The unit managers in Support Services, consisting of Acquisitions, Cataloging, Processing, the Delivery Team and the Clerical Pool, were trained in functioning as a selfdirected work team based on the principles of Total Quality Management.

It should be noted that in 1995 all of the units gained back some staff. The Catalogue Unit gained a half-time librarian, the Processing Unit added two clerical positions, and the MCDU gained a half-time librarian and a clerk, but not a Children's Material Coordinator. Outsourcing some support services functions was another way to reduce costs. Five outsourcing contracts were established in fiscal year 1992/93. The first was copy cataloging of direct orders and gifts. The second was for the provision of adult books including cataloging and processing services. A third contract was for the selection, cataloging and processing of bestsellers.

The fourth contract was for adult and juvenile audio-visual materials cataloging and processing, but not selection. The final contract was for selection, cataloging and processing of children's books. In 1995 both the copy cataloging and bestsellers contracts were discontinued when it was determined that staff could do the work more efficiently in-house. In Fall of 1999 the Assistant Library Director estimated how much it would cost to bring children's book selection and all cataloging and processing services back in house. She took into account the salary and fringe benefit costs to bring staffing back to the 1992/93 level.

Then she added the amount for processing supplies and OCLC fees. From that total she subtracted the amount currently paid for outsourced cataloging and processing services. Fort Worth Public Library has net savings of $212,825 due to outsourced services.

The decision to outsource book selection in fiscal year 1992/93 was made entirely for budgetary reasons. Selection of bestsellers was outsourced for two years, but discontinued. Administrators decided to outsource children's book selection after finding children's book collections to be more uniform from agency to agency with the major differences being in specific language and cultural needs.

Administrative staff wrote specifications for vendor selection of children's books to reflect the existing collection development policies. The selection criteria include review sources to be used for selecting books. Each unit also provides individual collection profiles. Profile information includes the book budget for the unit, a per item cost limit, a budget breakdown by Dewey classification number, demographic information, and a list of authors, illustrators and series titles to be supplied regardless of reviews. Unit profiles and budgets are reviewed and adjusted annually. Selection of children's audio-visual materials continues to be done in-house.

A collection development committee consisting of children's librarians was created to select media and identify books that were missed by the vendor or not reviewed in the journals stipulated in the specifications. Children's librarians remain responsible for identifying and ordering duplicate/replacement titles and are given their own budgets to do this. New children's books cannot be ordered until six months after the date of publication to avoid duplicating titles ordered by the vendor. Award winning books and books on lists such as the Texas Bluebonnet nominees are generally handled outside the vendor selection process.

The vendor also provides periodic reports of what materials have been selected for each unit. In the past eight fiscal years, three vendors for the children's materials contract have been used with varying degrees of success. One vendor lost the contract due to the inability to catalogue and processes the books according to specifications. Another vendor lost the contract due to extreme delays in getting the materials. Only one vendor has been able to keep the contract for more than one year and has had the contract for six of the last eight fiscal years.

Survey of System Children's Librarians

We surveyed staff to determine their perceptions of outsourced children's book selection. A structured survey instrument was used, the data was tabulated, and standard statistical software was used to produce frequency tables for each response. The sample was small consisting of 15 Children's Librarians and 3 Branch Managers who are former Children's Librarians for a total of 18 respondents.

All of the respondents have a Masters of Library Science degree and have a cumulative experience of over 155 years in the Fort Worth Public Library System. Eight respondents have more than 10 years experience each with the Library System. Eight also included narrative comments to the survey questions. The results of the survey indicate that timeliness of receiving materials, communication with the vendor, the ability to reject materials selections, meeting local needs, and the morale of the children's librarians are the biggest areas of concern. Over three-fourths of the respondents (77.8 per cent) found the receipt of books to be untimely.

This question resulted in the most written negative comments. One of the most frequent complaints being the six month waiting period before they can order a new book that may not have been ordered by the vendor's selector. Communication with the vendor elicited many negative comments as well. This issue is reflected in questions #5 and #9. A strong majority feels that they have little or no contact or input with the selector.

The narrative comments were somewhat contradictory with some saying they have annual contact with the vendors and others indicating no contact at all. They also expressed a desire for the ability to reject materials selected by the vendor.

Meeting the local needs of patrons and overall quality of the collection is another major area of concern and is reflected in the responses to questions #7, #10 and #13. Fifty five point six percent of the librarians believe that neighbourhood needs are not being met and 66.7 per cent believe that the quality of the collection has not improved due to outsourcing. One particularly insightful comment was "Keeping the same vendor over a period of years is important in building trust and understanding of libraries' needs, but is difficult in the current system of low bid wins. Changing out materials selectors several years running is ruinous to a collection as well as to morale." Someone also noted that "It is difficult to work on a 5 year plan of updating and filling in missing information when tied to vendor selection."

There is also a lack of confidence (55.6 per cent) in the ability of profiles to meet unit needs. Morale also seems to be an issue as stated in Question #15 with 66.6 per cent saying that outsourcing has not improved morale of the children's librarians. Only one written comment was made on this particular question, but when all the comments are reviewed there are definite morale concerns reflected elsewhere. On the more positive side, 61.1 per cent found that outsourcing allows more time for programming, 83.4 per cent feel that they are given time at work to keep up with new publications Question #2), and 55.5 per cent felt that outsourcing did not limit their ability to provide good reader's advisory.

Additionally, 44.4 per cent feel that working in a system that outsources children's books selection will not hurt their future marketability in the workforce, while 33.3 per cent expressed no opinion on this issue. Sixty-six point seven percent feel that the vendor has a commitment to the quality of the collection. There is a less clear majority as to whether there is an effective procedure in place for identifying and ordering materials not selected by the vendor. Fifty percent (50 per cent) strongly agreed or agreed with the statement while 36.4 per cent disagreed or strongly disagreed (16.7 per cent had no opinion).

A strong majority (77.8 per cent) feels that the selection of children's books by an inhouse coordinator would be more responsive than outsourcing. As for community awareness, 66.7 per cent feel that patrons are unaware that children's book selection is outsourced. Additionally, 55.6 per cent feel that outsourcing does not make a positive statement to the community about the library's commitment to children's services.

Thirty eight point nine percent (38.9 per cent) have no opinion on this question. Some of the written comments reflect a willingness to work with the system and offered constructive suggestions that bear consideration. One suggestion was that the vendor 's selectors make semi-annual phone calls to each children's librarian for input. This would be in addition to on-site meetings with the selector. Another suggestion is that the vendor provide selection lists for the children's librarians to mark for purchase. The results of this survey would serve as a good foundation to work from if Fort Worth Public Library decides to evaluate the outsourcing of children's book selection.

Study of Books Received – Methodology

Vendor selection of children's materials is controversial among staff, but its effectiveness has not been studied in depth. Historically, the contract has been monitored by checking that the correct discounts have been applied. There has not been a consistent method in place that monitors the timeliness of the materials received. Naturally, there are times when this is obvious. For example, one year the contract started with a new vendor in late November and virtually no children's materials were received until the end of the following April. Not surprisingly, this vendor lost the contract. It was decided that timeliness would be an appropriate issue to target in the context of this study.

We looked at both adult and children's materials to see if it is more timely to do selection in-house or to have materials selected by a vendor. We randomly chose 300 titles, 150 adult titles and 150 children's titles, that were ordered and received in the 1998/99 fiscal year to compare the length of time it took to receive the materials. It is worthy to note that both contracts are held by the same vendor. It should also be noted that the vendor both catalogs and processes the books so this is also a factor in the length of time it takes to receive them. Adult materials are selected and ordered by in-house staff using an automated acquisitions system.

Using this database, we were able to obtain the date ordered and the date received for each title. We then used *Book Review Index* to see when each title was reviewed in *Booklist, Library Journal, Publisher's Weekly* and *Kirkus*. Then we went to Amazon.com and Barnes and Noble online to determine the date of publication. Frequently, these databases only listed a month and a year of publication and not a specific date. For quantification purposes, we gave each a publication date of the 15th for the given month when the exact date was not provided. Thus, the resulting figures are not precise, but do provide comparative data. As the children's books were vendor-selected, we did not have access to when the materials were ordered by the vendor. What we did instead was look at when the titles were reviewed, the publication dates and the date received at the library.

Results - Adult Books

Fifty-five percent of the 150 adult titles studied were ordered prior to or in the week of publication. These titles were ordered an average of 5.23 weeks prior to the publication date. It took an average of 6.3 weeks after the date of publication to receive the cataloged and processed materials. The remaining 45 per cent of the adult titles surveyed were ordered after the date of publication. These titles were ordered an average of 6.43 weeks after publication.

It took an average of 8.6 weeks after the order date to receive these materials. The total average to receive all adult books was 7.35 weeks to receive new materials. There are many factors that can account for this length of time to receive materials. In FY 1998/99, the Acquisitions Unit did not have the capability to send purchase orders electronically, so they were mailed to the vendor.

Then the vendor has to input these orders once received. Once the books are in hand, they are cataloged and processed before shipping them out. The vendor sends out large shipments weekly rather than as materials are ready. All these factors must be taken into account when looking at this 7.35 weeks. It should be noted that none of these 150 titles are bestsellers which are handled on a separate contract. Orders for bestsellers are phoned in and usually received within 48 hours of release.

Results - Children's Books

As with the adult materials, 150 vendor selected children's titles were chosen randomly from FY 1998/99. Two of these titles were eliminated from the sample due to inability to find valid information. Thus, this sample actually consists of 148 titles. The average time to receive juvenile titles from the date of publication was 9.84 weeks. This time needs to be examined more closely. Due to the way the City's fiscal year is run, the vendor is told to have all funds encumbered by the end of June. Money is not available again until October or November when the new budget is approved. While the selector continues to identify titles for purchase between July and November, the orders are not released until the new budget is in place.

This resulting gap affects the availability of materials and the timeliness in receiving them. When we removed the figures for the 70 titles in the sample that were published between July and November 1998, the time to receive materials after publication drops to an average of 6.6 weeks. Another major difference found between the adult materials and children's materials is the fact that 78 per cent of the adult books sampled were reviewed prior to publication whereas only 27 per cent of the children's titles were reviewed prior to publication. This factor alone would account for children's materials taking longer to receive after publication since selection is largely predicated on the published reviews.

The Vendor's Selector's Perspective

In order to provide an additional perspective, we took the opportunity to talk to the individual who currently selects children's books for Fort Worth Public Library. There are factors that the selector cannot control, predominantly the budgetary cycle that creates a major gap in ordering. The selector commented that the easy part of her job is determining which titles are worthy of purchase. The hard and time-consuming part involves determining which agencies are to get which titles. She indicated that Fort Worth Public Library is unusual in that the vendor selector does it all. Most libraries that use selection services prefer to be provided with a recommended list of titles with reviews to select from. Generally, the children's librarians are satisfied with the materials selected for the library system.

It is the timeliness of the receipt of materials that is the major bone of contention. The current selector's credentials indicate an expertise that would be difficult to match within the library system, even in a materials coordinator position. She is an editor for the *Elementary School Library Collection* and is able to attend workshops and conferences that would be outside the typical children's librarian's realm. Her position also gives her access to review and galley copies. Although the contract specifies selecting from *School Library Journal, Booklist, Publisher's Weekly* and *Kirkus*, her scope is much broader than just these journals and she will select materials outside of these sources. Having worked with Fort Worth Public Library children's librarians for a number of years, she has established a rapport with them and seems genuinely interested in maintaining a quality children's collection for Fort Worth. Unfortunately, she has a small staff so when illness and family problems occur her work is just as likely suffer as it would if selection were being done in-house.

Bringing Children's Book Selection Back In-House

What would it take to bring selection of children's books back in-house? Assuming that the library continues to outsource cataloging and processing services, the very minimum additional staff needed would be a Children's Materials Coordinator to do the selecting and an additional clerk/typist to input and receive the orders. This would cost the library a minimum of $59,000 in salaries alone, not including fringe benefits.

It is difficult to determine how much the library spends for vendor selection services as it is factored into the book discounts. Currently, the vendor gives the library a 35 per cent discount for children's trade books. To get these same books from another source, the library would typically receive a 40 per cent discount. Thus, it can be assumed that the vendor is charging the library 5 per cent for selection services. In fiscal year 98/99, the vendor had a $200,000 contract for children's books. Five percent of this amount would be $10,000. This would not begin to cover the cost of additional staff. Even if the library could find the money, a major stumbling block would be the City's policy that permits staff to be added only if a new service is offered. Children's book selection would not be considered a new service. So, what are Fort Worth's options? The system is not perfect, but it is working. Tightening up the contract specifications and the monitoring of the contract could possibly improve the timeliness of children's books. For the adult materials, sending orders electronically to the vendor should speed up the process by eliminating mailing time and inputting data by vendor staff.

The major stumbling block for children's materials appears to be the gap in the ordering and budget cycles. Another problem seems to be a lack of a single spokesperson for the Children's Librarians. The Materials Coordinator's duties are primarily concerned with adult materials and only deals with children's materials peripherally. Similarly, the Head of the Central Library's Youth Center is generally not responsible for children's services throughout the system. Other than infrequent on-site visits with the vendor's selector, the Children's Librarians do not have much contact with her and are discouraged from contacting her directly. Concerns are reported to the vendor selector through the Materials Coordinator.

If Fort Worth Public Library wanted to bring children's book selection back in-house it would take some creative juggling of existing staff and their duties. One question to ask would be "Is the outsourcing of selection services that different from in-house centralised materials selection?" Both use profiles to determine which agencies get what materials. The main concerns seem to be timeliness and ease of communication. Results from the study of the time to receive adult and children's books show that ordering in-house was not all that much more timely than having a selector do it. Given that these materials arrive cataloged and processed, we do not know how much of that time accounts for cataloging and processing time. It appears that quality selection, whether done in-house or by a vendor, is a time-consuming process.

OUTSOURCING OF MANAGEMENT

Contracting out to manage an entire library or library system is the most extreme case of outsourcing. It is this type of contracting that has been most commonly labeled "privatisation," although technically management is no more "core" to librarianship than selection or cataloging, and perhaps it could be argued that it is even less.

Nevertheless, recent decisions by some communities to contract with corporations to manage the provision of library services have resulted in considerable consternation within the profession. In fact, management of library services by outside entities is a practice with quite a long history. Many firms in the corporate sector have secured essential information services by contracting with individuals, municipal libraries, or other corporations. Many communities have secured public library services for their citizens by contracting with other governmental entities—the county or the neighbouring community, for example—or with local not-for-profit organisations, like women's clubs or fraternal service organisations. Not since the demise of the social library after the development of publicly funded libraries in nineteenth century, however, have communities contracted with for-profit corporations to provide library services. This study focuses on two very different forms of contracting for the management of library services.

The first, the National Aeronautics and Space Administration, is a large and diverse federal government agency. While NASA's approach to securing library and information services is an extremely interesting and provocative example, circumstances of NASA's operation are unique, and very little of the

NASA outsourcing experience appears relevant to the general library situation. More central to the concerns of the library profession is the case of Riverside County, California. The decision of Riverside County in 1997 to contract with Library Systems and Services, Inc. caused many expressions of dismay within the library profession. This contract, together with the Hawaii Baker and Taylor contract, was the proximate cause for the establishment of the ALA Task Force on Outsourcing and Privatisation.

THE NATIONAL AERONAUTICS AND SPACE ADMINISTRATION CASE

In order to understand how outsourcing has impacted the governance, staff development and cooperative endeavors of American libraries, it is necessary to review the rare libraries that have always been outsourced, or outsourced for decades, for comparison. National Aeronautics and Space Administration (NASA) Scientific and Technical Information Administration libraries were selected for study because they are representative of those libraries that been contracted out for all, or almost all, of their history. NASA's policy of contracting for library services began before the Office of Management and Budget concluded in 1983 that federal library services qualified for privatisation.

After that, other federal libraries, including those in the system of the Environmental Protection Agency, the National Oceanic and Atmospheric Administration, Department of Energy, Department of Labour, the Bureau of the Census, and the Department of Housing and Urban Development have been contracted out to the private sector.

NASA History

NASA was created by the National Aeronautics and Space Act in 1958 and started with employees and facilities from the old National Advisory Committee for Aeronautics. Today, NASA consists of NASA headquarters, nine centers, the Jet Propulsion Laboratory, and several installations and offices in the United States and abroad. In 1958, the newly formed space agency's mandate from the Eisenhower administration was to lead the civil space effort. The agency's charter gave it broad latitude to contribute to the nation's general welfare and security and to preserve its role as a leader in aeronautical and space science and technology.

The agency was able to efficiently contract for labour and services, because in 1959, the General Services Administration authorised use of the Armed Services Procurement Regulations of 1947. This exempted NASA from the government policy of awarding contracts to the lowest bidder. This policy of contracting has continued and is supported by the Office of Management and Budget's *OMB Circular A-76 Transmittal Memorandum 20* which states that the government should not compete with its citizens. It requires that all government agencies contract "non-governmental" activities to the private sector. The Cold War and the flight of the Sputnik satellite fueled the agency's growth. President Kennedy challenged the nation in 1961 to send a man to the moon and return him safely, and the President and the Congress provided NASA with the funds to do so.

As a consequence of the rapid growth and preference for contract services, the agency's civil service personnel grew by a factor of three, while contract employees increased by a factor of ten. Throughout NASA's history, between 80 and 90 percent of its budget has been spent on goods and services provided through contracts. Because of its reliance upon contracting, the agency has developed efficient methods of soliciting and managing contracts. In 1993, NASA developed Acquisition Internet Service (NAIS), a web based electronic procurement information system for midrange contracts, to provide procurement information for industry and small business and to reduce contract administration costs.

The agency estimates that 80 to 90 percent of NASA's contract awards are in the midrange category. NASA employees at 10 field centers conduct the entire process of contract review and selections across the Internet. NASA has relied upon clearly written contracts and a corps of professional employees deeply involved in technical details to guide the work of NASA contractors. As the emphasis of who performed the scientific research for NASA changed, the original NASA scientists became contract administers.

In 1990, NASA asked for a study to be conducted on the consequences of contracting out the bulk of its research and development work. The National Academy of Public Administration's study made two significant suggestions. The first was that the government should not contract out decisions on what work is to be done, what objectives are to be set, what the results are expected to be, and the evaluation of the work. The second was that contracting out led to erosion of strength of an important NASA asset—a corps of experienced scientists and engineers. A subsequent change in contracting methodology has only increased the problem. Three years ago, NASA changed from contracts that specified a level of effort to be provided, a system requiring extensive monitoring, to performance-based contracting which monitors the contractor's activity. Performance-based contracting can save the government money because it does not require as many professional management staff for monitoring.

A concern has been expressed that skilled NASA engineers will leave to take private sector jobs, and the agency will lose its ability to monitor contracts. This loss of experienced personnel could also happen in other parts of NASA, as employees leave for other jobs or choose to retire. The agency has reduced its civil service staff by over 5,000 employees since 1993, and total employment will continue to decrease by 1,500 to 2,000 employees by 2002.

NASA Libraries

For NASA, and its libraries, contracting offered attractive advantages to supervisors and executives. NASA was able to acquire a high-quality labour force because contractors were not limited to government pay scales, could recruit employees more quickly than could be recruited in accordance with civil service rules, and could remove unsatisfactory performance employees from their positions.

Contract workers would have helped NASA administrators maximize the number of authorised workers in engineer, scientist, and technician classifications against employment ceilings. NASA's total employment has declined from 34,167 in 1967 to 19,259 in 1997, but the percentage of employees classified in engineering or technician positions has declined at a far lower rate. Herbert S. White, NASA Scientific and Technical Information Administration Executive Director from 1964 until 1968, has written about additional reasons for organisations in general to outsource library services.

The first is that it is cost effective to contract to an organisation that has expertise in specialised tasks and second, it is an effective way to reduce backlogs and eliminate repetitive and routine operations. Overall supervision of NASA libraries is by the Scientific and Technical Information Division that acquires, processes, archives, announces and disseminates information for the scientific community.

However, despite their common mission, NASA centers and facilities do not have a common organisational culture. This is because NASA combined three laboratories and two field stations from the 43 year old NACA, and rapidly added additional centers, each with its own history and traditions.

Instead of creating a uniform culture, the centers have been described as behaving like rival universities with their own set of contractors, long range plans, and interests. Since NASA libraries are governed by the center they serve, they also vary widely in methods of governance, population served, consortia participation, staffing, and collections.

The differences are evident in the following comparisons:

- Staffing Models Some libraries, such as Goddard Space Flight Center, have both civil service and contract employees, while others, such as Johnson Space Center Scientific and Technical Information Center, are entirely contracted out, with a NASA librarian serving as a technical monitor.
- Identity Not all libraries identify themselves as NASA. At least one library identified as NASA on the Headquarters web page maintained that it was part of another institution. The library and technical information center of the Jet Propulsion Laboratory, a contract installation operated for NASA but owned by the California Institute

of Technology, considers itself as an Institute/JPL library, and not a NASA library.

- Population Served They serve different populations. NASA Headquarters Library, founded in 1958, serves NASA and contract employees and permits public use of the reading room. In addition to serving contract and NASA employees, two others offer limited access to the public, and another library allows "qualified researchers" to visit.
- Archiving Records Johnson Space Center Scientific and Technical Center's records are archived at Fondren Library of Rice University in Houston, Texas. Sherikon Space Systems, Inc. archives records for the Jet Propulsion Laboratory library and technical information center offsite.
- Participation in consortia and networks NASA libraries participate in a variety of networks, but participation is also individual. Ten are members of Online Computer Library Center, Inc., six are members of PLC, four are members of the NASA Library Network, and one is a member of the AMIGOS group.

The agency's struggle against cultural change and centralisation has resulted in an aggregate of independent libraries with many contractors. There are several personnel management contractors for NASA libraries. The library staffing model with both civil service and contract employees has the potential of creating two separate and unequal pay and benefit schedules for employees performing similar work. Federal employees have established salary tiers, union representation, grievance procedures and perquisites such as time off for blood donations, while contract librarians do not have job security or perquisites. The Office of Management and Personnel listed 10 NASA librarians in 1997. And, while individual salaries are unknown, the 1997 biennial report on federal white collar employment shows that the government-wide average salary for librarians in Occupational Code and Title GS-1410 Librarian was $53,895.

Survey of Library Staff

A modified version of the survey instrument used by the research team that visited the Riverside, California County Library System was used to collect information about the NASA libraries. Basic data from the directory entry for each library that was found in the *American Library Directory, 1998-1999* was used for information about publications holdings, librarian and library assistant staffing, and to identify the supervisor or head librarian at each library. Each supervisor or head librarian was contacted by telephone and asked to participate in the survey. The survey form was sent by electronic mail to facilitate completion and return of responses. All but two of the responding libraries indicated that the questionnaire would have to be submitted to a higher level administrator for permission to complete and return the questionnaire. Only two responses were received to the questionnaire. The low response rate does not permit the survey data to be used or reported with confidence that the answers are representative of all NASA libraries and their staffs.

The evidence we gathered seem to support the following conclusions:

- Contract employment is likely to increase as government officials conduct more commercial activity reviews to fulfill mandates of the Office of Management and Budget's *OMB Circular A-76 Transmittal Memorandum 20*, which states that federal agencies should review activities that are performed by federal employees that are not inherently governmental and to contract with the private sector for the performance of such an activity.
- NASA has always contracted out services, supplies and projects. Thus they are not experiencing the problems that public libraries encounter as they begin to negotiate and administer contracts for the first time.
- Each NASA library has responded to its unique environment, and as a consequence, has differing methods of governance, staffing models, archiving, and participation in consortia and networks.
- The research team found that data and published research on NASA's libraries are extremely limited and suggest that further research should be conducted on the NASA library system. In addition, due to the small number of NASA libraries and librarians, comparisons should be made with other federal libraries for statistical significance.

THE RIVERSIDE COUNTY LIBRARY SYSTEM CASE

In June 1997 Riverside County, California, entered into a contract to with Library Systems and Services LLC (LSSI) to provide County library services. This event was widely reported in the library literature and generally decried as the first major instance of "privatisation" of public library services. Because the Riverside County situation is the first, largest, most visible and apparently most controversial incidence of outsourcing an entire library system, we deemed it important to examine the Riverside County Library System (RCLS) carefully, including not only a comprehensive literature review, but also a site visit.

Historical Background

When Riverside County established public library service in 1911, it opted to take advantage of a provision of the 1911 California County Library law to contract with the city of Riverside for library services. The contract between the two public entities called for the city library director to become the county librarian and the city's board of library trustees to become the county library's policy making board. County officials had little more to do than to hand over county funds designated for libraries to the City of Riverside to run the newly developed Riverside county libraries. Library services for Riverside County were provided under extensions of this agreement with the city of Riverside from 1911 until 1997.

In 1965, Riverside County Libraries was reorganised as a taxing district, and a dedicated property tax was established to fund the County Library. The city of Riverside chose not to join the county system, except as its contracted administrator. The city chose, instead, to retain the municipal library as a separate system since it could tax its citizens at a higher rate. Several other cities within Riverside County also chose to follow the city of Riverside's lead and create their own municipal libraries.

The county library system became known as the Riverside City and County Public Library in 1971. California's Proposition 13 was passed in 1978. This proposition set limits on the amount of property tax increases. Riverside City and County Public Library administration reacted to the cutbacks from Proposition 13 by closing seven small branches in the less populated areas of the county. Subsequently the county supervisors forced the library system to reopen the branches and distribute funds more evenly between both the highly populated and less populated areas of the county.

This was among the first of many contentious incidents that would later lead to the dissolving of the contractual relationship between the City of Riverside and Riverside County. Over the next ten years the population of Riverside County grew 76 percent.

The county and the Riverside City and County Public Library were hard pressed to keep up with the demands for public and library services placed upon them by the growth. The population, however, brought with it more funding.

The library needed to expand and update its facilities. In 1987, Moreno Valley Library became the first new regional facility built to accommodate the growth taking place within the county. Under the leadership of Linda M. Wood, who was the director during this period, the Riverside City and County Public Library was awarded LCSA grants and private funding for expansion. She also began construction on a new administration center, a move that became a severe drain on resources in the short term. Two more incidents occurred during the early 1990's that would spell the end of the Riverside City and County Public Library and force Riverside County officials to look elsewhere for administration and management services for the library.

In 1993, March Air Force Base closed. This closing caused the loss of military and civilian jobs that were a mainstay of the tax base in Riverside County. Property values plummeted as a result of the base closing bringing to an end the prosperity of the previous decade. As if this economic calamity were not enough, the California legislature passed the Educational Revenue Augmentation Fund in the same year. This act caused millions of dollars to be drawn from California counties, cities, and special districts to fund the state's failing educational systems.

The crisis in funding resulted in reduced library hours and services, layoffs, and several years when expenditures for materials in the 26 libraries were nearly zero. For three years running nearly all library staff received annual layoff notices, and though the cutbacks each time were less severe than announced, a number of library employees did in fact lose their jobs. Several branches became almost totally dependent on volunteers to be able to open their doors.

Some of the surrounding cities, sensing the difficulties, chose to withdraw from the county's library district, further depleting the library's funds. Public criticism of the new, costly library administrative center added to the woes of the beleaguered library system. Control of the meagre available funds became a critical political issue, one with significant emotional overtones. Lack of funding focussed attention on perceived inadequacies and misplaced priorities in the city's management of the county libraries. The issue was soon perceived by county elected officials, their constituents, and county staff as a lack of local control over funding and policy for county libraries. Disputes between the city and county culminated in the City announcing that it would no longer manage the libraries.

The Riverside City and County Public Library was dissolved in December 1996. County officials were faced with the need to find a new way to provide library services for the county.

Having little knowledge of the organisation of the library system and no expertise in running libraries, county officials determined to seek a new contractor to manage the county library system. A Request for Proposals was developed with help from key staff of the Riverside County Free Library System and the aid of Dallas Y. Shaffer, a consultant provided by the California State Library. In March 1997 Riverside County issued a "Request for Proposals for Administration and Operation of the Riverside County Free Library System." The RFP stipulated the funding that was available, and the scope of services desired.

Three entities responded to the RFP with proposals: the Riverside County Office of Education, the San Bernadino County Library, and Library Systems and Services (LSSI). After a thorough review of the three proposals, county officials selected LSSI as the best available alternative. Library service, under the management of LSSI, began on July 1, 1997.

In April 1998, LSSI issued an Assessment Report of the Riverside County Library System. The report focused on the improvements of the first year of library service provided by LSSI, and recommendations for the future. The management contract was renewed in 1998 and again in 1999. The details of the contract have varied slightly each year, but its essentials remain the same. The performance requirements focus on hours of service, staffing levels, and the materials budget. In the spring of 1999 the County Librarian commissioned an analysis of LSSI's Riverside County operations by an independent consultant, Ruth Metz, who reported that LSSI was meeting its contractual obligations in managing the libraries.

On-site Review of RCLS

In March, 2000, a three person site visit team spent three days in Riverside County, interviewing County officials, LSSI staff, and library users. We gathered data by means of structured questionnaire instruments. We also visited the Moreno Valley Public Library, a municipal library in Riverside County that is not a member of the RCLS, in order to ascertain what factors induced Moreno Valley to opt out of the system, and to determine how the RCLS is viewed by other libraries in the county. During our visit we received full and complete cooperation and support from both county and LSSI representatives. We were allowed to visit any location we chose, and to interview any individual we wanted.

LSSI and County officials encouraged LSSI staff to speak with us openly and to respond to our questions with candor. The site review team met with Deputy County Executive Officer Tom DeSantis and County Librarian Gary Christmas. DeSantis is the County Official who oversaw the RFP and contract negotiations throughout the period under review, and is perhaps the single person most responsible for the County's decision to outsource the management of the RCLS. Christmas is the sole library professional employed by the County of Riverside, and is responsible for overseeing the contract with LSSI and ensuring that the terms of the contract are met.

DeSantis offered a narrative description of the history of the RCLS contract. He emphasised the difficult and deteriorating relationship between the County and the City of Riverside in the mid-1990s. He stressed the difficulties in funding government operations, and especially a library district, under California's evolving tax code.

He pointed out that, as the population of the county increased while funding for library services deteriorated, it became clear to the elected officials of the County that they had no control over funding and policy decisions for the county library system. A city board made policy for the county. Moreover, under the terms of the contract, the city of Riverside charged a ten percent overhead assessment. In 1996 the county conducted an internal audit of library operations, and recommended that the county Board of Supervisors wrest control over the county library system away from the city. The city did not respond well to a proposed change in the nature of the relationship, and ultimately chose to walk away from it.

The decision to seek another vendor was thus not ultimately a funding issue, but rather a matter of structure, policy and governance. In assessing the three proposals received in response to the RFP, DeSantis noted that San Bernadino County utilised less qualified staff in its operations, and Riverside wanted to keep the professional staff already in place if at all possible. He also admitted that there were some political reservations about turning over library operations to a neighbouring county.

The proposal from the Riverside County Board of Education offered less service for the funds available. The proposal from LSSI, on the other hand, seemed to offer some creative approaches to managing services, and considerably more accountability than had been the case with the city of Riverside. LSSI was the unanimous choice of the county staff, and the contract was approved by an overwhelming majority of the Board of Supervisors. The period from January through June 1997, witnessed substantial uncertainty among the county library staff.

The city of Riverside "demonised" the county, resulting in substantial discomfort among the staff. County officials were prohibited by the city from directly contacting library staff, who were actually city employees. After selecting the LSSI proposal, the county negotiated a contract with the vendor. The contract firmly established that Riverside County would retain full governance of the library system, and LSSI staff would carry out policies established by the county officials. The contract ensured that the County would have final authority in the employment of key personnel, and established Zone Advisory Boards, citizens panels that would assist in developing policy in three management zones.

The county appointed as its sole library employee a county librarian who would serve as its in-house expert and monitor the contract. The contract specifies performance benchmarks in terms of hours of service, staffing, and collection development.

The county was able to achieve much of what it sought in terms of staff salaries and benefits. There ensued a difficult period of transition, in which LSSI sought with some success to assure county library staff that their jobs were secure.

Although some employees decided to remain with the city of Riverside, or to seek employment elsewhere, virtually all former city employees who wished to transfer to LSSI and continue to work in county libraries were given jobs at the same rate of pay. Several staff who had earlier been laid off were rehired. Branch hours of service were immediately increased, and staffing was increased from 67.09 FTE to 117.26 FTE. Funding for these improvements in services and staffing was made possible by the elimination of substantial administrative overhead built in to the management of the libraries by the City of Riverside.

In addition, LSSI trimmed the managerial staff, which under the city there had risen to twenty, down to only five. The controversial library administrative center was abandoned to other county uses. The county has been extremely satisfied with the services provided by LSSI. They have renewed the contract twice with only minor changes.

When asked what his advice would be to other public officials who might consider outsourcing management of a library system, DeSantis unhesitatingly offered these four suggestions.

- It is imperative to keep policy control with the elected public officials and representatives of the public;
- It is equally important to have your own in-house expert, a qualified professional, to manage the contract and oversee vendor performance;
- The contract must specify outcomes that are quantitatively measurable;
- Choose your service provider carefully; be certain they have the experience and qualifications to deliver on their commitments.

Further discussion with County Librarian Gary Christmas reaffirmed much of what DeSantis had described. Christmas offered more details, and more of a professional's perspective, but with essentially the same bottom line. Christmas emphasised again that LSSI does not set library policy; the county Board of Supervisors does that, with the advice of the Zone Advisory Boards. As an example, Christmas cited the RCLS policy on filtering Internet access. The Board decided to install filtering software on some of the public access workstations in some library branches, and LSSI implemented the policy. As County Librarian, he is involved in hiring decisions for the zone and branch managers. The Board scrutinises the budget, sets policies, and sees every contract. Christmas personally reviews book orders and has final say on all collection development decisions.

Christmas emphasised that increased services under LSSI come from their lean operation and organisational efficiency. The site review team also met with Gordon Conable, LSSI's Director of West Coast Operations, and the *de facto* project manager for the Riverside contract.

Conable stressed that, in his view, the RCLS contract did not constitute "privatisation" for two reasons:

1. The assets all belong to the county. While LSSI employees may purchase books or paperclips with county funds, the resulting materials are property of the county. "It's not our library—it's the county's" Conable says.

2. The library board makes policy decisions. LSSI is merely the contractor that carries out board policy.

Conable stressed that, under the contract with LSSI, the county has not saved any money. "We haven't contracted with anyone yet by selling ourselves as costing less," he pointed out. Instead, the county has decided how much it wanted to spend on library services, and asked LSSI what they could do with it. The LSSI proposal offered more services for the money. Conable suggested that improved hours of service and staffing have resulted from LSSI being able to run the system with less overhead.

Conable commented that the arrangement in Riverside would not work everywhere. He claimed that the strength of LSSI was its ability to "localise" and "customise." "We offer viable alternative with a level of accountability that is strong—we have a contract that could be terminated," he observed. Conable suggested that LSSI's potential future growth would be in communities that were looking for more local control and accountability.

While in Riverside County the site review team also visited nine of the 24 branches of the RCLS. At each location the team interviewed staff (including the branch manager when possible) and library users. We employed structured interview instruments customised for staff, branch managers, and library users. We also took the opportunity to briefly survey the facilities and collections at each site visited. Although all the facilities we visited were adequately maintained and furnished, they varied significantly in size and adequacy for the populations served.

The facilities ranged from renovated storefronts to magnificent new buildings, and included one joint-use facility. Although we made no effort to provide a quantitative analysis of collections, it was readily apparent that these too varied considerably from one community to the next. The primary cause for this variation in facility and collection adequacy appears to be the amount of local funding that is contributed to enhance the basic funding provided by the county. In some wealthy communities, that amount is apparently substantial; in other less affluent communities, there is little additional funding. Finally, while in Riverside County we also visited the Moreno Valley Public Library and interviewed its director, Cynthia Pirtle, and key staff. Moreno Valley is one of the largest and fastest growing municipalities in Riverside County, and one of the libraries that withdrew from the RCLS. We wanted to ascertain why Moreno Valley left the system, what the perception of the RCLS was in a nearby public library, and what issues (if any) might remain that were relevant to the study.

Survey Responses

We interviewed staff to assess their perception of changes in library services and management following LSSI's assumption of the management role.

We used a structured interview instrument, we tabulated the data and, using standard statistical software, produced frequency tables for each response. The total number of staff interviewed was small (N=23), and we therefore hesitate to make generalisations. But some strong indications do emerge from this small sample. On the whole, RCLS staff is satisfied with conditions working for LSSI.

More than eighty-two percent thought that their current salary was satisfactory and comparable to others in the area. Seventy-eight per cent said they had received a salary increase since they started working for LSSI. Seventy-three percent thought that they had adequate opportunities for continuing education.

Ninety-five percent found their branch manager approachable and open to their ideas. Eighty-two percent felt that the collection in their library had improved since LSSI took over, and seventy-eight percent felt that the hours of service at their library were good for the community they served. Some areas of concern also emerge. Forty-three percent expressed no opinion about their benefits, while more than a quarter each thought that their benefits were better or worse, respectively, than they had been before.

Clearly there are some concerns that the benefits they had as public employees were better than those they now had as corporate employees. Only fifty six percent thought that their work schedule enabled them to get their work done in a professional manner; apparently a substantial minority have concerns about there being more work to do than they can manage. And forty-three percent of those surveyed clearly felt that funds for collections were inadequate to address community needs, while another thirteen percent had no opinion. Newer staff hired by LSSI generally appear to be paid less than staff who had been employees of the City of Riverside.

There are unanswered questions about staff turnover, though it appears to be significant among newer employees. This raises questions about the potential impact on compensation in other libraries in the region if arrangements like this were to become commonplace. It is not clear, however, that either of these issues is related to LSSI's management of the library system. In most organisations newer staff receive less remuneration than the former City of Riverside employees, who are now the senior staff in RCLS. It is not clear that turnover among the newer employees is any greater than in other libraries of comparable size. In its operation of RCLS, LSSI has demonstrated a willingness to hire staff without professional qualifications to perform function that had previously been performed by professional librarians.

It must be noted, however, that this is not merely a local trend in Riverside. There is ongoing discussion in the library profession at large about appropriate staffing levels for various library functions, and there appears to be a trend to focus professional librarians on truly professional tasks while increasing the number of paraprofessionals to carry out work that can be rendered routine.

Non-traditional staffing patterns, instigated in part by increasing competition for a shrinking pool of librarians, appears to be a national trend. We also interviewed library users at nine branch locations. We used a structured interview instrument, we tabulated the data and, using standard statistical software, produced frequency tables for each response. The total number of patrons interviewed was small (N=74), and generalisations from such a small sample should be made with caution. Nevertheless, some strong patterns do emerge.

On the whole, the citizens of Riverside County who use the libraries there are generally satisfied with their library services. Sixty-three percent think that library services have definitely improved in the past three years. Ninety percent think the staff is very helpful. Eighty-one percent think that staff is readily available to help, while seventy-three percent feels they don't have to wait to check out materials. More than sixty-eight percent get what they need when they come to the library, and seventy-three percent are satisfied with the results of known-item searches. Almost two-thirds of the library users are satisfied with the hours the library is open. On the other hand, only forty-three percent of the users find the library's OPAC easy to use, while an equal number have no opinion.

This suggests that the OPAC is a problem, and that many users simply avoid it and go to the librarian for help in finding things. In fairness it should be pointed out that the OPAC is a legacy system, inherited by LSSI, and that the corporation has significantly upgraded the system at its own expense. Almost a third of those surveyed had no opinion about the availability of computers in the library, while almost another third felt that they had to wait too long to get access to a computer. There was similar lack of consensus about the quality of the reference collection available.

The instrument we used did not include a question about the public awareness about the outsourcing of library management in Riverside County. It became clear, however, in the course of our investigations, that few people were aware of it or concerned about it. Indeed, many library users seemed even unaware that their community library was part of the county systems, perceiving instead that it was an operation of their own community. County officials indicated that they were pleased that the change had gone essentially unnoticed, and saw no reason to make any effort to inform the public about the change. In short, both staff and patrons seem to agree that, in general, library services are improving, but that more money for collections is needed. Surprisingly, both groups seem to think that the hours of service are adequate.

Findings

The overall condition of the libraries in Riverside County continues to be poor, but most of this is due to the effects of California's maze of restrictive tax measures rather than any effect of privatisation of library management. Funding levels for Riverside County libraries remain at desperately low levels, barely more than a third of the national average on a per capita basis. Materials budgets have increased each year, rising from $180,000 in the first year of the contract to a projected $700,000 in 2000-01. Nevertheless, they are still inadequate to maintain the branch library collections, which are in the main too small for the populations they are intended to serve, and are generally old and worn.

The few branches whose collection appears in better condition have clearly benefited from infusions of additional local funds. None of this can improve significantly until a larger source of revenue can be found. Riverside County has pinned its hopes for overall improvements in funding for library services on a package of impact fees that will provide significant revenues as long as the current growth boom continues. Two cities in Riverside County have withdrawn from the county library system since LSSI assumed management control of the system. Both withdrawals were underway before LSSI was selected to manage the library system, and there is no evidence that the withdrawals were in any way a result of privatisation. An interview with the three top staff at Moreno Valley indicated that the motivation for the withdrawal was the city's desire for local control, combined with the opportunity to capture a local tax revenue stream sufficient to provide better library services than the county is able to fund.

It is significant to note in this context that six other cities were contemplating withdrawing from the county system prior to the arrival of LSSI, and none of them appears at this time interested in pursuing the course further. This can be attributed in part to several factors, including service improvements instituted under LSSI, a perception of greater equity in resource allocation and increased local control, and a realisation of the high costs of providing better library service with exclusively local funding, The County of Riverside has made great efforts to give local communities a sense of greater local control.

They instituted three zone advisory boards of citizens to provide input on the allocation of fiscal resources within regional zones. They have focussed on trying to return tax funds to the zone in which they were generated, and in doing so have calmed many concerns about inequitable funding. However, the issue of "return to source" with regard to tax revenues remains. It is a difficult one to manage in an area with great disparities in both wealth and local property tax base.

There is reason for concern that this issue may be a potent force tending to pull the county library system apart over time. Based on a number of interviews, the staff of the Riverside County Library System apparently has no reason to feel that their professional values or standards are in any way compromised by being employees of a private corporation that manages their public libraries. Most staff members interviewed seem to feel strong sense of loyalty to LSSI because the company has restored a measure of stability to their jobs. Staff has perceived relatively few changes of policy or procedure at the branch level since LSSI assumed control. This may point to a possible problem in leadership or direction due to the division of responsibilities between the county and the contractor.

The County Librarian is fully occupied in administering a large number of contracts and interlocal agreements, and takes care not to become involved in the details of running the libraries. Much of his administrative effort is currently being focussed on an ambitious programme of building and improving facilities.

The contractor, LSSI, is charged with providing day-to-day management of library operations, but is not responsible for strategic planning for the library system. It appears that responsibility for long range planning may have fallen into the cracks between the contractually stipulated responsibilities of the respective parties. It is open to question if a single county employee, the County Librarian, can be expected to manage so many contracts, continue an aggressive building programme, and effectively provide vision and direction for the system.

The County needs to either hire additional staff for that purpose, or else contract for that task as well as for day-to-day operations. The staff reports that there appear to be several advantages in private sector management of the library system. Among these advantages are reduced red tape in getting things done, ranging from the ordering of supplies to the furnishing and equipping of a branch library. In interviews some staff noted, with an obvious show of relief, that it was easier for a private contractor to discipline or discharge employees who weren't performing well.

Overall, the evidence we gathered leads to the following conclusions:

- The county acted judiciously in contracting the management of Riverside County Library System to LSSI. County officials took care to retain policy control, and have developed detailed and enforceable contracts. A capable and experienced library professional, who is an employee of the county, manages these contracts.
- The decision to contract with LSSI has apparently enhanced local control over library operations and increased the accountability of library management to public officials.
- The outsourcing of library management to LSSI can not be considered "privatisation" under any reasonable definition of the term because the County retains full and complete control over the assets of the library and over library policy matters.
- The citizens of Riverside County feel that they are receiving better library service now, with the LSSI management of RCLS, than they were receiving when the system was managed by the city of Riverside.

- Funding for collections and hours of service have both increased since the decision to outsource management of RCLS to LSSI. These issues both remain a significant concern for County officials, and further improvements are expected.
- Staff feel that, overall, LSSI is a better employer than the City of Riverside, and are generally satisfied with their compensation and working conditions. They do appear to have concerns about the benefits they receive, and about work schedules.

CONCLUSIONS AND RECOMMENDATIONS

This study has been limited to a comprehensive review of the literature on outsourcing in general, an in depth analysis of the literature on outsourcing of cataloging, followed by a detailed examination of a four selected specific outsourcing cases. This is a rather limited set of cases on which to generalise, but nevertheless the evidence does point to some tentative conclusions about the impact of outsourcing on the three specific areas identified in the RFP.

LIBRARY GOVERNANCE AND FIRST AMENDMENT ISSUES

We found no evidence that outsourcing *per se* represents a threat to library governance, or to the role of the library in protecting the First Amendment rights of the public. Library staff in organisations where the management was contracted to outside vendors expressed little concern that their values were in conflict with those of their employers. Likewise, surveys of library users revealed no concern about the practice.

Elected officials and county officers in Riverside have found that by contracting out the management of the public library system to a commercial vendor rather than a municipality, they have significantly increased their control over policy matters and resource allocation decisions and enhanced the accountability of the library to the people it serves.

MAINTENANCE OF A QUALITY WORKFORCE

With regard to outsourcing of cataloging and selection, this issue is elusive and difficult to determine. There appears to be legitimate cause for concern that, with increasing reliance on vendors for cataloging and selection, the expertise of local library professional staff in these areas way dwindle and atrophy. One the other hand, this is a logical by-product of the managerial choice to direct local staff resources towards other activities and functions, enhancing staff expertise in these other areas. These represent the difficult choices managers must make in the face of limited resources and increasing demands for services.

In the Riverside case, we uncovered some vague indications of increasing workloads and decreasing compensation—especially in terms of benefits—that might lead to diminished workforces over the long term. There was also a clear indication of a change in the staffing pattern in some libraries, with non-professionals handling tasks that had formerly been carried out by professionals. Some observers might interpret this as the cynical manipulation of labour by a for profit employer.

An equally valid view, in our opinion, is that this represents a specific instance of a much larger trend in library management, involving innovative approaches to staffing patterns in order to find more effective allocations of scarce resources. The evidence is equivocal and the conclusions by no means certain. More study is needed, and perhaps more time to develop a discernible pattern of activities.

THE COMMUNITY OF LIBRARIES AND THEIR COOPERATIVE ENDEAVORS

We also found no evidence that outsourcing *per se* had any significant impact on interlibrary cooperation. Conceptually, there is the possibility that library collections developed by vendors rather than local selectors might tend to become homogenous over time.

This, in turn, would limit the diversity of library collections as a whole, and vitiate the rationale for effective library resource sharing. It is not clear from the evidence at hand, however, that the scale of outsourced selection justifies concern about this theoretical evolution. Nor is it certain that, given emerging patterns in publishing and information distribution systems, such homogenisation is not more or less inevitable in the long run. Far from being a threat to library cooperation, outsourcing of cataloging is in fact facilitated by widespread access to shared cooperative cataloging efforts. Outsourced library management, on the other hand, more logically might pose a threat to interlibrary cooperation. We found, however, no evidence that it fact has as yet made any impact. In Riverside, the surrounding communities appear to view LSSI as a good neighbour, and one with whom they are more than willing to work for common improvements.

GENERAL CONSIDERATIONS

While we found no evidence that outsourcing *per se* represents a threat, there are to be sure a number of issues which might deserve sobre deliberation by the library profession. There are clearly instances in which outsourcing has led to undesirable— perhaps even disastrous—results. In seems apparent, however, that these debacles are less a consequence of outsourcing than of poor management; in other words, outsourcing badly done. It is clear from these examples, as well as from consistent admonitions in the literature that, a decision to outsource is one that should be made very carefully, with deliberate consideration of all of the factors and ramifications.

It would be perhaps useful to reiterate the suggestions of Riverside County official Tom DeSantis about things to be sure to do before outsourcing.

- Keep policy control with the elected public officials and representatives of the public;
- Have your own in-house expert, a qualified professional, to manage the contract and oversee vendor performance;
- The contract must specify outcomes that are quantitatively measurable;
- Choose your service provider carefully; be certain they have the experience and qualifications to deliver on their commitments.

The first two of these are clear and unambiguous. We might elaborate further on the second two. From the third suggestion it can be noted that a key element in successful outsourcing projects is the quality of the contract: a poor contract will likely result in poor performance. It is imperative, therefore that librarians and library managers become experts at developing, monitoring and administering contracts. It seems equally obvious that model contracts and guidelines for developing proposals be created by appropriate professional organisations to aid librarians in negotiating their way through the contracting wilderness.

The final suggestion leads to another observation: one of the greatest impediments to successful outsourcing is the limited pool of qualified and experienced vendors, especially in the area of library management. The most important handicap that Riverside County has in negotiating with LSSI is that there are few alternative vendors from which to chose. If there were a half dozen qualified and experienced vendors from which to chose, contract negotiations with any single vendor would take on a completely different complexion. Michael Gorman is one of the most outspoken critics of outsourcing in the library literature. He has written that library managers who decide to contract with outside vendors for cataloging, selection or acquisition services "are saying, in effect, that professional library skills and experience can be replaced by distant vendors who probably lack the former and certainly lack the latter". We would certainly agree that library managers should not contract for *any* services with vendors who lack relevant professional skills or adequate experience. We would assert, however, that many vendors can offer skills and experience equal to the professional staffs of many libraries.

The evidence we considered indicates that, in many cases, the skills and experience of vendor staffs may far exceed those of the local library staff—*for specific activities and functions*. The key to success in outsourcing is knowing when to outsource, and negotiating a workable contract with a capable vendor. This in turn results from careful analysis and planning, establishment of measurable objectives, and vigilant monitoring of contract performance.

RECOMMENDATIONS

The following recommendations are offered to the American Library Association to improve the use of outsourcing as an effective management tool in American libraries.

- The American Library Association should encourage the inclusion of data documenting the extent of outsourcing in libraries in the regular annual data collection activities of such agencies as the National Center for Education Statistics.
- The American Library Association should foster regular treatment of outsourcing trends, vendors and services, and other issues related to outsourcing, in the journals published by the divisions and units of ALA.
- The American Library Association should foster, through its Divisions and other units, the development of guidelines and model contracts to aid librarians in making decisions about outsourcing.
- The American Library Association, working collaboratively with other appropriate agencies such as the Council on Library and Information Resources and the Institute of Museum and Library Services, should encourage and foster further research into the impact of outsourcing on library services and management.

4

Change Management Process

CHANGE MANAGEMENT STANDARDS

- All substantive changes to the IT Environment must adhere to the XX change Management process. A substantive change has the potential to affect the ability of users and systems to interact with each other.
- All changes must conform to the published guidelines that dictate the 'look and feel' of the XX web environment.
- All web page content changes must have the approval of the web page owner prior to change implementation.
- All changes to the production systems within IT will have a corresponding set of documentation that describes the change, the business reason for the change and the disposition of the change. This includes emergency and exception changes.
- The risk and/or impact ratings of the requested change will determine which of the four phases of the change workflow will be required to promote the change into production. For 'minor' changes only Analysis and Implementation will be required.
- Anyone with a valid XX Notes access will be able to enter a change into the Change Request process. Only authorised approvers will be able to accept a change request into the Change Management process.

STATUS OF CHANGES

The following status codes are used to reflect the status of a change request:

- *Open* – The change has been received and accepted but has not been assigned
- *In-Progress* – The change has been received, acknowledged and assigned. Work is in progress to fulfill the change request.
- *Approved* – The business and technical assessments have been completed and the change has been approved and committed to the change scheduler.

- *Rejected* – The change has been rejected and will be routed back to the Request for Service process and sent back to the customer with an explanation and a recommended course of action.
- *Closed* – The change request has been closed.
- *Canceled* – The change request has been canceled.

TYPES OF CHANGES

The Change Management Procedure applies to all types of changes related to the XX IT environment.

The following is a description of each of the types of changes that can take place and the rules that apply to each:

- *Application Changes:* Changes to any application code that is running on or linked to by any hardware or software in the XX IT environment. These changes are typically made to enhance the function or performance of or to fix a known error in the IT application environment. These changes cannot be implemented without approval of the owner of the application and cannot be requested by any programmer other than the one assigned to the programme. Assignment of Risk Category Level of the change is to be a joint effort of both the owner and the Change Implementer.
- *Hardware Changes:* All XX IT and IT support equipment installations, discontinuances and relocations are controlled by the Change Management Procedure. This activity can be requested by anyone but must have the approval of the Operations Manager.
- *Visual Image Changes:* Changes to the 'artistic' presentation of web pages are not required to make entries into the Change Management system. Changes to 'Active' areas of the web page are required to use the XX Change Management procedure.
- *Software Changes:* The criteria for entering a software change into the Change process are based upon the effect that the changes may have on the IT support resources. If the changes affect the system, users or the support staff there is a requirement to enter it into the Change process. If the change is made for the exclusive benefit of the requester and if failure could not affect anyone else, that change would be exempt from the Change Process. For example, a change made by a programmer affecting a procedure or a programme under development on a test application requires no entry. However, when stand-alone test time is required on a production system, a change request form is required.
  - — Typically, software changes would include changes to the Operating System, Vendor supplied Programme Products, e.g.,

Visual Studio, Java, etc., or common application support modules. However, during the last two and first five workdays of each month changes are restricted to emergency and critical necessities as determined by the Director of Information Technology.

- *Network Changes:* All installations, discontin-uances and all relocations of equipment used for IT teleprocessing communications are entered into the change process. This includes all routers, switches and telephone lines as well as Personal Computers if they are connected to the network.
- *Environmental Changes:* Environmental changes normally involve the facilities associated with the IT Installation. These facility changes include items such as air conditioning, chilled water, raised flooring, security, motor generators, electricity, plumbing and the telephony system for voice and data. For example, when there is a planned weekend power outage initiated by the local power company this information is submitted to the Change Management Process a minimum of two weeks prior to the scheduled outage and communicated to management, staff and the user community.
- *Documentation Changes:* All procedural changes to the standard operating procedures will be implemented through the Change process. Also, all permanent deviations from the published schedule time for running of production applications will be communicated through the Change Management system.

CHANGE LEVELS

The following guidelines for definition of Change risk levels are provided for consideration during the planning cycle. It must be clearly understood that these requirements are the minimum for each of the defined levels. The Requester may wish to plan additional lead times, documentation or reviews to insure that targets can be met and planned implementation schedules can be achieved. All changes are tracked, correlated and used for management reporting, statistics, trending, etc., to identify when and where additional resources should be provided.

For any change that fails, the Change Requester must enter an explanation in the comments section of the Change Record for that change and notify the Change Coordinator. The Change Coordinator will then close the change with the appropriate close status. If the change is to be attempted at a later time, the Change Requester should re-enter the change with the new date. Changes that cause a Platform outage will be reviewed at a Quality Measurement Meeting.

LEVEL E CHANGES

Emergency changes are those changes that are vital in order to ensure that IT's committed service levels are maintained. An Emergency change should not be used in order to bypass the appropriate lead-time for a change that has been entered into the system.

Exception changes are those changes that are a result of a business need and must be installed prior to the required lead-time. These types of changes proceed to the implementation phase when the requester's manager and the Director of Information

Technology acknowledge that an Emergency or an Exception situation exists and authorise the modification planned. These changes will be post-reviewed to assure successful implementation, along with identification of any external impacts or new requirements. Post-review will also evaluate the reason for the Level E change request and try to determine a way of eliminating this requirement in the future.

The post-review will also evaluate if, in fact, the change addressed a real or a perceived emergency condition. In all cases, the review must determine if additional action is required, what that action should be and who will be responsible for the action. Documentation requirements for Emergency changes are the same as any change. The Requester is responsible for meeting all requirements for the change documentation within one week of the implementation.

For non-application changes:

- Is the change needed to restore immediate service to the end user.
- Is the change necessary to fix an existing problem immediately.
- Is this a change that must be installed immediately but the need for it was not recognised early enough to be approved through the regular process.

For application changes:

- Must this change be done immediately to fix problems for jobs that ABENDed during the previous night or are required to run in order to bring up on-line systems.

What Types of Management Approval is Required for Level E Changes

Approval required by:

- Director of Information Technology or her designee.
- Change Management Process Owner or his designee.
- Manager of the user department requesting the change.

Depending on the scope and impact of the proposed change, approval by one or more of the following individuals may be required.

- Operations Manager.
- Application Development Manager.
- Network and Technical Services Manager.

LEVEL 4 CHANGES

A Level 4 Change would have a major impact on IT services if a problem occurs during install. The install time is lengthy and the backout is very difficult or impossible. Level 4 Change Requests are to be entered into the Change Management Data Base at least thirty business days prior to the planned implementation date. The Requester or representative for a Level 1 change is required to attend the Change Communication meeting immediately prior to implementation so that any questions or concerns may be addressed.

Whenever a Level 4 change must be expedited to address a critical timing situation, a special meeting must be held. To expedite a Level 4 change, all parties that may be affected by this change must be present or represented at the special meeting. It is the responsibility of the change requester to arrange the meeting and assure attendance by the required groups or individuals. If the required groups or individuals cannot be assembled, the change cannot be expedited and an escalation will be required.

How do you know that the Change Falls Under Level 4

For non-application changes:

- From the end user's eyes, is it possible for the change to have a major impact on services if problems occur.
- Is the change visible to all end users.
- Is this a high-risk change.
- Is this the first time this change has been done.
- Is the change difficult or impossible to backout.
- Is it extremely difficult to install the change.
- Does the change involve a lengthy install time.

For application changes:

- Would failure of the job being changed stop the flow of all jobs for critical files or an application system.

What Types of Management Approval is Required for Level 4 Changes

Approval required by:

- Change Review Board.
- Manager of user department requesting change.

Depending on the scope and impact of the proposed change, approval by one or more of the following individuals may be required.

- Operations Manager.
- Application Development Manager.
- Network and Technical Services Manager.

LEVEL 3 CHANGES

A Level 3 Change may impact a large number of end users. It is a high-risk change that requires a significant effort to backout. Level 3 Change Requests must be entered into the Change Management database fifteen business days prior to implementation. All Level 3 changes will be communicated via the Change Management reporting system. The requester or representative for a Level 3 change is required to attend the Change Communication Meeting immediately prior to implementation so that any questions or concerns may be addressed.

How do you know that the Change Falls Under Level 3

For non-application changes:

- Will the change be visible to a large number of end users.
- Is this a high-risk change.
- Has the change been done only infrequently?
- Will a significant effort be required to backout the change.
- Is it difficult to install the change.

For application changes:

- Would failure of the job being changed stop the flow of jobs for non-critical files or applications.

What Types of Management Approval is Required for Level 3 Changes

Approval required by:

- Manager of user department requesting change.
- Network and Technical Services Manager.
- Change Review Board.

LEVEL 2 CHANGES

A Level 2 Change is not transparent, but is minimal in risk and impact. It is the responsibility of the Requester to notify any areas of a potential impact. The change is a Level 2 if it requires an IPL of a system, subsystem or the restart of a critical component on a production system. Level 2 Change Requests must be entered into the Change Management database prior to the Scheduled Change Window being requested. The Requester or representative for a Level 2 change is required to attend the Change Communication meeting immediately prior to planned implementation so that any questions or concerns may be addressed. All Level 2 changes will be communicated via the Change Management reporting system and will be tracked and reported by the Change/Problem Coordinator.

Examples of Level 2 changes:

- Single fixes—APAR, PTF, etc.
- Low usage programme product upgrades, installations.
- PARMLIB updates which require an IPL to implement.
- Regular maintenance updates to system or application libraries.
- Hardware Preventative Maintenance.
- Data management to critical volumes.

How do you Know that the Change Falls Under Level 2

For non-application changes:

- Will the change have only minor impact on services provided to the end users if problems occur.
- Will the change be visible only to a small group of end users.
- Is this a moderate risk change.
- Is the change relatively simple to install.
- Has the change been implemented successfully a number of times before.
- Does it require only a moderate effort to backout the change quickly.
- Will it require only an IPL, recycle of major application or reloading of an NCP to implement or backout.

For application changes:

- Is this the first time the job has been installed.
- Must this job be fixed to run tonight.

What Types of Management Approval is Required for Level 2 Changes

Approval required by:

- Manager of user department requesting change.
- Change Review Board.

LEVEL 1 CHANGES

A Level 1 Change has little or no external visibility, no external dependencies or no operator intervention. There is no associated risk or impact with the change, either to the system if the change is incompatible or to the Requester if the change implementation is delayed. The change does not require an IPL or recycle of an application to implement or backout. Level 1 changes are entered into the Change data base and will be communicated daily to any affected areas where impact or interest can be identified outside of the Requester's own area.

How do you Know that the Change Falls Under Level 1

For non-application changes:

- Will the change have only minimal or no impact on services provided to the end users if a problem occurs.
- Is the change familiar or common to those who will implement it.
- Is the change reliable and low risk.
- Is the change easy to backout if a problem occurs.
- Can it be backed out without an IPL, recycle of a major application, or reloading of an NCP.

For application changes:

- Would failure of the job stop just this job.
- Is this a low priority job.

What Types of Management Approval is Required for Level 1 Changes

Approval required by:

- Manager of user department requesting change.
- Change Review Board.

CHANGE REQUEST FLOWS

ASSIGN CHANGE IMPLEMENTER FLOW

Description:

- The Assign Change Implementer flow begins once a change request has been documented and selected for the change management process. During this workflow, a change record is assigned to an appropriate owner, the change record is updated with this assignee information, and the change is sent to the assignee.

Scope Inclusion:

- All changes reviewed by the Change Review Board.

Scope Exclusion:

- Changes not accepted by the Change Management process or Changes not reviewed by the Change Review Board.

Goal:

- To ensure that change requests are assigned to appropriate implementers.
- To ensure that the change management workload is allocated by area of expertise.

- To balance workload within an area of expertise.

Start Trigger:

- Initial change record.

Stop Trigger:

- Initial change record is assigned to an owner.

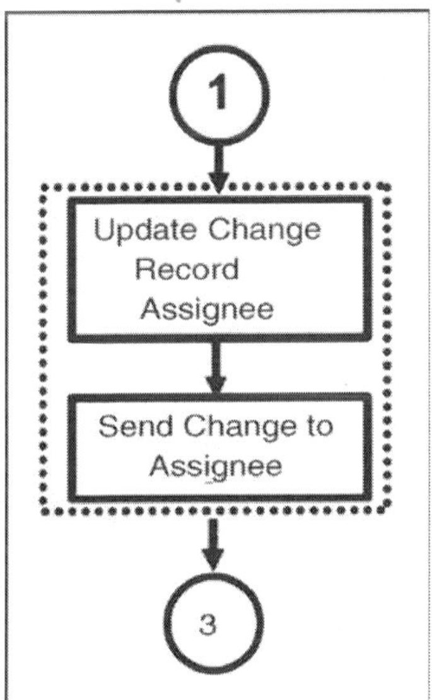

Fig. 2.1 Workflow Diagram for Assign Change Implementer

Workflow Details for Assign Change Implementer (fig. 2.1):

- *Update Change Record Assignee:* Assign the change an owner based on the classification of the change.
- *Send Change to Assignee:* Place the assignee information into the change record and send an e-mail notification to the assignee.

ENTER CHANGE REQUEST FLOW

- *Description:* The Enter Change Request flow begins when a change request is submitted.
- In this activity, all required information about the change and supporting documentation is entered into the Change Management system. The change request should be submitted in accordance with the time frame required by the initial impact assessment.
- *Scope Inclusion:* All changes, including software, hardware, control mechanisms, configurations, environments, facilities, databases, business applications, processes, and procedures.

- *Scope Exclusion:*
  - — Development activities that produce the actual change content.
  - — The coordination of sets of changes.
  - — Testing of the change package.
- *Goal:*
  - — To introduce changes into the environment with minimal disruption to information technology and its users.
  - — To communicate such that all affected users are aware of changes.
  - — To log all changes into the change management system.
  - — To ensure all pertinent change information is collected.
  - — To ensure all changes meet lead time criteria.
- *Start Trigger:*
  - — Change Request.
- *Stop Trigger:*
  - — Fully documented and approved change request.

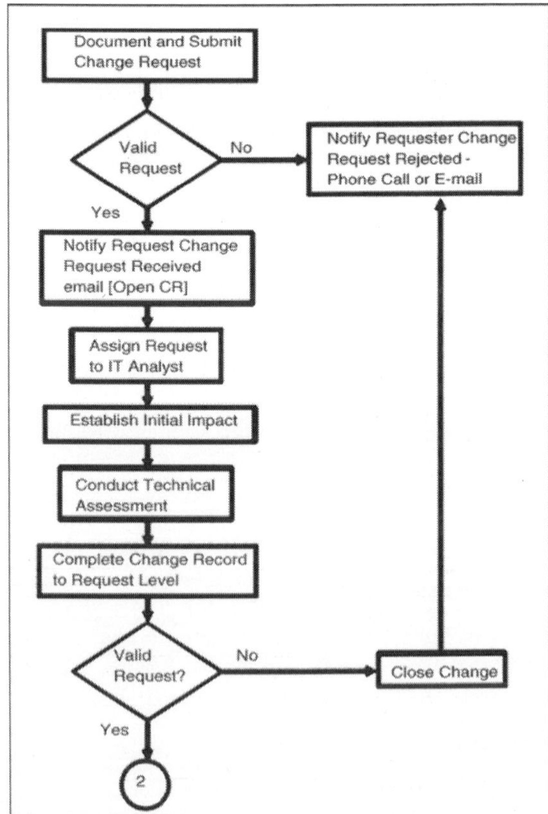

Fig. 2.2 Workflow Diagram for Enter Change Request

Workflow details for enter change request (see Fig. . 2.2):

- *Document and Submit Change Request:* Collect system change request and begin preliminary review of the change.
- *Valid Request:* Determine whether or not to submit change request into change management system based on whether the request form has a managers signature, it is within IT responsibility, and filled in correctly.
- *Notify Requester Change Request rejected – phone call or e-mail:* If change request is rejected, provide a form of notification.
- *Notify Requester Change Request received – e-mail:* If change request is approved for the change management system, a change record is opened and a change number is assigned. A notification is auto-sent to the change requester by Peregrine.
- *Assign request to IT analyst:* Assign the change request to an initial analyst to review the change record.
- *Establish Initial Impact:* Determine impact of the change to the customer community. This will include times when service is not available, testing time, new procedures, new support requirements, and any other impact that may occur as a result of the change.
- *Conduct Technical Assessment:* Determine the feasibility of the change from a technical perspective. This assessment will include the amount of resources, level of knowledge, and skills necessary for the change.
- *Complete Change Record to Request Level:* Based on initial impact and technical assessment, determine the type and category level of change, and complete all descriptive fields. Additionally, the completeness of the change success criteria is validated.
- *Valid Request:* Based on the initial assessments, determine whether to perform this change. This decision is based on the change conforming to the strategy, resources being available, and whether or not it is already being worked on.
- *Close Change:* Mark change record as closed when it doesn't pass validation requirements.

MONITOR CHANGE CALENDAR FLOW

Description:

- The Monitor Change Calendar flow determines the scheduling for changes to be deployed. During this workflow, changes are penciled into a calendar, and the schedule is monitored for changes that are completed or have run out of time in their scheduled change deployment window. If time has expired for a change then it can be escalated and rescheduled based on escalation standards.

Scope Inclusion:

- Changes that are formally put into the change calendar.

Scope Exclusion:

- Changes that are not formally put into the change calendar.

Goal:

- Monitor the change calendar for changes that have not been completed and have run out of time for the purpose of change escalation.
- Allow for changes to be rescheduled.
- Allow for changes to be removed from the change calendar upon completion.

Start Trigger:

- A change request has been assigned an owner and has been sent to that assignee.

Stop Trigger:

- A change is complete and removed from the calendar.

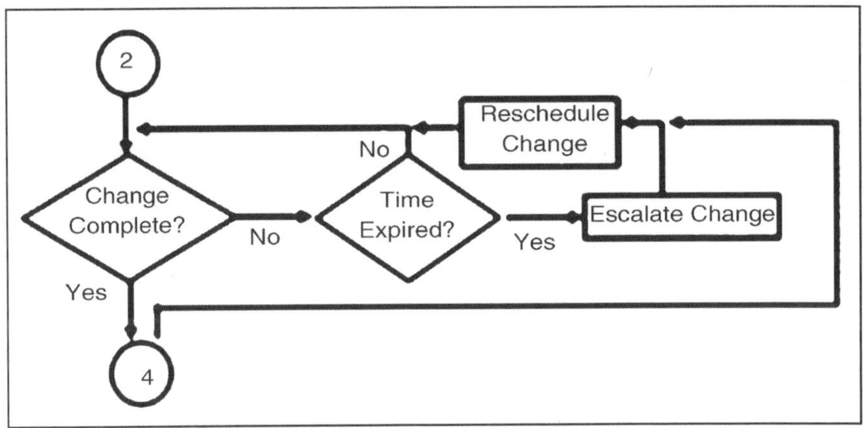

Fig. 2.3 Workflow Diagram for Monitor Change Calendar

Workflow Details for Monitor Change Calendar (fig. 2.3):

- *Change Complete:* Monitor the change calendar for change work that has been completed.
- *Time Expired:* Determine whether a change record that is incomplete has run out of time.
- *Escalate Change:* Reclassify the change to a higher change category level if time has expired.
- *Reschedule Change:* Update the calendar with a schedule for the change after it has been escalated or if the change package is incomplete.

PERFORM ASSESSMENTS FLOW

Description:

- The Perform Assessments flow involves conducting both a business and technical review of the change package. The assessments determine if the change package is complete and can therefore continue through the change management process.
- Specifically, the perform business assessment flow involves validating the impact of the proposed change on XX from a business perspective, evaluating the completeness of the success criteria and communication plan and reviewing the backup/ backout/ recovery plans. The assessment looks at the proposed timing of the change and ensures that the customer's management has given the agreement necessary for the change to be approved and scheduled. Standards, business requirements, and SLAs are reviewed and a recommendation is made to approve, reject, or reschedule the change.
- The perform technical assessment flow reviews the completeness of the change plan, test plan, backup/ backout/ recovery plans, platform impact assessment, estimated install time, etc., from a technical perspective. The change success criteria are validated and the impact of the change to the environment is reviewed to ensure it has been accurately evaluated. Technical standards are enforced and a decision is made to approve, reject, or reschedule the change.

Scope Inclusion:

- All documented changes with a change category that requires a formal business or technical assessment.

Scope Exclusion:

- Changes with change categories that specifically do not require formal business or technical assessments.

Goal:

- To ensure that all factors have been taken into consideration in terms of the business aspects of the change.
- To ensure that all factors have been taken into consideration in terms of the technical aspects of the change.
- To ensure that everything required to deploy the change and to maintain service is included in the change request.

Start Trigger:

- Fully documented change record.

Stop Trigger:

- Assessed change.

Workflow Details for Perform Assessments (fig. 2.6):

- *Business Review of Change Package:* Review the change package for the following points:
  - — Ensure that the business requirements will be met.
  - — Verify existence and completeness of backup/ backout recovery plans.
  - — Verify existence of test plans, including the testers names and expected results.
  - — Ensure that the change conforms to business standards and policies.
  - — Determine whether the change conforms to service level agreements.
  - — Review communication plan for change.

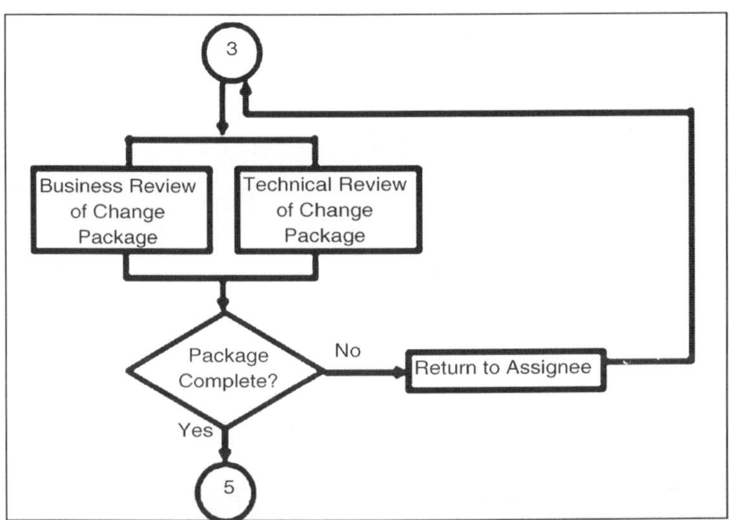

Fig. Workflow Diagram for Perform Assessments

- *Technical Review of Change Package:* Review the change package for the following points:
  - — Determine the impact on the technical environment.
  - — Ensure that the change conforms to technical standards.
  - — Verify the completeness of the change plan.
- *Package Complete?:* Make a decision on whether the package is complete based on the results of the business and technical reviews.
- *Return to Assignee:* If the package is determined not complete than the change is returned to the assignee and can be rescheduled.

APPROVE CHANGE FLOW

Description:

- The Approve Change flow is initiated as soon as both the business and technical assessments have been completed. If the change is approved, it is passed on to the next sub-process to finalise scheduling. If the change is rejected or determined to be rescheduled, it may be sent back to the business or technical assessment subprocesses once the necessary actions are taken. All parties that have been involved to this point in the process should be notified of the approval, rejection or rescheduling.

Scope Inclusion:

- All changes that have been forwarded for approval from a business and technical perspective and whose change categories indicate the requirement for formal approval.

Scope Exclusion:

- Changes with change categories that specifically so not require formal approval.

Goal:

- To ensure that appropriate approval is obtained for change requests.
- To ensure that the change record is properly updated.
- To minimize service interruption.

Start Trigger:

- Completed change record with business and technical review including recommendation.

Stop Trigger:

- Approval for change deployment.

Workflow Details for Approve Change:

- *Final Change Review:* Final review of change prior to acceptance and scheduling.
- *Accept Change:* Based on the result of the final change review, determine whether to go ahead with or close the change.
- *Close Change:* If it is decided not to continue with change, then change record is closed by change coordinator.
- *Notify Requester Change Request rejected – phone call or e-mail*

IMPACT OF INFORMATION AND COMMUNICATIONS TECHNOLOGY

Information and Communications Technology (ICT) have transformed Library and Information services globally. The Internet has provided universal access to information. Technological innovation has dramatically increased the rate of conversion of knowledge, information and data into electronic format. Developments in the software arena has generated powerful knowledge management software which has transformed the way knowledge is organised, stored, accessed and retrieved.

The digital revolution driven by ICT innovation has transformed academic libraries fundamentally. It has impacted on every sphere of academic library activity, e.g., the form of the library, collection development strategies, library buildings and consortia. Information and communications technology have changed the academic library in a profound way. Computers and networked electronic resources had become an integral part of the academic library the past decade.

This has been underscored by the phenomenon of knowledge or information commons in academic libraries, which refer to a specific environment in the library where a designated number of PC workstations, networked to databases and other e-resources, are made available to students. Every sphere of the academic library is being affected by ICT quite radically.

No longer is the library the untouchable custodian of information. It is being shaken to its very foundation, in fact its existence is being threatened. The academic libraries' traditional role of information custodian had been reduced to that of being one of many information providers. Of all the information and communication technologies the Internet and particularly the World Wide Web with its graphical user interface, has had the greatest impact on the information revolution. The number of electronic resources available on the Internet is growing at a phenomenal rate.

One of the major search engines Alta Vista has reported in 1996 that it has indexed 30 million Web pages. By 1998 the number of Web pages indexed by this search engine has leaped to 90 million. According to Farrow wide spread publicity has lead to assumptions that the Internet will meet all user information needs and that there will be no need for professional librarian intervention in future between user and information resources. Moyo states that student expectations that all their research needs will be met online are on the increase. Not only do students expect to find the information they need online, they also expect it to be available in full text. According to Tam and Robertson these assumptions have lead to a reluctance to use the physical library materials and to a decrease of visits to the library.

This phenomenon has fuelled fears of potential future job losses amongst librarians. Cheng explores the impact of information technology from an information ecological perspective. In information ecology the focus is not on information technology but on the human activities that are served. Cheng cites Nardi and O'day who draw a parallel between the explosive growth of information technology and the consequential Information explosion and a volcanic eruption. This eruption is impacting on everyone existing with the information ecosystem. Cheng emphasise the importance that we as academic librarians are clear about the challenges posed by this situation and also the opportunities offered.

Cheng highlights some of the changes that took place within the information ecology:

- The way we gather information, organise it, disseminate and use information has changed.
- The evolution of the Web has lead to availability of masses of information, electronic journals and databases.
- The way information is being published is evolving rapidly, e.g., it is threatening current practices.
- New problems have come to the fore, e.g., the issue of intellectual property rights of e-resources.
- User expectations have changed. Users expect full text delivery to the desktop.

Researchers are of the opinion that the changes that library and information services face are of an unknown and unpredictable nature. He states that it is impossible for library managers to predict future trends accurately. He feels traditional change management techniques are inadequate to deal with the changing environment that libraries are facing. For him it is a scenario where one has to brace oneself for whatever occurs. Under these conditions it is crucial that libraries make optimal use of the entire workforce.

It is of fundamental importance that customer service be given top priority. It is also essential that flexible organisational structures be created where workloads and responsibilities are shared and trust and responsibility are the norm rather than control. For library and information services in academic libraries to prevail under these conditions real leadership and real changes in management styles and organisational structures are necessary.

CONCEPTS DEFINED

Change

Robbins and Coulter defines change as any alterations in people, structure or technology. Change involves moving from the current state of things, the status quo, to a new state of things. It is therefore a process of moving from what is known to the unknown.

Information and Communications Technology (ICT)

Adeyoyin cites Bayode who defines ICT as "the acquisition, processing, storage, and dissemination of information by means of computers and other telecommuni-cation equipment." The Wikipedia free Internet encyclopaedia defines "information technology (IT) or information and communication(s) technology (ICT)" as the "technology required for information processing. In particular the use of electronic computers and computer software to convert, store, protect, process, transmit, and retrieve information".

From the definitions it is clear that the terms IT and ICT are used interchangeably and has the same meaning. According to Jimba information technology is rooted in three sectors namely information technology, telecommunications and the media and these sectors are converging on one another.

TYPES OF CHANGE

Researcher define change along a continuum ranging from low-scope to high-scope change.

Evolutionary Change

Evolutionary change is incremental by nature. Incremental change is smooth and happens gradually in an organised and predictable way. Incremental change tends to be small changes that lead to improvement but does not alter the operational structure of the academic library.

Strategic Change

Strategic, revolutionary or transformational change leads to radical transformation and often changes the general organisational structure. Transformational change tends to be very traumatic by nature. It can be generated as a response to a major crisis or a complete change in organisational strategy or purpose. The outcome of this type of change can lead to organisational transformation to the effect that the organisation might look completely different from what it used to be.

Discontinuous Change

The academic library is confronted with change that is unlike anything it has been exposed to before. Management theorists use the term discontinuous change. Pugh notes that discontinuous change is different from revolutionary change that is change undertaken to generate rapid results. Discontinuous change is unique in the sense that established management practices are inadequate to deal with it, in fact there is no model, paradigm or pool of experience that managers can fall back onto.

Researcher describes discontinuous change as turbulent, complex, traumatic, uncertain and of a revolutionary nature which requires different management skills to survive, supported by highly trained, motivated, flexible and multi-skilled staff that can be redeployed quickly and effectively if necessary. There is a stark contrast between the clearly defined boundaries of businesses in the 1960's and 1970's and the postindustrial era that is characterised by volatility, complexity and uncertainty. "This type of random, discontinuous change—which, by definition, is fast, traumatic, and revolutionary – requires very different management and leadership skills if the challenges it presents are to be handled innovatively and opportunistically." What organisations need in order to survive is highly committed, skilled, informed and trained staff which is willing to give their all.

Until 15 years ago change was incremental. One could build on lessons learned before. Since then change had become discontinuous. In this climate old management behaviours are inadequate. New ways of doing things are imperative which questions the practices that worked in the past. Information services in the academic library are driven by ICT with all its uncertainties and instability. Change is occurring at a greater dimension than ever before.

The volume, pace and complexity of change is increasing at an unprecedented rate. A comparison between 1970 and to-day reveals that in 1970 only 5 per cent of changc within organisations was of a continuous nature. Currently 75 pcr ccnt of all organisational change is of a continuous nature.

IMPACT OF ICT DEVELOPMENTS ON STAFF

Managers often introduce drastic change without considering its impact on people. People respond to change in a myriad of ways. Any significant change will impact on people's self-esteem, their motivation to do well, their status or the stress they experience be it positive or negative. It is of vital importance that managers do not overlook people when dealing with an ever-changing environment.

According to Morgan research suggests that 90 per cent of change initiatives fail because people are not taken into consideration. Change is good for academic libraries but its adoption requires tremendous input of physical, mental and emotional energy. After having to make intense inputs to accomplish change people expect to reach a plateau, a period for review and restoration of energy. The problem is that in the academic library this plateau had become non-existent because one peak follows after the other.

Phases People go through when Exposed to Radical Change

Elizabeth Kubler-Ross has identified 5 stages that patients experience when confronted with personal loss or death. These stages are denial, anger, bargaining, depression and acceptance.

Conner has used Kubler-Ross's 5 stages as a basis and extended it to 8 stages:

1. *Stability:* This is the phase just prior to change where everything is still normal.

2. *Immobilised:* When confronted with radical change people initially experience shock, confusion and become disoriented. During this phase people are out of touch with reality.
3. *Denial:* Conner defines denial as a refusal to accept reality. According to Fossum denial is a psychological defence mechanism that kicks in when individuals are confronted with radical change. It is a refusal to accept reality while the person's internal resources are being mobilised to eventually face a situation. To help staff to deal with this phase managers should use techniques designed to promote awareness that change has occurred or is in the process of occurring. The denial phase is a critical stage in the change process and people experience it differently. While some people are still dazed and out of touch with reality others may be ready to move on. Spending time on an individual bases with people struggling with this phase can be very useful.
4. *Anger:* During this phase people experience anger and outrage. They become emotional, irritated, frustrated and hurt and may often lash out at those supporting them.
5. *Bargaining:* This is a negotiation phase with a view to avoid the negative aspects of change. A typical example would be negotiating an extension of a deadline one is facing. This phase indicates the person is reaching a position where he or she can no longer avoid reality. This phase also demarcates the beginning of acceptance.
6. *Depression:* It is normal for people to become depressed when confronted with major change that affects them negatively. This is a very unpleasant phase but is an indication that the individual has come to complete realisation of the negative change being faced. It is an unpleasant phase but indicates another step towards acceptance.
7. *Testing:* At this point a sense of control is regained. A person might explore how to set new goals.
8. *Acceptance:* At this point people accept change. To go with an employee through the negative response model can be a costly exercise because people need support at every step of the way. However the cost of an employee failing to go through the process can be more costly to an organisation.

Resistance

Managing change within the academic library is essentially about managing people since it is people that effect change. People who are such a critical factor in change implementation can also be a stumbling block to the change process by resisting change. Change initiatives are often shipwrecked because of resistance. Resistance leading to escalation in costs often delays change processes.

Resistance is such a central element in change management that it deserves serious attention in the change implementation process. Researcher states that one must neither fear resistance nor make efforts to avoid it. The inertia of systems which have relied on doing things as they have always been done and achieving objectives through well-tried methods is not to be underestimated. It is part of the organisational instinct for survival and as well as comfort and complacency and it breeds resistance.

The successful implementation of change in the academic library is by and large dependent on the attitudes of people to the change process. People respond in different ways to change. Whereas some people will experience change as an exiting and stimulating event others may find it frightening and intimidating and consequently resist change.

Causes of Resistance

Pendlebury identified the following causes of resistance:

- Lack of realisation of a problem.
- Not grasping the implementation of a solution.
- Outright rejection of a solution as it is seen as the incorrect option.
- Fear of the outcome of change.
- Lack of interest.

This kind of behaviour is often the result of a vision not clearly communicated or staff's unwillingness to face up to the demands of change.

Researcher identifies the following additional reasons why people resist change:

- *Security:* Fear of potential job losses.
- *Financial:* Fear of loss of income.
- *Pride and satisfaction:* Technological innovation might make jobs and skills redundant.
- *Freedom:* Structural changes might impact on freedom of decision-making.
- *Authority, responsibility and status:* Restructuring might lead to a loss of authority and respon-sibilities.

Resistance tends to manifest itself in many different ways. Conner distinguishes between overt and covert resistance. Overt resistance is open and can be constructive. Covert resistance is submerged and can gain momentum unobtrusively and ruin a project. Fossum describes covert resistance as a passive-aggressive form of resistance. It is difficult to manage because on the surface a person appears to do nothing but is often busy sabotaging a project through negative statements. In major change there will always be resistance. Creating an environment where people can openly express their fears will go a long way to minimize resistance. Managers need to be aware that resistance often manifests itself in an increase in absenteeism, reductions in quality, decreased productivity, strikes or slowdowns and increase in grievances.

STRATEGIES TO FACILITATE CHANGE WITHIN THE ACADEMIC LIBRARY

The prevailing organisational culture will determine how easy or complex it will be to communicate the need for change, share the vision and get people's opinions and participation. In an open culture communication is easiest.

The leadership style, the trust people have in top management and the extent to which people are able to openly express themselves is of cardinal importance. Managers who have successfully implemented change understand that resistance is a natural reaction and would encourage it rather than suppress it. They would even reward people for open resistance in a constructive manner.

Fossum states that clear and open communication about pending change is crucial. Managers must not allow people to hear via rumours or the grapevine or the media about pending change. They should be open and upfront about pending change. Hearing from a third party will undermine trust and credibility. When communicating change it is important to send out positive and optimistic messages. Conner is of the opinion that effective leaders can change people's mindsets to a realisation that meaningful change is not only essential but also possible.

Morgan argues that buy-in is crucial in change management. If staff can take ownership of change, it will bolster commitment and assist in overcoming any obstacles.

It is also crucial to involve staff in the decision making process. Participation will break the management versus staff syndrome. Instead of letting management do the problem solving it is useful to involve staff at all levels in this process. Managers must be careful not to make assumptions about the acceptance of change. It is better to get accurate feedback through interviews or surveys.

Techniques to Make Change Positive

Change creates conflict but the negative energy generated can be turned in constructive energy. Managers should realise that conflict in itself is not necessarily negative. It creates an opportunity to do creative problem solving with the staff. Conflict must never be taken personally. If people disagree managers should see it as an opportunity to find a more elegant solution that more staff members will find acceptable. People should be encouraged to be honest about how they feel and support one another. Managers should maintain their sense of humor. It is essential to cultivate an atmosphere that will transform negative issues of conflict into positive constructive energy.

Celebrate Success

It is important to sign-off change to ensure closure and enable people to move on. It need not be a celebration in the real sense. It could be a scenario where the team is thanked for their contribution. In that way they will see smaller change events as temporary unpleasant things to deal with and move on. If change events are seen as individual unrelated events it can lead to resistance.

ACADEMIC LIBRARY STRUCTURES

Organisational structure can be defined as "one of the interrelated components that define any organisation referring to the definition of individual jobs and their relationship to each other as depicted in organisational charts and job descriptions." It clarifies how information is distributed, and jobs are organised.

For decades the hierarchical structure of management was regarded as the most efficient way of managing an organisation. This system worked well in and environment where the future was predictable and librarians were in the driving seat. Hierarchies were not designed to foster creativity and lead workers to self-fulfilment.

It is therefore very difficult to introduce fundamental change within hierarchical structures which are naturally resistant to change. In an effort to bring about reorganisation within organisations institutions try to either modify the existing hierarchical structure or replace it with something else. Deming as cited by Mullins states that management systems still prevalent today have had a destructive impact on people.

According to Deming "people are born with intrinsic motivation, self-esteem, dignity, curiosity to learn... " Qualities such as these are undermined by a management style that reward top achievers and punish those that do worse. Managers that exhibit such management styles use disapproval as a negative control measure. This approach leads to a climate where staff performance is primarily directed at pleasing their superiors and that inevitably lead to average performance.

According to researcher managers have a natural tendency to maintain the status quo. They would instinctively fall back on models and practices that worked in the past. The volatile nature and unpredictability of information services is forcing managers to adopt new management styles. It is beginning to dawn on people that the bureaucratic way of management is becoming outdated and that change will be more effectively achieved through education, sharing, motivation, teamwork and coaching.

Moran states that unprecedented change has forced managers to re-evaluate structures. Customary practices designed to maintain organisational stability are being questioned. To cope with change, organisations have started flattening structures to induce more flexibility within those organisations. These new structures being adopted have decreased levels of hierarchy, increased flexibility and resulted in diminishing boundaries between departments.

Issues to Consider when Introducing New Structures

Management theorists are very reluctant to prescribe to a particular structural model but advise that structure should rather be designed to meet organisational needs and goals.

Organisations should try and learn as much as possible from others who have implemented organisational change. They should never introduce a structure simply because it is being used elsewhere but always to meet specific organisational needs. Of cardinal importance is to determine how people within the organisation will adopt the new structure. Researcher shares the following points learnt from a process of restructuring:

Before implementing a process of restructuring it is important to have clear vision, goals and objectives with the focus on service delivery. It is useful to establish a core team to lead the restructuring process. It is vitally important that senior management support the process, e.g., a deputy vice-chancellor. It is important to involve the entire staff component, listen to their inputs and concerns since ownership by the staff is vital for successful change implementation. Staff development programmes should be part of the process to prepare staff for new functions or roles they may be involved in.

After implementation it is important to critically analise the performance of the academic library within the new structure. Managers often do not adapt easily to the flatter less bureaucratic structures that are generally being adopted. Even staff members at lower levels experience this problem. Generally it is very difficult to introduce change that goes against prevailing organisational culture. Proper planning is needed to take the organisation from the existing structure to the new one.

Employee input in developing such a strategy is crucial. Research indicates that organisational transformation had been most successful in scenarios where employees had maximum input. Finally evaluation is necessary after change implementa-tion to determine its success. In reorganised libraries structures are always flatter resulting in manager's roles reverting from directing to coordinating. The prime purpose of reorganisation is to create a more effective organisation. Reorganisation results in academic libraries becoming learning organisations.

The learning organisation is characterised by staff empowerment, is team based, decentralised, practices participative management and information sharing. In the learning organisation the person closest to a problem has the responsibility and authority to deal with it. Tom Wilson as cited by Moran states that the academic library is in bad need of reconstruction. To Wilson academic libraries were essentially designed to manage physical artifacts. The rise of the Internet has completely transformed the way information is created, distributed and accessed.

The e-journal is a typical example. Johansen and Swigart as cited by Moran states "we had outlived the usefulness of models from the Industrial era but don't yet have robust organisational models for the information era". It is therefore of paramount importance that academic librarians continuously re-evaluate current structures and through an experimental process adopt new models. Moran states that for people who advocate restructuring there is good and bad news.

The good news is that people understand that technological change will compel fundamental organisational change. The bad news is that there is a lack of urgency. Generally organisational change appears to be incremental rather than radical.

IMPACT OF ICT CHANGE ON ACADEMIC IBRARIES

The Internet has made information access and retrieval both simplistic and complex. Information retrieval systems are being designed to suit the needs of end users and therefore try to simplify the process. Simultaneously however the user is overwhelmed with so much information resources and choices that the process becomes complex. This creates a situation where the users need skills and knowledge in terms of search strategies and conceptualisation. Herrington is of the opinion that information literacy instruction at the point of need can be very effective. Wood and Walther is of the opinion that unlike popular believe the Internet will not completely replace the skills of professional librarians but rather make them indispensable.

Changes in the Job Description of Academic Librarians

An overview of the core competencies required by academic library and information workers gives one an idea of how dramatically information and communications technology has changed the library profession.

Cheng identifies the following core competencies needed by the future librarian:

- Good communication skills.
- Should be more than just computer literate and should have a good understanding of ICT and its relation to information resources.

- Should have an in-depth understanding of organisational and user needs that is research based and should organise library resources to satisfy those needs.
- Competent in Web publishing techniques.
- Skilled in manipulating metadata to organise digital information.
- Skilled in training users in the use of e-resources.
- Skilled in filtering, evaluating and appraising Internet information.

Researchers identifies another quality required, an in-depth understanding of what information resources are available on the Internet, as well as insight in terms of its reliability and scope.

The Changing Nature of the Academic Library

ICT is busy transforming the nature of academic libraries. A variety of terms such as hybrid, digital and virtual library are used to refer to the academic library. A digital library can be defined as "a managed collection of information, with associated services, where the information is stored in digital formats and accessible over a network".

The virtual library has been defined as "remote access to the contents and services of libraries and other information resources, combining an on-site collection of current and heavily used materials in both print and electronic form, with an electronic network which provides access to, and delivery from, external worldwide library and commercial information and knowledge sources". Hybrid libraries are libraries that provide access to both electronic resources and paper-based resources.

From the definitions it is clear that most of today's academic libraries fall in either the hybrid or virtual category. The library of the future is unlikely to be a physical entity as we know it but would probably be a Web portal providing access to information.

The emphasis will be on access to information rather than physical ownership. Akeroyd supports this view and states that as a physical space entity the library, as we know it is unlikely to prevail in a digital environment. One reason for this is that because of Web access the digital library is accessible from anywhere.

Changes in the Information Seeking Behaviour of Users

Academic librarians have a good understanding of the tremendous value of printed and electronic resources available to students at academic libraries. Academic library users do not necessarily share this insight. New generation academic library users have a preference for Web resources rather than visiting the library. Research done on undergraduate engineering students in 2004 revealed that they would turn to the Internet as the primary resource for information for their projects. Moyo refers to a scenario where users were asked what they expect from an academic library service.

They responded as follows:

- All resources should be available in full text and be printable.
- The library service should be fast and easily accessible.
- 24/7 availability of a virtual reference service.
- Wish to do all library transactions online.
- Web resources that is easy to use and Web search engines that meet information needs.

What is clear is that new generation academic library users prefer the convenience of digital access above reliance on assistance from librarians. This preference for the Internet poses a serious challenge to the academic library which has to move from a paradigm of the library as a physical entity to a library where the users do not have to come to physically to make use of it's services.

Electronic access to information resources does have many advantages, e.g.:

- Multiple access which implies more that one user can access a resource simultaneously.
- Lots of resources are available in full text.
- 24/7 access which means users can access resources remotely, e.g., from off campus or from dormitories.

One of the disadvantages of remote access from an academic library point of view is that users are not always aware of the fact that they are using library resources. One user stated: "No, I don't need to use the library, I use Internet resources".

Despite the apparent preference for digital content the need for access to high quality digital content remains constant. Greater cooperation between library and faculty is necessary to develop ways to connect users and high quality digital materials.

IMPACT OF ICT ON COLLECTION MANAGEMENT

Collection development can be defined as the selection and acquisition of library materials based on current and potential user needs. Collection management goes beyond this. It is concerned with managing the utilisation, storage and accessibility of a collection. Collection development can thus be seen as a subdivision of collection management. Academic librarians find themselves in an era of unparalleled access to information.

The latest edition of Uhlrich's has indicated the availability of more than 1,72,000 journal titles. Although this appears to be a most ideal situation it is not because the financial resources available in acquisitions departments have not necessarily increased. The sheer volume of information available also makes selection of the most suitable information a complex task. The impact of electronic resources has made collection management a very complex and challenging task. There are budgetary constraints, numerous formats, ever changing user needs. Collection management implies involvement in tasks such as analysis of needs, negotiation of contracts and evaluation of resources. There was a time when the size of an academic library collection determined its stature. At that time the library's resources were generally adequate to meet most of its users needs. Since then the academic library has exchanged the ownership model for an access model where physical location becomes completely irrelevant.

Access versus Ownership

Information and communications technology has had a fundamental impact on library collection development policies. Academic libraries had traditionally applied an ownership or just-in-case approach to collection development. The premise was that users would need the material and make use of it. Having the material available in the library would also provide immediate access to it than having to borrow it from a third party. The cost of maintaining collections and increased demands for more information had forced academic libraries to reconsider the ownership model and adopt another model. Unparalleled price increases and shrinking budgets had ushered in a new model called access or just in time where the focus is to give the user the information that they need when they want it.

Cost

Technically it is more cost effective to produce an e-resource, for example an electronic journal, because the first copy costs are reduced. There is also savings in terms of packaging, delivery and storage. In practice these savings have not lead to reductions in the cost of e-journals. It has been suggested that the academic library adopts a pay-as-you-use approach. This make sense according to research done in 1997 that indicated that 22 per cent of science articles published in 1984 were never cited for the next 10 years. In the social sciences this figure goes up to 48 per cent.

Storage Space

With the access model there is no need for storage space, *e.g.*, back copies. Moahi cites Cooper who states that the storage cost per single copy is between $25 and $40. Calculations to determine JStor pricing lead to the conclusion that the cost per single volume was between $24 and $41. When costs for re-shelving and maintenance were included, the estimated cost rose to $45 per title per year for a core journal and $180 per title per year for a large research library.

Enhanced Access to Information

One of the benefits of ICT is enhanced access to library services and resources. The academic library can expose its users to a much larger collection than it can house physically because users can access information remotely. With online access it is possible to accurately measure utilisation of e-resources and that is invaluable in determining which resources to purchase. It is easier to search e-resources and access speed is greatly enhanced.

Other advantages are that users can simultaneously access the same resource, and there are no incidences of lost copies or mutilated issues. Singh is of the opinion that a paradigm shift is taking place within the academic library as more academic librarians are doing collection management rather that collection development. The focus is rather on interpretation of information rather than selection. Librarians are becoming knowledge managers rather than collection managers.

Digital Preservation of Data

One of the major costs facing the academic library is the cost related to the conversion and preservation of information in digital format. The cost of this process amounts to $1 per page. This does not include the cost relating to the annotation for indexing purposes and the cost of conversion of audio-visual material. One of the problems with converting records into digital image is the fact that the technology used to store these pages as a digital photograph results in large files which have storage implications and place demands on band-with. Funding allocated to preservation of digital material is generally inadequate. This has to do with expectations that the costs of digital preservation over length of time might be very high. It is also difficult to forecast cost in terms of how long to retain digital material in an archive and computer architectures needed to access material. Preservation of digital materials poses many challenges. It is further complicated by the fact that computer technology changes at an unprecedented rate.

There are concerns that changing interfaces, standards, formats and operating systems will render it impossible to read today's computer discs at some point in future. The implication of this is that one needs migration strategies to move data to new operating systems and structures or have scenarios where computers can simulate data structures and operating systems of previous eras. This scenario will make digital preservation prohibitively expensive. A great deal of current research into digital preservation is based on overcoming the technical issues to ensure long-term preservation of digital content. The issue of digital preservation initially came to the fore as an impending crisis. Fears were expressed that large portions of our cultural heritage were in danger of disappearing forever. Examples were cited of Web sites available today that might be gone to-morrow.

Although digital materials are more fragile by nature than analog materials the risk varies within different categories of digital materials. Although it is true that a Web site currently available may disappear overnight, the same does not apply to electronic journals.

This realisation has transferred the focus from the immediate rescue notion to an approach that sees digital preservation as part of a carefully planned digital access management process. One way academic libraries can deal with digital preservation is through cooperation.

Through cooperation various institutions can share costs. Another advantage would be that it would reduce redundancy. Because of the fragile nature of digital materials libraries cannot put off decisions to preserve digital information *ad infinitum*. Time is of the essence.

Unlike a book that can be repaired or rebound, once a digital file becomes corrupt it may be impossible or prohibitively expensive to restore the data. Another problem facing the academic library is the long-term preservation of digital information.

There are questions concerning the long-term stability of digital information stored on disks and tapes. There is the potential of these media deteriorating over a period of time. Another way digital preservation is approached is by letting the vendors do the preservation.

These days there are also escrow repositories, e.g. Elsevier has agreed to provide the National Library of Netherlands with a copy of Science Direct which the National Library will maintain and make available should Elsevier be unable to do so.

ELECTRONIC RESOURCES

ICT has fundamentally changed academic library collections. Forever gone is the era when an academic library's physical collection determined its stature. In the modern networked technological era the emphasis has shifted from ownership of physical resources to access to electronic resources that are globally accessible.

Internet Information

There are huge amounts of unedited information on the Internet. There are countless Web sites and no single listing of them all. There is also the phenomenon of Web sites disappearing overnight that create problems in terms of access.

The Invisible Web

Academic library users make use of search engines such as Google and Altavista to find information on the Web. As a result they are only exposed to a small portion of the Web called the 'Publicly Indexable Web' These students are only exposed to Web pages accessible via hyperlinks. Search engines do not index Web pages that requires authentication or Web pages behind search forms. The Web consists of two components namely the 'Publicly Indexable Web' also referred to as the visible Web and the invisible Web. The invisible Web refers to all those information resources available yet not indexed by conventional search engines yet accessible via the Web.

Masses of information available via the invisible Web are found in subject databases. Most of the databases that academic libraries make available to their users resort under the invisible Web, e.g. EbscoHost and Eric. Conventional search engines can find databases such as EbscoHost but cannot access them. Search engines can only find content that was indexed by their software called spiders or crawlers.

The problem is that they only index Web content available in formats such as HTML and PDF. Michael K. Bergman in year 2000 in a paper on the invisible Web for an Internet Search Company called Bright Planet suggests that the invisible Web is 500 times larger that the visible Web with approximately 550 billion documents.

The Issue of Quality of Resources Available on the Visible Web

The Internet had become a very important research tool for academic endeauvour. Slaouti as cited by Stapleton notes that the relevance and importance of the Web as a research tool should not be underestimated. There is a stark contrast in the way resources are published on the Web versus traditional publishing. In the traditional print environment publishing generally was done by a publisher hence a controlled environment that impacted on quality as well as the scope of the audience being reached. The open nature of the Web, the development of sophisticated search engines, browsers, Web creation and publishing software and easy access to networks via low cost connectivity has developed the Web into a tool that can be easily utilised by the masses for publishing purposes, people who were formally shut out of the publishing process.

This has lead to a flood of Web publications of variable quality. During the 1990's library scholars recognised this dilemma and suggested criteria to evaluate Internet resources, *e.g.*, authority, purpose, coverage and objectivity and accessibility.

These days a single search can yield hundreds of thousands of items. The unfiltered nature of Web resources has made evaluation of these resources essential. One often finds that unlike in traditional printed media, e-resources found on the Web often lack important criteria such as author or date. Web pages because of its non-linear textual nature has added new effects to the search process such as sound, videos and access to thousands of items by clicking a mouse. These new elements imply that new sets of skills are required on the part of the researcher.

Reference Works

According to Moyo reference statistics in academic libraries are plunging. At the same time electronic access of these resources are increasing. This tendency can be ascribed to the fact that users can access these resources remotely via the Internet. Internet connectivity and e-resources had become absolutely essential for the new reference service paradigm. One of the key elements of e-reference service success is that the service is available at the point of need. The tremendous growth in the use of online reference works has created a need within the academic library to develop services to support this type of service.

Academic libraries are turning to on-line real time reference tools also referred to as ORR to support students remotely. The Pen State University library has more than 300 databases that students may access. On-line real time reference support is used to assist students at the point of need. E-reference works share all the benefits of e-resources, e.g., 24/7 remote accessibility, concurrent access for multiple users and the potential for online updating to keep content up to date. Electronic communication had become the primary mode of communication in e-reference services. Online chat had become the method of choice. Some e-reference application providers have added *Voice over IP* (VOIP) to their products which enable voice dialogue with the library user.

E-reference services have many advantages, e.g.:

- Availability via the Internet.
- Service at the point of need.
- Easy for people who are unable to come to the academic library, e.g., the physically disabled.
- 24/7 availability.

Moyo cites Stormont who states that online real time reference support is very labour intensive. In order to cope academic libraries have adopted a distributed staffing model where the load of the service is shared among various libraries.

E-Journals

The e-journal can be defined as "a version of the traditional print or paper-based journal which is disseminated electronically in some form or other directly to the end user." Although e-journals had been in existence since 1976 it became prominent during the 1990's. Since it's inception in 1665 the printed journal remained the primary vehicle for communication among academics and researchers.

The advent of the Internet transformed publishing radically as it made it possible to publish cheaply. Internet also made access universally available. Because of the Internet academics and researchers became more creative and productive.

Cost Factors

There had been major increases in the cost of journal subscriptions during the last two decades. According to researcher between 1986 and 1996 the average increase per journal subscription had been a whopping 147 per cent. This state of affairs had been laid at the door of the commercial publishers. Moahi states that simultaneously there had been a significant increase in the number of science and engineering journals published. Because of ever decreasing budgets academic libraries are unable to purchase the titles they deem necessary.

Falk cites McCabe of Georgia Institute of Technology stating that publishers offer libraries bundled packages of e-journals under the pretense that it is cheaper but these deals actually inflate prices.

Moahi is of the opinion that a consequence of these bundled deals is that academic libraries end up with titles they do not want or need. Despite the fact that publishers have substantial cost savings on first copy production of e-journals and also save on distribution costs, these savings are not passed onto their customers. Cost of e-journals tend to be similar or higher that their printed counterparts. What further complicate matters are the fact that provision has to be made for connectivity and desktops, which means additional costs. Aggregate publishers also tend to drop titles without prior consultation with academic librarians.

Academic Library's Response to Publishers

Despite general expectations that e-journals should be cheaper than printed versions publishers maintain the status quo by maximizing profits. Publisher's attitudes have forced academic institutions to take a tougher stance against them. Recently the Senate of the University of California instructed the library to sever all ties with Elsevier, *e.g.*, cancel subscriptions and cease submission of research papers if negotiations with them fail to obtain a reduction in the price of subscriptions.

Harvard University has cancelled their Elsevier subscriptions of bundled journals. The Senate of North Carolina State University urged that excessive prices from publishers be resisted.

Four North Carolina universities had signed a deal for a bundle of 1300 journals in 2003 with the proviso that no titles are dropped. When these institutions wanted to renew subscription for 2004 the price was so exorbitant that they all cancelled the deal. Cornell University and the University of Missouri also cancelled subscription with Elsevier for the same reasons. Three

North Carolina universities have drafted policies to only forward research to publishers whose journals are reasonably priced and widely accessible.

In the event of this not being possible they will include an "authorisation to publish' clause in contracts that empower the author to retain copyright to reproduce research for academic and research purposes. Kansas University includes a clause in their contracts that give them permission to use their research for teaching and research purposes and retain the right to make it available on public accessible Web sites.

Open Access Journals

The open access initiative is aimed at making scholarly research freely available via the Internet. Open access journals are journals available on the Internet for academics, researchers and the general public. The open access journal philosophy received a tremendous stimulus with the birth of the *Public Library of Science* (PLoS). At its conception 30,000 scientists promised their support in terms of submitting research. The first open access journal to emerge was PLoS Biology in the year 2003 which was received with great enthusiasm. In the publishing arena the Biomed Central publishing house embarked on free access to peer-reviewed journals. Recently the *Directory of Open Access Journals* (DOAJ) made open access journals available covering different languages and subjects.

Open Access Archives

Many leading universities are setting up electronic archives as depositories for their research output and are granting access to it. There are plans in progress to use theses archives as a platform to provide open access journals. The *Massachusetts Institute of Technology* (MIT) has made software freely available for managing electronic archives. Currently there are approximately 140 universities that have established open access archives. The number of journals held in these archives have increased from 20,000 in 2001 to 1.3 million in 2003. Although this is still fairly insignificant compared to the 2 million peer reviewed journals printed annually it nevertheless sends out a clear warning signal to commercial publishers of what is to come. In Europe the Open Archives Forum was established. The goal of this forum is to establish electronic archives and make it globally available.

e-Books

There are various definitions for e-books but e-books are essentially published books and reference materials that were digitised and are distributed electronically. In the year 2000 e-books were heralded as the new publishing revolution. One market research company predicted that by 2005 there would be 1.9 million users. Forrester Research predicted that income generated from e-book sales would increase from $9 million in 2000 to $414 million in 2004.

Unfortunately e-book popularity never rose to expected heights. Despite the negativity surrounding e-books it had not demised completely. There are still some companies dealing with e-books that are profitable and experiencing growth. One of the first commercial e-book services, NetLibrary, was established by OCLC in 1998.

The NetLibrary collection has since grown to over 400 000 titles. The shortcoming in the NetLibrary system is the fact that an e-book can only be used by one user at a time. Questia, another commercial e-book service went live in 2001. Their target market was students and they employed librarians to manage collection development. By 2003 Questia had more than 400 000 titles from more than 200 publishers.

Advantages of e-Books

E-books have numerous advantages. There are no printing, storage, warehousing and shipping costs. Consequently e-books can be published at costs much lower than conventional books. Additional advantages are online availability, keyword-searching capability, cross-referencing, adjustable fonts, electronic bookmarks and imbedded audio. Updating e-books will be easier than re-editing conventional books.

From an academic library point of view benefits would include cost savings in terms of shelving, binding, circulation, overdue notices and management of fines. All needed would be a person to maintain the collection and a person to manage user accounts.

Print collections in academic libraries are very expensive to acquire and maintain. E-books are also environmentally friendly in the sense that no tree pulping is necessary to for its production. The flaws in current e-book technology will be overcome. When that day dawns e-books being much cheaper to produce and publish than printed books as well as economies of scale will tip the balance in favour of e-books.

Disadvantages

The devices needed to read e-books are relatively expensive, *e.g.*, hand held devices, PC's and laptops. In order to minimize piracy publishers use proprietary hardware devices and software platforms. This lack of universal standards is a problem.

The question many ask is whether e-books pose a threat to libraries. Can it eventually put libraries out of business. Although e-books did not take off as well as expected within the public domain, the use of e-books at schools, colleges and universities are rapidly increasing.

Use of e-Books

Falk refers to research done by Forrester that indicated that 4 million e-books were sold at campus stores in year 2000. Forrester forecasted that by year 2005 e-book sales should have increased to 140 million. Research indicates that students are developing a preference for e-books above printed books. At the University of Rochester Rush Rhees Library course reserve section students were exposed to printed books and their e-book equivalents. Statistics compiled on a weekly base indicated a three to one preference in favour of the e-books.

SOME OF THE PROBLEMS RELATING TO ELECTRONIC RESOURCES

Online full text implies availability of articles rather that the entire content of a particular journal. The complete contents of a publication are seldom put into a full text database. This implies that an author one might have seen in a physical publication may not be traceable in electronic format. This predicament also applies to archiving where there is uncertainty about the percentage of a journals content that is archived in digital format.

Another concern is that the academic library in a sense has lost control over the resources it make available to its users. When academic libraries subscribe to aggregator databases, *e.g.* EbscoHost or ProQuest they subscribe to a service, a list of titles bundled together of which many are useful and many not so useful. One of the problems is that aggregators sometimes drop titles. Typically this would happen when publishers withdraw all their titles.

The Chronicle of Higher Education has reported in 2003 that Elsevier has been removing articles from aggregator files because of various reasons, *e.g.*, scientific misconduct, plagiarism and errors. On the Web there are masses of information available.

With search engines, *e.g.* Google or Yahoo one may find useful information and record the URL or title. There is however no guarantee when one wants to revisit the site that it may still be available. Sites on the Web sometimes disappear overnight. An organisation may have merged with another one or the host server might have become dysfunctional.

The quality of information available on the Web is also sometimes questionable. Any individual with access to the Web and basic hardware and software can publish on the Web regardless of whether the person's views are factually correct. On the Web are more than an estimated billion Web pages and this create problems for users of the academic library to distinguish between what is useful or not. Another problem is that search engines cover only a small portion of what is what is available on the Web. There are lots of information behind firewalls and thus inaccessible. Many crawlers of search engines only focus on html and ignore graphics. Generally ASCII files will not be found. To assist users academic library services should try and inform users when sites have relocated or are no longer available.

CHANGES IN THE EDUCATIONAL ENVIRONMENT

ICT have changed every fibre of society including education. Lifelong learning has become essential. A very competitive working environment has influenced this. Even educational methodologies have changed. Greater interaction between learner, educator and material is becoming the norm. Learners have greater choices in terms of curricula. The 24 hour networked classroom became reality leading to the birth of the virtual library.

Network technologies and new educational methodologies have empowered learners, given them a greater measure of control and participation in the learning process and enabled network interaction with both fellow students and lecturers. Change in institutions of higher education will compel academic libraries to change accordingly. The most dramatic change according to visionaries will take place in distance education. This was a direct influence of the Internet. When the day dawns when distance education becomes the norm, universities the way we know them may vanish and virtual libraries may become a reality. Recently an author warned that the railroad managers overlooked the fact that they were in the transport business. He noted that universities must remember they are in the education business and not the campus business. If campuses disappear libraries will disappear.

There are already examples of cyberspace universities, e.g. Phoenix. If academics should fail to restructure their institutions' external forces will do it. Of cardinal importance is to focus on what education wants to achieve and how one can fulfill it. Survival of the academic library will depend on its ability to continuously reshape and reorganise.

Distance Education

New technologies driven by ICT innovation have enhanced the virtual delivery of academic programmes and stimulated unparalleled growth of distance education at institutions of higher learning. The phenomenal growth in distance education technologies has lead to an escalation in the availability of online academic programmes and a tremendous increase in remote users. In order to support these programmes academic librarians have developed excellent portfolios and programmes for remote students. One aspect that is neglected is evaluation of these programmes.

What is of critical importance is to establish how these programmes are used, which ones are used more frequently than others and why. Monash University library in Australia provides online curriculum content to their students all over the world. The university library provides online access to more than 440 online databases, 140,000 e-books and 20,000 e-journal subscriptions. Apart from full text databases and e-books the university library also provides digital audio recordings of lectures that become available minutes after conclusion of lectures.

According to Ho Monash University library has made a paradigm shift to a complete new service module that utilises e-commerce technologies. Moyo is of the opinion that the transformation in distance education has created a need for distance librarianship.

Changes in Scholarly Communication

The rising of the Internet and subsequent Web during the 1990's has resulted in the decline of the printed journal as the principal medium of scholarly publication. The costs of journals have increased dramatically driven by commercial publishers trying to control research content. This resulted in depriving many researchers of access to needed resources. The Web has also made fast and easy electronic publication possible and has increased direct communication between researchers.

Publishers immediately started making electronic versions of printed journals available on the Web. This was however seen as perpetuating the status quo in a new medium. Scholars started seeing in the new technology the potential to develop a new model for publishing research and an opportunity to return ownership of scholarly output to the rightful owners of the research.

These sentiments were driven by shortcomings in existing scholarly journal publishing which were:

- The time to publish an article was to too long.
- The existing model demanded transfer of copyright to the publishers.
- A too rigid peer review system that tends to favour publication of authors from the more prestigious institutions.
- Journal prices had become unaffordable.

One of the outcomes of this dissatisfaction was the birth of the e-print which is essentially an electronic version of a research paper. E-prints lead to the development of e-print repositories that are an archive of e-prints accessible to the public. Some of the advantages of e-print repositories are the reduction of publishing barriers, increased visibility of research and rapid dissemination of research results to a wide audience.

Consortia Collaboration

Initially libraries got involved in consortia in order to reduce costs particularly with regard to the acquisition of e-resources. Consortia development is thus an attempt to maximize limited resources through co-operation and resource sharing. In the consortia scenario the emphasis is on access to information rather than ownership. Consortia collaboration provides more power when it comes to negotiating contracts. It also provides a platform for libraries to co-operate in terms of services. Nowadays libraries also turn to consortia to provide advice and guidance in complex decision-making. The input of consortia is also valuable in terms of evaluating e-resources in terms of quality, different options, e.g., whether to subscribe to journals or pay article-by-article.

The South African Scenario

In terms of network infrastructure South Africa is not on par with first world countries where consortia cooperation is very effective. For the establishment of an information society in South Africa proper connectivity infrastructure is an absolute prerequisite. There is an uneven distribution of telecommuni-cations infrastructure across South Africa stemming from the political ideologies of the apartheid government. This inequity is also prevalent in South African academic libraries. Institutions for the privileged white people were well financed and resourced under the apartheid regime. Institutions for blacks were under funded and thus under resourced; hence the distinction between advantaged and historically disadvantaged institutions. Because of this there are great differences in wealth and the collections of academic libraries.

In South Africa there are five academic library consortia.:

1. CALICO (Cape Library Cooperative) based in Cape Town.
2. ESAL (Eastern Seaboard Association of Libraries based in Kwazulu-Natal.
3. FRELICO (Free State Libraries and Information Consortium) based in Free State.
4. Gaelic (Gauteng and Environs Library Consortium) based in Gauteng.
5. SEALS (South Eastern Academic Libraries System in the Eastern Cape.

Essential for the development of successful consortia is low cost tariffs coupled with high bandwith connectivity. Academic institutions constantly engaged with government agencies to achieve this ideal. Library consortia can also be invaluable in assisting member libraries with change management because "An organisation needs external coaches to catalyse, guide and facilitate a change process", the reason being that people within the academic library are sometimes to closely involved with daily activities to see things objectively. An outside view often helps to see things in the right perspective.

ICT MANAGEMENT ISSUES

Libraries are caught midstream between print versus a digital setup. To navigate the transition from print to digital remains enormously challenging.

Rapid ICT development had resulted in lots of incompatible systems being used within libraries. To manage ICT is a complex and daunting task. To select the right ICT technologies is a major management issue. It is very difficult in a world where hardware and software changes at a phenomenal rate.

The shift in the academic library from printed resources to electronic resources that are accessible via campus networks or remotely and the fact that users can even request services via the network has lead to a decline in users visiting the library. The growing electronic nature of the academic library is resulting in it becoming less visible as a physical entity to its users.

What is also disturbing is the fact that users are often oblivious to the fact that they are using library resources because of the seamlessness of access. Users are not aware of the fact that to make those resources available are costly in terms of subscriptions, infrastructure and staff. Academic libraries need to find a way to reverse this scenario of the library loosing its visibility. Hooper suggests that the academic library should use ICT to stimulate interaction between user and the library. It should be done in such a way that the user could identify with the academic library providing the service and experience a sense of ownership.

As a starting point the academic library can interact with the user relating to loans, database searches and other services available. It is also important to create an environment where the user can provide feedback relating to service shortcomings and suggestions that could lead to improvement. Stakeholder relationships are also very important. It is of vital importance for the academic library to ensure that their operations dovetail with the strategic goals of the university it supports.

In these days where accountability is becoming the norm it is essential to run operations in such a way that the academic library at any point is in a position to provide proof of the value of its services as a return on investment made by the university authority.

MANAGERIAL CHANGE FOR THE SURVIVAL OF LIBRARY

DIGITAL LIBRARY AND ITS IMPACT

The origin of ICT has changed the performance and service pattern of every institution and organisation, library is not excluded from it. Impact of ICT has transformed the 'traditional library' into 'automated library'. 'Digital library' and 'virtual library' are also the gift of ICT. Many libraries have been serving as hybrid libraries. A library digital is an organised collection of electronic resources. Digital library is a very complex and dynamic entity.

It has brought phenomenal change in the information collection, preservation and dissemination scene of the world. It is a complex entity because it is completely based on ICT systems and the concept is of recent origin. Its main aim is to provide ready access to the required information at a right time to the right user with right information.

The collection of digital library are not limited to document surrogates they extend to digital artifacts which cannot be represented or distributed in printed formats. Therefore, digital library is not a single unit, but a complex of multiple units that provide instant access to all information, for all sectors of society, from anywhere in the world.

Therefore, in this context, the digital library must cope up with the changing technology, information seeking behaviour of its user, user needs, etc. The day has come to adopt change management at par with information management in the library.

CHANGES IN LIBRARY AND INFORMATION CENTRE MANAGEMENT

Due to fast-paced technological change and new skill requirements, information professionals are increasingly required to renew their skills and practice in order to gain an awareness of technological advances. As a result, the profession itself exists in a state of flux alongside these emerging technologies, with traditional roles being increasingly subsumed by new skills and working environments, and, therefore, job descriptions. Thus, information professionals are now expected to be aware of and capable of using and demonstrating emerging ICTs.

There is a need for additional training to augment the traditional skill and knowledge base with a competency in ICT use. Information professionals must be flexible, and adopt traditional skills to incorporate the requirements of technological advances.

Given the current situation, wherein ICTs are being continuously updated or introduced and traditional formats are being replaced or supplemented by digital formats, it seems likely that there will continue to be a need for regular training for information professionals. There is also an increased focus on communication skills, with more people involved in the electronic information environment. Information professionals are being called upon to work closely with ICT users and providers - including IT staff - and to work in collaboration with others in the profession. Some groups of users lack the necessary IT skills to obtain quality information and information professionals will therefore be called upon to act as both educators and intermediaries.

Given these circumstances, information professionals are required to have additional teaching and communication skills. Thus, it is vital for those in management positions to recognise the imperative of *continuing professional development* (CPD) and ensure that the staff is proactive in maintaining up-to-date levels of expertise. The significance of CPD in this milieu has been acknowledged by both the United Kingdom's *Chartered Institute of Library and Information Professionals* (CILIP) and the United States' *American Library Association* (ALA).

Certain active roles are necessary for change management to:

- *Establish the quality goals of the library:* Library and Information Centres (LICs) should aim to establish the quality goals for qualitative service to its user community.
- *Provide the resources to their library:* LICs should provide all necessary resources suitable in the ICT era to manage the LICs in a better way.
- *Provide the quality-oriented training to the library staff:* New generation library staff are almost trained with ICT applications to LICs but old staff and others who are novices in such applications need quality training because without quality training library staff are unable to provide automated services.
- *Stimulate quality improvement in the day to day activities of library:* This is the age of competition. Like other organisations, to survive the LICs, top management should stimulate the staff for quality improvement in the day to day activities of LICs.
- *Review progress of the library activities:* Higher management should review the progress of library activities to maintain the quality and quantity of assigned job to the staff.
- *Give recognition to library staff:* Top level management should recognise the operational level library staff for quality performance, without which they will be demoralised to perform the job in a better way.

With the change in environment the objectives need to be revised to face the challenges of future. Over a period of time, due to the impact of technological advances, research and development, economic, social and political factors, the objectives also tend to change. To adopt these changes, it is essential to state objectives and functions of information system in changing context. For this purpose the following steps should be followed.

Structure Related Changes

The structure related changes in libraries and information centres may include:

- *Change in the work design:* The work design of a traditional library is not similar to modern automated library, so a change in the work design is compulsory for the success of automated library.
- *Change in the basis of departmentalisation:* There are various departments in university and research libraries. In case of automated

library, book acquisition, classification and cataloguing, circulation, serial control assignments are being done through computer with specific software instead of doing manually. Besides these departments, modern library has other departments like barcoding, RFID tagging, OPAC/web-OPAC, e-journals, e-books, CD-ROM, digital library, touch screen kiosk, server maintenance etc.

- *Change in the number of operation levels to perform various activities, routine work of library staff:* As there is a major change in the processing and service departments a change in the number of staff in the lower level or operational level management has become essential.
- *Change in the plans, programmes, policies and procedures to and improving integration among various sections:* Due to changse in the pattern of service; plans, programmes, policies and procedures and integration within various departments it is very essential to cater to the service in a better way.
- *Change in the span of management and levels of management for effective co-ordination mechanism and flow of task:* Since the nature of job of modern automated library is more complex than traditional library, it is very difficult to manage large number of operational level staff under one middle level manager. In view of this span of management should be narrow and levels of management should be changed because top and middle level management have to be directly linked with every department to perform each department's functions in a better way as well as for effective co-ordination mechanism with every department.
- *Change in line-staff and functional authority, work group relations between people and functions to improve their ability:* Line positions are responsible for accomplishing the organisation's primary objectives; they have final authority to make decisions. Staff positions, on the other hand, provide suggestions and advice for the line positions but cannot, theoretically make decisions for the line positions.
- An organisation seeks to keep authority for decision making in the positions accountable for results and to preserve a clear chain of command from the top to the bottom of the organisation. But in the automated library system there should be no hurdle between line and staff position because anyone who is aware about a particular system can give his advice. It helps to improve the work group relation as well as the ability of the all levels of management.

Structural changes affect relationships among the organisational positions and in the interactions among internal departments, the reporting mechanism, interactions of all sections in the library and the functional relationships.

Changes for Technological Advancement

The technology refers to the sum total of human knowledge providing ways to do the things in a better way with the help of techniques. It may include inventions and techniques affecting the ways of doing things.

Thus, technology related changes may include:

- *Use of new machines and equipments for developing new services or modifying existing services:* Many new machines and equipments, *e.g.*, computer, server, barcoding equipments, RFID tools are necessary for developing new services or modifying existing manual services. So the awareness about the use of new machines, equipments and tools is very essential.
- *The procedure of doing things which may result in change of work process:* The methods and procedures of doing new tasks should be changed in context of old library system. So that the work process is not disrupted.
- *Introduction of technological devices like computers and computer related technologies:* Introduction of technological devices like computers and computer related technologies is necessary for automated library. Without computers and related technologies, we are unable to cater to services in automated library system.
- *Change in the existing techniques for making or doing the things in effective way or adoption of new techniques for creative work:* Automated library is ICT oriented and some technique is involved in every work. So existing techniques of traditional library management should be changed and adoption of new techniques is very essential to carry out every task and service in automated library environment.
- *Change in the methods of using new tools equipments and products:* In the traditional library system, there are only a few equipments like fumigation chamber, catalogue cabinet, book rack, cardex, journal display rack, etc.
- But now computer terminals, server, barcoding equipments, RFID tools, etc., equipments and products are being used, so it is very natural to change the methods of using new tools, equipments and products.

The change in the technology affects the nature of work and activities, organisational structure, the processes and the people's behaviour.

Task-related Changes

Technology related changes determine the ways to complete the task effectively and efficiently. Task related changes helps to achieve major gains in terms of cost, service and time.

Task related changes may include:

- *Identifying the steps involved in performing tasks:* It is very necessary to organise meeting with library staff at all levels to identify the steps to perform the tasks effectively.
- *Task identification:* Every task should be identified to depute the staff who is efficient in that work. So, proper task identification is the key factor to perform the task properly and to serve the user community in a better way.
- *Significance of task related changes in attaining the organisational and institutional objectives:* As the nature of library has been changed so it is very significant to change the task which is relevant in changed atmosphere to attain the organisational and institutional objectives.
- *Identifying the skills and abilities required for the changed task:* It is very natural to identify the skills and abilities required for the changed task and to assign the specific job to the specific staff that is suitable for that particular job.
- *Improving both quality and quantity of work/ service:* For the satisfaction of our customer we should improve our quality as well as quantum of day to day work/service.
- *Bringing cost-effective solutions through maximum use of available resources:* Cost-effectiveness is concerned with the value. It asks, "This is what the service costs. Is it worth it?" So effectiveness of the resources is the key to maximum use of available resources.
- *Improving the work performance:* Quality training of staff is very essential to aware the task of each and every personnel effectively which improves the work performance.

People-related Changes

Change in any factor has an impact on human resources and human behaviour. In the context of Library and Information Science, the people-related categories include:

- *The library staff:* In case of library staff, it requires the corresponding changes to be made in the skills, abilities and the performance of the employees.
- *New investment in training and development activities so that employees acquire new skills and activities:* New skills and activities are required in automated library system so new investment in training and development is essential. Library can get the fund from UGC for this purpose by making a systematic and comprehensive proposal
- *Socialising employees into the organisational structure so that they learn the new routines on which organisational performance depends....':* Top

management should meet with middle and operational level management to become aware about the every bit of work with theory and practical and to assign the job to every personnel as well as time required for this purpose. Through socialising the employees organisational efficiency can also be increased.

Accordingly the change may also include –

- *Change in skill levels of the workforce:* Skill levels of each and every employee should be changed to cope up with new task.
- *Change in the training programmes to improve performance levels:* Training programme should be organised in a scientific way to sensitise the employee about every practical aspect of work and service. So change in training programmes is essential to improve performance levels of the staff.
- *Change in attitude and values:* Change in attitude and values is a must for better performance in work and service in the changed library environment.
- *Change in behaviour and interaction pattern:* As the library scenario has changed from traditional to automated one, behavioural and interaction pattern regarding work and service should also be changed.
- *Change in technology requires different skills of the operator:* Presently, library is technology controlled. To cope up with this change, the library personnel requires different skills to carry out their own task because it is very difficult to work properly for a unskilled staff.
- *Change in the structure requires change in their position, their authority, responsibility, etc.:* Due to shift from traditional to automated library, structural change is required. For this purpose positional, authoritative and responsibility change is necessary for better performance.
- *The readers:* Readers/users/customers are our prime focus. To serve the right user to the right information at the right time, we have to organise our resources systematically through which they can collect their information himself/herself. Such a systematic arrangement helps us to work and serve the users with less human resources.

Any change in the processes demands that it should be communicated to the readers to enable them to adjust to these changes. Readers are ultimately getting the benefits of all the technological advances, procedures, services, activities as well as other resources for their satisfaction in the libraries and information centres.

Changes in Library Policies

Change in the objectives and functions of the library and information system by the planning body would directly impact the existing plans and policies of the library. Accordingly, change in plans and policies become essential. The developmental plans and policies should be in conformity with the objectives and functions of library and information system as well as the institution it serves.

Changes in Objectives and Functions of Information System

The information system in the changed environment shall aim at:

- *Ensuring maximum use of all available resources:* Top management should ensure maximum use of all available resources through cost-effective solutions.
- *Promotion and development of all units in the library:* In the automated library, to cater the service to the users in a right way, it is very essential to develop all units in a proper way.
- *Better communication of ideas to achieve the objectives in an ever changing environment:* To communicate every new ideas to all levels of management is essential to achieve the objectives in constantly changing environment of library work and service.
- *Minimising the time, cost and efforts involved in all the activities, processes and functions:* Top level management should plan with with staff at middle and operational level for proper coordination of every function with minimum time, cost and efforts because duplicity of activities, processes and functions increases the time, cost and efforts.

In order to achieve the newly stated objectives as per the requirement of changing circumstances, certain functions are to be carried out. These functions may relate to adoption of latest technologies, use of modern tools and techniques, updating professional skill, ability and knowledge through education and training, future prospects of change in goals, objectives and functions, etc.

Librarians will need to be ready for competition and prepared to find new ways to make their skills and services distinct from those offered by the competition from media companies, publishers, internet companies, intermediary service providers and also from technologists parking on traditional library territory with technical names for old fashioned library ideas.

PROCESS OF MANAGERIAL CHANGE IN LIBRARIES AND INFORMATION CENTRES

The various steps involved in a planned change are:

- *Identifying need for change:* In the changing scenario of library, it is very essential to identify every need of users for effective planning and execution.
- *Elements to be changed:* It is very natural that the elements in traditional library and automated library are different. So top level

management should foster awareness about every element of change and communicate the relevant elements to every unit.

- *Planning for change:* Every organisation/institution plans the total work procedures for proper execution. So, for the sake of efficiency all the steps for success in the changing scenario.
- *Assessing change forces:* It is very essential to assess the change forces for success of the new project/assignment.
- *Change actions:* Each and every action should be changed for proper functioning of every unit for better work and service.
- *Feedback:* This is very important aspect of every organisation/ institution. Without feedback system, an organisation/institution cannot assess their customer needs and information seeking behaviour as well as their satisfaction level.

Above steps in a planned change can be applied for managing the changes in libraries and information centres.

Identifying Need for Change

Various external and internal factors necessitate change in libraries and information centres.

This change may be made in staff, library building or internal layouts with infrastructural facilities, the hardware and software requirements, activities and services, etc.

While identifying the need for change, the following should be considered:

- How the change will have an effect on the system, space, staff, services, activities, etc.
- What will be the frequency and nature of change.
- How it will impact use of information sources for study, research and development.
- How it will impact users information requirements.
- How it will have an effect on the procedures, policies and programmes.

Identification of need for change depends on:

- Readers' expectations;
- Changing objectives of libraries and information centres according to changing environment;
- Policies and programmes to be implemented to achieve these objectives; and
- New challenges created by change in technology.

These steps will determine the rationale why change is essential and if change will be made, whether it will create problems or not?

Elements to be Changed

What elements of the libraries and information centres should be changed is to be decided for managing the change. It will be decided on the basis of the need for the change as well as the objectives of the change.

The identification of need for change will determine the base for why change is essential whereas this step will specify what elements in the system are to be changed.

Generally change is required in the structure, technology, hardware and software requirements, database design, IT infrastructure, skills of the staff, and nature of library services, etc. The nature and extent of change in the elements will further depend upon the nature of problems being faced by the libraries.

Sometimes a change in one element may require change in another element, e.g., a change in any activity from manual to machine may require change in staff and their skills but at the same time change in the structure of the libraries may also be required.

Planning for Change

Planning for change includes deciding in advance about:

- When to bring change.
- Who will bring change and
- How to bring change, etc.

In the libraries and information centres change is usually required in the structure, technology, staff and services. Careful planning for bringing change in these elements is essential because "Planning looks at how the librarians and information scientists can develop the means to locate the resources which are most relevant to the need of users community, integrate these resources into their infrastructure, adopt the necessary technology and finally to anticipate the future trends in changing circumstances".

Accessing Change Forces

Various internal and external forces enable us to bring change. To manage the change effectively, it becomes necessary to ensure the co-operation of the people to create an environment in which change will be accepted by all. Change force, both internal and external, is an important consideration to anticipate and respond properly for the problems in the existing system.

Success in managing the change is possible only when we assess change forces and their impact on the efficiency and effectiveness of the existing system. If the effect of these change forces can be accessed, it becomes possible to take necessary actions for change.

Actions for Change

A distinguished social psychologist, Kurt Lewin, developed what he called 'Action Research' which happens to be a more motivational approach and a more evolutionary one.

According to him 'since most change efforts flounder because carefully expected plans are ignored or sabotaged', this first step is critical:

- Seek change when the people who are going to have to effect the changing are distressed and feel they have a problem.

The next step involves getting them to accept some procedure for exploring how the problem can be solved.

The manager . . . gets the department to establish a study or mini research project on the problem:

- What kind of information is needed?
- Who will collect it?
- Who should analyse it and how; what is secret and what can be openly discussed?

The manager may have to help to get the project underway. It may require some outside technical aid, a survey, a review of old records, interviews with people in the departments.

This step means the manager must:

- Get consensus on what kinds of data and what method of collection and assessment the group will accept as valid for evolving a solution to its problem.
- Make feedback then, the critical element; it becomes a catalyst to the people who will have to change, emphasising the discrepancy between what they believed and the reality of the situation.
- Aid people in coping, skill transfer, experimenting with new methods.
- Then the cycle is repeated.

Usually, the initial efforts won't be roaring successes; there will still be unresolved problems, and some innovations won't work as planned or hoped.

So the group which is the focus of change is encouraged to continue:

- Research/study the work flow problems – by collecting data.
- Evaluate and feedback.
- Consider further innovations.
- Get help in implementing these.
- Then check how these are working.

The manager's role is one of felicitato, so that the individuals will be motivated to change, in contrast to being told to change; Further, the process is, or ought to be, a continuing one'. The Lewin model has suggested that every change requires three steps – "the first step is unfreesing - individuals who will be affected by the impending change must be laid to recognise why the change is necessary. Next, the change itself is implemented. Finally, refreesing involves reinforcing and supporting the change so that it becomes a part of the system.

These steps can also be effectively applied in library and information centres to manage the change. At first step, the library staff as well as the reader community have to be informed about why change is essential to improve efficiency of services. At second step, they have to be made aware about new methods of working, new procedures adopted, their expected roles in changed environment, etc. We have to conceive them to recognise the basic purpose of change and ensure that they fit into the new organisational change for the benefit of all. At third step, integrating change into actual practice, the staff as well as readers has to adapt to the new environment with improved performance. They have to be protected from reverting back to the old and traditional behaviour.

Feedback

Feedback is essential to ensure that changed pattern is going to achieve the objectives with minimum time, money and energy and determine whether follow-up action is essential to ensure success of change in management. The impact of change is to be measured in terms of attainment of objectives, improvement of services, readers' increased satisfaction, employee motivation and increased level of efficiency and effectiveness of each activity, product and service.

5

Management and Marketing

Leadership and management are two terms that are often used interchangeably. In fact, they describe entirely different concepts, as leadership is more than a component of the functions of management. Management is the process of administering and coordinating resources to ensure than an organisation accomplishes its mission and goals. *Library and information science* (*LIS*) has a managerial focus; librarians manage the infrastructure of a library: its collections, staff, technology, and facilities. For this reason, the interconnection between management and leadership is the domain of LIS theory and practice.

The purpose of leadership is to challenge the status quo as libraries undergo a transition in organisational culture, the services they offer, and workforce restructuring as they try to better fulfill the organisational and broader institutional mission. Management, on the other hand, prepares the infrastructure for that transition. As early as 1950s, the term *managerial leadership* was coined, but its definition was imprecise. "No definition of the phrase 'managerial leadership' has gained general acceptance. In fact, it is often referred to but left undefined" or merely equated to particular leadership theories and styles.

The term recognizes that leadership is not exclusively a top-down process between the *boss* as a leader and subordinates. This paper, which aligns with the programme in managerial leadership in the information professions at Simmons College, views managerial leadership as encompassing an examination of leaders, followers, the interaction between the two groups, and, in this context, leadership becomes a process whereby people influence others to develop, accept, and carry out a shared vision that guides future actions of the organisation.

As a result, that process is longitudinal and involves events. Because leadership is not always effective or positive, it should not automatically be assumed that goals and events are always successfully met or that staff members are sufficiently motivated or inspired to challenge themselves and others. The purpose of this paper is to build on the international research agenda that Candy

Schwartz and I presented in 2008 and that illustrates that LIS research needs to go beyond a preoccupation with under-standing the style, personality, traits, and other characteristics of the boss and that person's influence on organisational dynamics and performance.

LEADERSHIP

In addition to focusing on a shared vision, leadership is about giving people confidence to meet organisational expectations and to serve as change agents. It also encourages them to seek, be given, and benefit from team coaching and mentoring aimed at enhancing their knowledge, skills, abilities, effectiveness, and commitment to the transformation process. A library's staff might consist of both followers and leaders who are willing to collaborate with other institutional partners.

As well, the director, if that person is truly a leader, might be more so within the organisation than in representing the library to other stakeholders. With so many libraries organised into teams or small groups and involved in managing change; with new staff members expected to work together to plan, implement, administer, and evaluate services; and with libraries forging new partnerships at the institutional, local, and other levels, more librarians are becoming increasingly interested in knowing about and applying leadership theories, styles, traits, and roles.

They are also trying to develop their leadership potential. Within this context, there is much interest in transformational leadership and emotional intelligence, which helps leaders move beyond basic 'people skills' to understanding how one's own reactions and feelings impact how one is perceived by others.

Leaders and managers need to understand their own emotions and recognize and understand the feelings of those around them. Leaders are more successful when they pay attention to their social interactions with others in the workplace and the impact they as leaders have on those around them. It is also important for leaders to understand the impact that others' emotions have on them. When leaders are aware of the emotional side of the workplace, they are better able to create a working environment that encourages excellence.

As librarians gain an understanding of such theories, it is important to remember that, as Peter Northouse points out, leadership has 'many different meanings;' this is evident when people "finish the sentence 'Leadership is....'" Their responses might ignore social influence, add new elements, or confuse leadership with someone holding a managerial position. They might also fail to recognize that there are also spiritual, legacy, moral, ethical, charismatic, and other types of leadership. Each of these areas actually produces separate leadership theories that have been long investigated but rarely connected to LIS.

CONTEXT

Even though this paper focuses on topical areas for future research and selected methodologies, it is important to remember that methodologies do not frame a research study. Research, which engages in problem-solving, is shaped by a reflective enquiry. These components, as well as the study procedures and data quality, comprise a framework in which each component should be bonded to the others through, what David R. Krathwohl calls, a 'chain-of-reasoning.' That 'chain,' he points out, 'is only as strong as its weakest link' and 'all links...should be built to about the same strength.' He further explains that, "as the work load is picked up by the first link and passed to successive links, the work load—and therefore the nature of each link—is determined by the previous links."

Furthermore, "where several links together join those above and below them, there may be trade-offs to compensate for weaknesses. It is beyond the scope of this paper, however, to present and relate the entire chain-of-reasoning. Still, I would be remiss if I did not underscore the importance of the theoretical framework. Vincent A. Anfara, Jr. and Norma T. Mertz provide an excellent overview of theatrical frameworks and the impact of 'good and useful' theory on the chain-of-reasoning. In the case of managerial leadership, like other areas within LIS, there are numerous theories, some of which fit a given problem statement and set of objectives better than others.

One such theory might be constructive-development theory, which relates directly to leadership and which offers a way to view the complex problems that organisations face from multiple perspectives. This theory describes "how adults develop more complex and comprehensive ways of making sense of themselves and their experience." Another concept relates to trust, which is an essential component in motivating or inspiring others and which is more than a trait.

RESEARCH DESIGNS

As a prelude to methodologies, research designs for leadership research might call for a longitudinal study and a comparison of several organisations. Widely used research designs centre on either a case study or the application of grounded theory. A case study is a means "for learning about a complex instance, based on a comprehensive understanding of that instance obtained by extensive description and analysis of that instance taken as a whole and in its context."

Grounded theory, on the other hand, "is a method for discov-ering theories, concepts, hypotheses, and propositions directly from data, rather than from a priori assumptions, other research, or existing theoretical frameworks." Theory emerges from, and is grounded in, the data themselves.

DATA-GATHERING TECHNIQUES

This part focuses on some of the most prevalent methodo-logies used in leadership research, especially within LIS. As such, it builds from Karin Klenke's work on leadership research. It is increasingly common for researchers to apply qualitative methods. The accompanying table offers examples of some methodologies applicable to the study of leadership in LIS that will not be discussed in the body of this paper. The sources in that table came from an extensive review of the vast literature on leadership produced outside LIS.

The largest number of research studies related to leadership involves the distribution of a self-report survey or questionnaire. Such surveys are often in paper-and-pencil format, although more recently Web-based surveys have appeared with increasing frequency. The survey might involve the use of a predeveloped, behaviour-based leadership assessment tool that is distributed to those heading the organisation or to subordinates who are asked to evaluate the director or boss as a leader or their immediate supervisor.

As an alternative, surveys might probe respondent preference for a particular leadership theory or style and ask them to rate themselves or identify the most important attributes for individuals in their position. Complementary to a questionnaire that is mailed or otherwise distributed, investigators might use personal or focus groups interviews.

Responses to open-ended questions might be subjected to content analysis, which "is a set of procedures for transforming nonstructured information into a format that allows analysis." On occasion, biographies of people identified as leaders have been developed and their content subjected to analysis for discussions of leadership.

Available historical records, however, might focus more on their accomplishments than the story behind those accom-plishments: how did the individual co-opt and navigate different stakeholders and the staff to bring about that change? If a shared vision emerged, how was it developed? Some other means of data collection include an analysis of citation patterns of a body of works on leadership and a characterization of the most cited works and authors, as well as the age of the cited material. Additional insights might be gained from a consideration of the journal's impact factor and the number of copies of a work that libraries hold.

Assuming the availability of a body of independent studies focused on the same aspect of leadership and that describes the research design, the methodologies and data-collection instruments used, information about the population and sample, and so on, meta-analysis might be appropriate. Such analysis refers to a set of statistical procedures used to summarize and integrate those studies. It reveals sources of bias and is helpful for posing research questions for future study.

Among other things, it cannot exceed the limits of what the researchers report. Another method, known as the Delphi study or technique, is a procedure relies on the use of sequential questio-nnaires in which experts share their perspectives on issues. The Delphi technique is not necessarily designed to generate consensus, but it does involve a systematic refinement of prior responses. It has been applied to seeing which leadership attributes are most critical for future managerial leaders.

Concept Mapping

Concept mapping is both a process for representing data in the form of pictures or maps and a structured methodology for organising the ideas of a group or organisation.

The goal is to bring together groups of multiple "stakeholders ... and help them rapidly form a common framework that can be used for planning, evaluation, or both." The maps represent the groups' thinking about a topic, show how their ideas are related to each other, and, in general, indicate "which ideas are more relevant, important, or appropriate."

Interviews and other techniques might produce datasets that might be examined by the use of concept maps. These maps provide a graphic illustration of patterns among the findings. Jan Schilling, for instance, takes interview data about negative leadership and produced maps that show the antecedents of such leadership, negative leadership behaviours, and the consequences of negative leadership.

Simulation and Scenarios

A simulation study, as G. Yukl explains, involves a realistic task that continues for several periods of time and asks participants to assume the role of top executives in an organisation and to engage in team and organisational learning. Simulation "is also relevant for understanding how collective learning occurs among people whose decisions and actions affect organisational processes and performance." Instead of doing a simulation exercise, researchers might develop scenarios that make projections for the next fifteen years; forecaster Joseph P. Martino indicates that the accuracy in predicting what will likely occur declines dramatically with a longer time frame.

Scenarios, as a prime technique of future studies, have long been used by government planners, corporate managers and military analysts as powerful tools to aid in decision making in the face of uncertainty. The idea behind them is to establish thinking about possible futures which can minimi[z]e surprises and broaden the span of managers' thinking about different possibilities.

They recommend that the number of scenarios not exceed four and that any scenario should meet criteria such as:

- *Plausibility* (each is capable of happening),
- *Differentiation* (each differs from the others and together they offer multiple futures),
- *Decision-making utility* (each offers insights into the future that help in planning and decision-making), and
- *Challenging* (each challenges conventional wisdom about the future).

RESEARCH AGENDA

The accompanying figure, which updates the depiction that Schwartz and I created, centres on three broad areas that relate to planning:

- Accomplishments (translating vision into effective organisational performance);
- People (creating an organisational climate that values staff and inspires them); and
- Transformation abilities (focusing on the change process that brings people together to accomplish the organisation's mission and goals—preparing the organisation of the future).

These areas match those that guide the doctoral programme in managerial leadership in the information professions (Simmons), which the Institute of Museum and Library Services has funded since 2005 with two multi-year grants. Those areas, originally modeled by the National Centre for Healthcare Leadership, cover twenty-five distinct leadership competencies. Under each of the broad areas, numerous topic areas emerge.

At the same time, relationships among the areas might be probed. As directors or other members of the senior management team retire or depart, their replacement might be someone who serves on an interim basis. Are such people leaders or caretakers? The answer might take into account the library but also engagement beyond the library, transformation abilities, mentoring, and talent management. Focusing solely on talent management, many businesses engage in succession management or planning, but do libraries?

Succession planning and management are not synonymous with mentoring. In some countries, if there is leadership, it might be characterized as autocratic. Such leadership merits analysis. Finally, various aspects of the figure might be probed in the present recession as libraries make significant decisions about collections and staff that will likely have a long-term impact. Turning to other topics, James G. Neal discusses 'feral library professionals,' which refers to the hiring of more people into traditional and nontra-ditional library positions who do not have the credentialed degree from an accredited library school programme.

Comparative case studies might analyse the emergence of leadership in organisations that employ both feral and non-feral professionals and that include staff who represent different generations. How cohesive are staff within and across departments? Do they share a common vision—do they need to share one? Studies might probe LIS educational programmes and see whether they incorporate leadership as a student learning outcome, one that reflects what students have learned throughout their programme of study and demonstrates what they can apply upon graduation.

Some other possible topics include the role of power in effective leadership, the major trends in making leadership effective, the communication networks of leaders, transformational leadership and its relationship, for instance, to

- Emotional intelligence, which deals with one's ability to manage emotions and relationships and to use this ability to advance the organisation's mission and goals. Emotional intelligence presumably requires *sense-giving* or shaping how people understand themselves, their work, and others engaged in that work.
- Resonant leadership, which focuses on self-awareness and self-renewal, and which enables individuals to recognize and cope with work stress.
- Distributed or shared leadership, which views leadership as more than a top-down approach. Leadership moves up the organisation as well and is distributed among a number of people working in teams and groups.
- Servant leadership, which recognizes that leadership is not confined to those in formal managerial positions and who lead as a way to extend service to others. The servant leader focuses on the needs and the development of followers.

Recognizing that libraries serve multicultural communities, employ a diverse staff, and deal with myriad stakeholders, it is critical to assess different leadership theories, recognizing the strengths and weaknesses of each. Many of the prevailing theorists have not considered how multiculturalism influences what they propose. Perhaps the best illustration of this comes from Linda Sue Warner and Keith Grint, who adopt a historical perspective and compare American Indian and western approaches and perspectives on leadership. There are differences between the practice of leadership in a tribal setting and in other organisational settings.

EXAMPLE

Although library directors cannot be equated with the president of the United States and other heads of government, political commentators have identified areas in which the leadership of those aspiring to be president might be probed. Prompted by the lack of penetrating questions raised in presidential debate and the quality of the responses, David Gergen and Andy Zelleke identify a series of important questions that deal with leadership and that require answers of more than a number or brief response. Their categories and questions have been reorganised and combined with the categories that Jack and Suzy Welch would like considered.

The revamped questionnaire was pre-tested with one university library director and one library consultant. Based on their comments the questionnaire was revised. As of this time, the author of this paper is conducting a study to fine-tune the instrument and to gauge the responses of some library leaders. Instead of presenting preliminary data, this part probes relevant methodologies that might be used to address the open-ended questions and determine the relative rating of the categories. The methodology part of a hypothetical study might be based on a survey that is most likely administered in the form of an interview, either in-person or by telephone.

Directors might be unwilling to devote the time necessary to complete a paper-and-pencil survey or be unwilling to write detailed responses to each question. It might be difficult to find a time when five to ten directors could meet and participate in a focus group interview. For additional data collection, the inves-tigator might ask for historical documentation or visit the institutional repositories of selected institutions to gather data for event history analysis, assuming such information has been gathered and is publicly available.

Interview results might be analysed in terms of grounded theory and content analysis. The rating of the categories on a seven-point scale might be visualized in terms of concept mapping, and such mapping might also apply to the responses to the various questions within a category, especially if responses can be gathered from the same scale. A follow-up study might concentrate on selected categories and probe responses more deeply.

For instance, under 'Coalition Building/Advocacy,' partici-pants might meet and be asked for an example of when they became a catalyst who brought groups with polarized opinions together so that all voices were at the table. The examples generated might be cast in terms of a concept map, or the investigator could make the topics recurring most frequently and pursue them more with the Delphi technique. A different study might recast question responses to the initial study or one focusing on selected categories as scenarios or as simulation exercises.

It is also possible to take selected responses from the first study and select particular sites for in-depth case study analysis. That instrument, however, is framed in such a way that the research focuses on leadership as events and assorted methodologies are applicable. Leadership, after all, "is a process, a series of activities and exchanges engaged in over time and under varied circumstances." As such, accomplishments might be viewed as events in that leadership is an ongoing, never-ending process.

To gain a more complete understanding of the phenomena under investigation, it is common for studies on leadership, like other topical areas, to incorporate more than one method of data collection. Mixed methods, which are most prevalent with case studies, integrate quantitative and qualitative methods into one study and therefore strengthen the chain-of-reasoning presented in study findings. While it is important to expand the methodo-logical tool-chest that researchers within LIS use, it is also important to shift from studying leaders to investigating leadership events.

Many aspects of leadership presented in the figure have not been addressed, and a need emerges for a fuller body of evidence-based research relevant to change management within libraries and similar complex organisations on a global basis. It is also important that those within LIS contribute to the broader literature on leadership and that their works be recognized by those in other disciplines.

LEADERSHIP AND SERVICE PROVISION IN PUBLIC LIBRARIES

In USA and Western Europe, we do witness the same types of developments in public libraries and we see very similar themes of discourses independent of the national and local culture in which these libraries operate. Some of the themes concern the manage-ment structure and organisation bur more important is probably the current think about service delivery in a broad sense. Service delivery concerns the activities. It is areas like collection and collection management, the allocation of resources to the different part of the collection, the interplay and relationship between national internet-based delivery and the local service.

Another important theme is the effort concerning the public library and its integration into the community taking up different forms of citizen services, cooperation and partnership with the local community, but also a focus on playing a new and more active role in the cultural scene by for example emphasising learning activities, lifelong learning, internet courses and different forms for events and exhibitions. The ambition is to become a local meeting place, a third room; a common intended to generate social capital.

This discourse and many of the activities resulting from it like 23 thinks, the libraries in the second world and experiments with various forms of social technology appear to have great appeal in the library profession. However, both library statistics and numerous studies of users and their preferences give a more differentiated picture. In most countries, the public libraries face economic hardship. They witness stagnating or decreasing numbers of visitors and the issues of traditional materials also tend to decrease. The public appear to value especially the services and products that suffer due to economic pressures and the internal priority setting in libraries.

Overall, it appears—at least at the surface–that users do have a rather traditional view of the public library and their stated preferences also seems to be very traditional as they are oriented towards books and information and to a lesser degree towards new services and delivery forms. It is of course of paramount interest to investigate possible discrepancies between the discourse and the practices in the professions and the users' preferences, priorities and level of satisfaction.

There is probably no right solution to the problem, but it is of both a practical and theoretical significance to investigate which factors influence the development of the discourse and the activities in the professions and in the public libraries and is also important to be able to measure users perception of the significance and importance of the service delivery and to which degree this is connected with measures of satisfaction. The paper further discusses the factors behind the profession's discourse and practices.

The concept of an organisational recipe is introduced in relation to organisational culture as two factors that have influence on the way libraries tend to adopt different forms of innovations. Of course, leadership plays an important role and the keynote also introduces measures of the personality traits of library directors and discusses this in relation to the innovation and development process but also in relation to the 'sense' or construction the profession is creating of the user.

This paper departs from 2 different theoretical perspectives of pertinent interest for management of institutions. One of the perspectives is concerned with the question about how manage-ment information and management recipes are adopted and interpreted in organisations like libraries.

The other perspective concerns the role of the directors' personality in this context especially how they acquire management information and how they value and use management information in relation to organisational change processes. This paper is built on several studies into leadership in libraries in Denmark and United Kingdom. The paper also builds on several user studies.

LEADERSHIP AND PERSONALITY

During the last couple of years, the interest in leadership and management topics has increased very much. This is also the case in library and information science. It is due to the very fundamental changes that takes place overall in the public sector. Many of these changes are connected to requirements concerning accountability, user orientation, outsourcing, quality, information technology and staff-related issues. It is a widespread notion that the requirements in relation to leadership and management have become much more complex.

The complexity is connected to environmental turbulence, change processes and to the amount of vast information that leaders need to deal with. Information in the form of management tools or recipes is one way to confront the organisational problems arising from the changes. Leadership is an important element in the configuration of organisational culture and both leadership styles and the leaders approach to innovation, change, and competency development are of importance in relation to the directions of the organisation. Leaders are both part of an organisational culture but they also have the possibility to be change agents in relation to the culture. The relationship between leadership priorities and organisational culture are important.

One can argue an interesting relationship between the directors' personality and preferences and the direction and change processes in libraries and this is exactly the focus for this paper. The Revised NEO Personality Inventory is one of the most widespread personality tests based on the Five-Factor model and it was employed in this investigation. Besides allowing for both a general and detailed description of personality, the test is also build up in such a way that it takes into consideration the characteristics of the specific test-person in focus. Specific norms for groups of people and profiles have been developed from research to help validate the testresult.

The NEO-PI-R measures five broad personality factors. Each of these is a summary and an average of six facets. Each of the five factors and their associated 6 facets is measured through 48 statements, implying that all 30 facets are measured through 240 statements. The result of the 240 statements is distributed into low and high scores on the 5 factors and the 30 facets, hence demonstrating a personality profile. As suggested, now turn to a short profiling of the 8 library directors.

The profiles of the directors as a whole are very congruent with modern expectations of leaders and managers. They tend to possess emotional stability. They are extroverted and open to change. They all score high on the facet assertiveness. They score high on conscientiousness. Overall, the profiles of the library directors appear to be very far away from the traditional stereotypes of librarians as shy, introverted, a bit oldfashioned, nervous and timid.

The factor named openness is often considered as an important factor in relation to chance processes and it is clear that all directors except one scores high on this factor. One director is distinct from the others, scoring rather low. It is director B that scores low on 3 of the 6 facets. What is more interesting is probably that all directors score high on some of the more important facets related to get things done. All score from middle to very high on actions, ideas and values indicating openness to new ideas.

Common for all the directors have been the fact that they have been involved in change processes. These change processes have focused on both the provision of services and on organis-ational development implementing more flexible and democratic structures. They have all succeeded to change the libraries both internally and in relation to the users. One of the reasons that change processes have been successful overall can possibly be attributed to the assertiveness of the directors, their overall openness to experience and change and their general high degree of conscientiousness.

The organisational culture is a very important mediating factor both in relation to how information in the form of recipes are adopted and translated both also in relation to the actual possibilities the director possess for implementing change. But the style of change management varies. This can be partly explained by situational factors like the local political climate, restrictions due to the building and economy, the organisational culture and other important factors.

The relevant facets or traits that relates to interpretation and adoption of new standards are some of the traits that relate to the factors named openness and conscientiousness. The facets under openness can possibly give an indication of how willing the director is to seek and implement new recipes in the organisation and the facets related to conscientiousness can indicate how through the process of implementation is conducted. These facets will also relate to the directors' sense of the usefulness of own participating in leadership courses and development.

We emphasise that it is broad hypotheses. Another more general aspect is how the directors value innovations or changes. A comparison of D with H indicates the usefulness of analysing behaviour using all the facets and not only the factors. It is evident that the profile of H indicates a person oriented towards actions and change. H also possesses a high degree of impulsiveness and a middle orientation towards ideas. H is more of a doer than a thinker and this is also the way H comes forward in the interview and in interviews with the staff.

Things must happen and failures—both own and staff failures—are accepted as inevitable. Some of the change processes are conducted nearly on the spot and many traditional activities are set in motion. In some ways, the change processes runs in a very goal directed manner but there is a high degree of acceptance of a chaotic nature of some of these processes that involves staff very much because the director delegates much based on both trust and on a disposition to take up new challenges.

The change processes that have taken place in D's library are conducted in a very different way. They are just as goal directed and strategic but they are much slower and much more deliberated and it is evident that the D places a very high value on bringing the staff along. The disposition for activity seeking is much less here than in relation to H. It results in a 'flavour' of the library as a bit more old-fashioned and a bit slower or a bit more cautious in change processes.

The implicit formulated hypotheses about the relationship between personality traits and profiles indicated that the director's openness to especially intellectual experiences or practical innovations and changes influenced the process of implementation of both structures and processes of competences. It also influenced the way the recipes and standards were conceptualised in the organisation. The integration of the recipes was influenced by the perseverance of the director with cultural factors as a mediating factor.

DISCOURSES AND ORGANISATIONAL RECIPES

These figures contrast to a certain degree to the dominant discourses in the public library profession. The dominant discourses are concerned with modern topics and issues like library as a place and libraries as generators of social capital and societal trust on a more general level. In relation to services the emphasis in the discourses are on issues like lifelong learning, information literacies and integration of the physical library into the digital services. The discourse also contains strong elements of the need for permanent change for example in relation to continuing professional development.

There is also much debate on phenomena like 23 things, facebook and other digital services. A discourse is characterised by dominant themes but is also delimited by themes that do not occur and these absent themes signifies the themes in the discourse. In the 80'ies and 90'ies, the library profession had focus on collections and collection management and especially the concept of immediate availability was a central topic.

Today, these themes of discussion are missing from the professional debate. There existed also a rather interesting debate or discourse concerning the proper relationship between supply and demand in relation to the collection. It is interesting that these topics seldom are covered in the present discussion because the different digital possibilities emphasise new turns of these central concepts. Just to give a few hopefully illuminating examples one can ask questions about the links on libraries' websites and enquire if a link is part of the collection or not.

The answer to that question is interesting because if the answer is yes it follows that the libraries have the responsibility for dead links and for the misinformation contained in some of the links. Another interesting question is the transformation of topical needs into specific needs due to the way people search the digital databases. Librarians are not discussing the increase in the selling of books and the reasons behind this interesting fact. Is it because of an increasing affluence in society or is it because of a want for instant gratification?

Many of the elements in a given dominant discourse relates to organisational recipes or standards. A recipe or a standard that becomes a trend has the following characteristics: It often originates in an academic setting but very often it is created in cooperation with the professional world—be it libraries or business. It is blueprinted by leading members of the academic and professional communities and it is taken up also by the consultancy industry.

Prestigious firm and companies use it. The recipe incorporates the promise to solve serious problems in the companies and in the institutions they are interesting to work with. They are marketed and they are frameworks for actions but most of all they are interpretable meaning that institutions can adopt them, change them according to the national and organisational culture. They are very often connected to stories of success and the story behind the recipe often takes the form of a drama.

Successful recipes tend to hit a trend in the time and use this as a kind of vehicle for its travel across boundaries and cultures. Some recipes like the balanced scorecard have a rather long life. Other—not as successful like for example business process reengineering—have a shorter lifespan. It does not mean that they are not used. It could mean that they are incorporated in the organisational operations but people have stopped talking about it.

Finally, all recipes have dimensions of both content and symbolic aspects. It is of course extremely interesting which recipes become dominating themes in the discourse of a profession. It is also of huge interest which recipes a given profession does not include in its arsenal of themes in the discourse. There is no doubt that the profession as a whole has a very determined focus on change and the need for change.

The catch phrase that the libraries stand on a burning platform has been brought forward several times in the discourse and this catchphrase has been used as a kind of rationale for changes. This is of course the consequence of a special or peculiar interpretation of the environment. However, there is no doubt that the ideology of change and the need for change is deeply integrated in the professional identity of public librarians and leaders in the public libraries. It is an interesting question if the interpretation of the environment is in accordance with other indicators of changes in the environment.

USERS AND PREFERENCES

One aspect of organisational effectiveness is a system's ability to cope with users and non-users expectations and needs enabling the system to deliver services appropriate to satisfy needs and expectations. Organisational effectiveness has been one of the ultimate goals and objectives for the performance measurements endeavours for many years. Organisational effectiveness is related to processes, products or services and the customer or the user and it is normally seen as an important element in the quality of a service. The importance or significance for the users of the single services is of course a very important element for the libraries' planning process and assessment of how to proceed.

Libqual is a measurement instrument that is often used for this kind of investigation as it specifies the minimal level of service people would like. However, Libqual has not been employed in these surveys. We have simply asked people to attach the significance or importance for themselves on different services.

The end result is a kind of ranking that probably is rather robust. The importance or significance is calculated on a scale from 0 to 100 and it forms the basis of the ranking. The ranking of the importance or the perception of the significance of the public libraries' services follows:

Table. The Users' Perception of the Significance of Different Services in Two Surveys

	High School	Rank	Aarhus	Rank
A kind and polite service	72	1	90	2
Distance to the library	67	2	91	1
Ambience	64	3	84	3
Collection of non-fiction	62	4	66	5
Quite and peaceful place in the library	59	5	65	6
Collection of fiction	55	6	78	4
Places for relaxation	43	7	51	8
Collection of music	41	8	46	10
Wireless network	40	9	21	14
Collection of film	37	10	47	9
Group work facilities	35	11	15	15
Computers	34	12	28	12
The Library's homepage	34	13	63	7
Study places	33	14	21	14
Exhibitions, lessons	28	15	45	11
N	978		243	

Translated into normal text, one can say that the high school students and the 'traditional public library users' prefer a kind and polite service in nice quite rooms in library with ambience not too far away and filled with books. There are differences between the preferences and significance attached to services among the two groups but rank correlation analysis shows a Spearmans Rho of 0,81 which indicate a very high degree of similarity in ranking the services. The ranking between the two groups are more or less similar, but there appears to be differences in the importance attached to the service.

One explanation for this discrepancy is simple and it is, that the group of high schools students consists of students relying heavily on public libraries and groups or segments that rarely, seldom or never use the public library. This composition of the total group tends to decrease the average figures. In comparison, the respondents from the Aarhus group were all public library users. In the 2006 investigation in Furesoe, we also asked questions about preferences and significance, but we employed a measure-ment tool based on forced pair-wise ranking.

It is impossible to make a direct comparison, but one can look at the trends and compare these with caution. The most striking feature of the answers to this question is the similarity in preferences. The respondents were asked on a forced scale where they had to prioritise alternatives. Overall, the users preferred present openings hours more than longer opening hours with less staff service. The preferred more books in favour of longer opening hours or music.

The preferred more film than more music. They preferred a broader range of literature more than additional copies of the popular books. We did not find any differences in pair-wise preferences in relation fiction versus non–fiction, computers versus more reading places or more reading places versus more places for relaxation or social interaction. The conclusion is that users–even the young age group—want more documents. It is a very clear first priority.

We do see that this priority and preference increase with age, but it is still a very striking result that young people that rely heavily on and use the library's collection of film and music much prioritise books and documents more if they had to choose.

The preferences and the prioritising are probably an expression of the perception of what a public library is—and ought to be. It is obvious that the structure of preferences in relation to public libraries is rather traditional. The nationwide study of high school students also showed some interesting features of the significance they attached to the services in relation to different demographic factors.

Table 10.2 The Students' Perceptions of the Importance of Services and Facilities in Relation to Demographics

	Type High School			Gender	Study Year			
	G	B	T	Female	Male	1	2	3
A kind and polite service	77	69	63	76	66			
Distance to the library	74	61	61	72	61			
Ambience	68	61	59	67	60			
Collection of non-fiction	70	54	52	66	56	56	61	68
Quite and peaceful places in the library	63	55	51					
Collection of fiction	61	49	49	63	44			
Places for relaxation						49	44	36
Collection of music						45	36	38
Wireless network						45	40	35
Collection of film Group work facilities						41	35	28
Computers				32	37			
The Library's homepage	37	28	33			28	36	37
Study places						38	30	29
Exhibitions, lessons								

First of all, there appears to be differences in perceptions of significance and importance dependent on the type of high school. There are 3 types of high schools in the country. The general high school is the classic one. In the table it is called G. There is also a high school oriented towards business topics called B and at last a technical high school called T. The general picture is that the high school students from the general school place more significance on most of the library services than students from the other two hig schools do. We also notice marked differences between male and female high school students.

Female high school students tend to value the collection of fiction an non fiction much more than the male students. It is also interesting to note that the students through their study process tend to place less significance to the library as a place to be and work in.

However, overall the ranking of the single services is not hugely affected by this segmentation, but the segmentation indicates that the different groups have very different preferences and strength of preferences attached to the single services.

LIBRARIES AND POTENTIAL USERS: METHODOLOGICAL APPROACH, THE CASE OF GREEK LIBRARIES

Libraries in the fast communicative environment they live, implement three spaces of interaction:

- Between librarians who decide the offered services, the resources, the manuals and every necessary equipment for users satisfaction and the exploitation of the service.
- Among users and librarians who are responsible. The communication aims to identify the users' needs and the relevance of the resources to them.
- Between Library and users community as a whole. Users receive modified information that can be used to their work. This is the step that library proves its usefulness and illumine its image.

Libraries are social places, where individuals, teams, social groups interact. Social theories, behaviourism, socio-psychological analyses drive to the recognition of special characteristics of libraries and of every target group they refer. Libraries are also one of the key factors that can impact the development and the prosperity of the social entity they refer. Consequently, we can say that they involve competitiveness and entrepreneurship.

They take into account the following factors before decision making:

- Target focusing;
- Strategic planning;
- Efficiency and effectiveness;

- Resources saving;
- Cost-benefits analysis.

The coupling of these different options, social and business, designates the communication methods and the policies that libraries choose on occasion. The synthesis and the identity of the unity that we call 'library users' is a continuing changed variable, as it strands upon the dynamic of human mobility, potential individual needs, and behavioural rules of societies. Users can turn into non-users, actually without caution, but not without any cause. Equally non-users could turn into new, enthusiastic users.

THE RESEARCH AND THE METHODOLOGIES

The questionnaire consists of items that derived from:

- The subject as come up for discussion in the literature;
- The marketing plans of business;
- The adjustment of them to library context.

Needless to say that the findings analysed by qualitative methods. There is an integrated combination of qualitative and quantitative methods, what is referred as mixing methods. Libraries need to know the synthesis and the characteristics of the population they refer to, in order to successfully appeal them.

The major problems on this face the public and the special libraries, which the target groups are fuzzy and random. The social stratification is a matter of research of specialized organisations that collect data on the population structure, family synthesis, economic activities, education, leisure etc. The data is completed by using qualitative methods like interviews of opinion leaders, structured observation, discussions with famous public people. The target is to be ensured that the concept, the structure and the procedures of a service are harmonized to the target group.

MARKETING AND LIBRARIES

Marketing is the wide range of activities involved in making sure that you're continuing to meet the needs of your customers and getting value in return. These activities include market research to find out, for example, what groups of potential customers exist, what their needs, are, which of those needs you can meet, how you should meet them etc. Marketing also includes analysing the competition, positioning your new product or service pricing your products and services, and promoting them through continued advertising, promotions, public relations and sales.

Marketing is connected with library's operation itself. Value added works such as cataloguing and classification corresponds to the product packing, embodied also the concept of the product: in this case is knowledge, research, information, entertainment. Shelving, Abstracting and Indexing, bibliography compilation correspond to the promotion. Regarding the users training programmes, the location of material in the library correlates with marketing practices, such as study of consumer behaviour, product promotion etc.

The mission and the objectives of libraries are modified according to the conditions; services, procedures, rules and operation follow the change. Consequently the Marketing Mix changes too. To catch the alterations, a marketing plan is necessary in order to define the policies, the promotional practices.

On the other hand and because of the 4P balance differs for every target group, it is necessary the research on the groups of population that are the potential clients of the library.

4 Ps of Marketing Mix of libraries:

- Product is the value that librarians add through their knowledge, expertise, and informational, organisational, and retrieval skills. Product is library's services. Collections consists the basis of the 'product', but the main one is an *Idea, an intangible product,* in which the tangible good, the services and the processes are incorporated;
- Place is the space of the library, either physical or virtual. Place is an important factor that can appeal the potential users. Another factor relevant to this is the location of the building, how easily accessible is it. Relevant to this point is the mention that the place nowadays is both place and space, equally physical and virtual;
- The Price of library services or products consists of both the staff time spent in ensuring that resources and services are available and accessible and user's time in finding and using resources efficiently. Libraries do not Price their activities and decisions. However they assess the cost of services, of acquisitions, of operation. The main interest of libraries is the best exploitation of their resources, the advancement of their services, the improvement of their quality, without increasing of their cost;
- The communicative policy of the library is the Promotion policy and its part of the strategic marketing. Promotion consists every positive action, even the politeness of the staff, but in practice, promotion targets to explain to users and non-users why they need the library in their everyday life.

THE SURVEY AND THE RESULTS

The questionnaire contains questions for collecting quan-titative information, questions for seeking behaviours and attitudes scaled to 4 degrees. The third unity contains questions on the organisational level of the library, its resources, its finance and fund raising. The stratification of the sampling of libraries who participated to the survey is analog to the number of libraries that belong to every type. The questions and the analysis follow the structure of a marketing plan.

Mission and Goals of the Library

The diagrams show the weak idea that Greek libraries have on the strategic management:

- More than half of the libraries have a fuzzy idea of their mission;
- Only 37, 5 per cent has written specific explicit mission.
- Only 11,4 per cent writes down the strategic plan, shared to the whole staff; and
- 21,5 per cent of libraries share the plan to employees relevant to the its content.

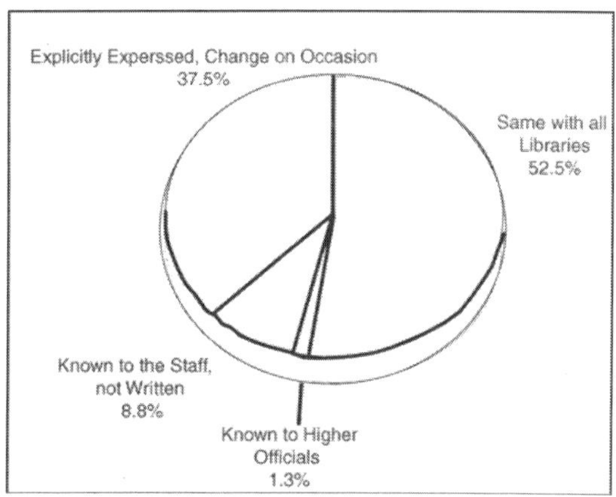

Fig. 10.1 Library's Mission

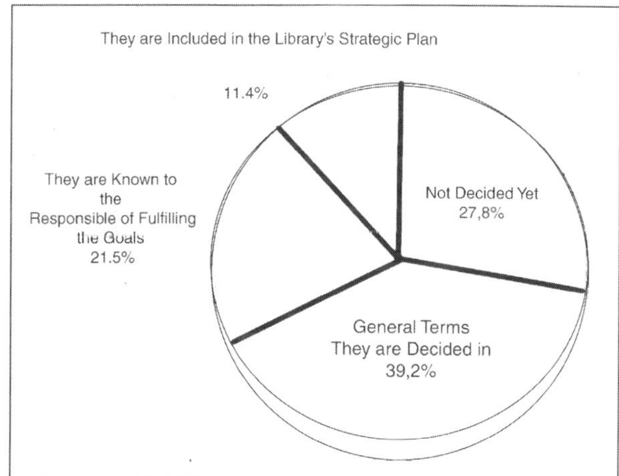

Fig. 10.2 Means for Achieving Library's Goals as they are Ordered by its Purpose and Strategy

Furthermore, as usual, the 56 per cent of Libraries deny to set economic goals, but the 57, 5 per cent of libraries set non-economic goals, which they achieve and sometimes they overcome.

Needless to say that an economic goal is not a business goal: it could be a cost effective goal, or the better exploitation of the resources or the decrease of operational expenses etc. Libraries are negatively biased on economic and public relations actions.

Marshall mentions some causes for academic libraries that seem to be common to every kind:

- Argument that academic libraries have a captive audience in members of the academic community who need to use the library in order to be successful in their academic areas of teaching and research;
- Library funding is not a concern because it is linked to overall institutional funding;
- Promotion is not a part of the library's purpose;
- Promotion of the library and its services will crate expectations and demand that are beyond the library's capabilities;
- Reliance on the university's communication or development office to perform a public relations role will suffice.

Product (Life Cycle, New Life Design)

Because of the lack of strategic thought and promotional vision, libraries gave the following answers:

- 69 per cent declare that the strategic planning is unofficial, and
- 54, 5 per cent answer that there are no procedures for the creation of new services.
- Not users but other factors determine the orientation and establishment of new services.
- The questions on the life cycle of the services reveal that libraries mainly operate as traditional organisations and low communicated.

Market (Target–groups)

- Most of the libraries (86, 8%) know their population and their mobility;
- They study the attitude of people; and
- They try to form a special policy for every group.

The kind of libraries that answered explain it:

- 44,3 per cent does not examine the target group, and
- 30 per cent systematically focuses on numerous groups of the population.

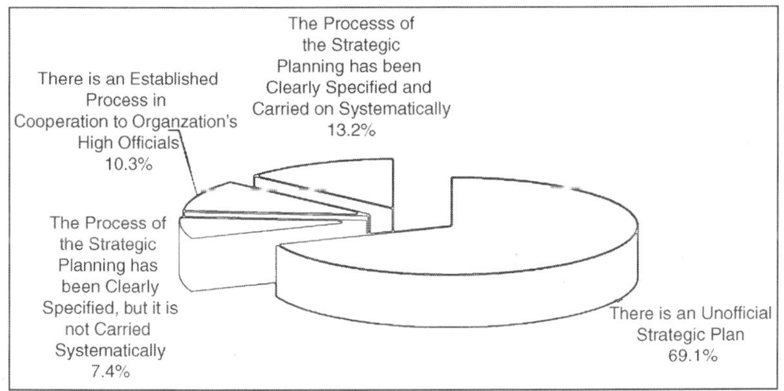

Fig. 10.3 Is there Any Strategy for Developing Library Services

The Library's Image and the External Relationships

As it is clear up to now, libraries operation is mainly collection oriented than users-centred. The modernization steps parallel to technology, without harmonizing processes, management, and services. They use technology without innovative processes.

The following answers confirm the lack of a strategy for appealing new groups of population and new users.

- Only 1,4 per cent collects systematically data on users' and groups' behaviour; and
- 7, 8 per cent focuses on the appealing of new target groups.

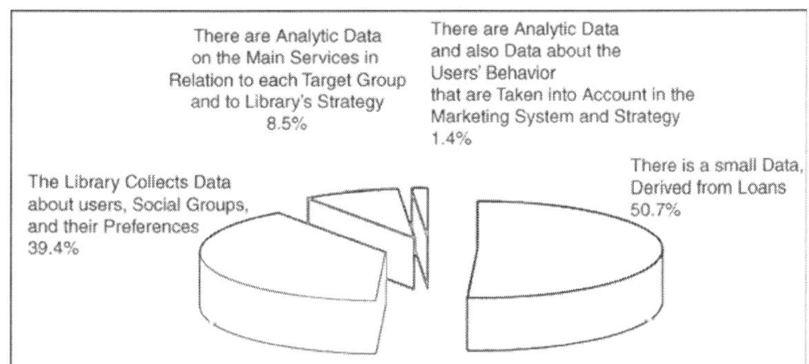

Fig. 10.4 Information about Users and Potential Users

External relationships:

- 8,3 per cent agree that strategic alliances increase the users and advertise their services, and
- 52,8 per cent agrees to evaluate cooperation proposals that could cause the increase of the users;
- Lack of active, systemic promotion of the library;
- Uninterested in communication.

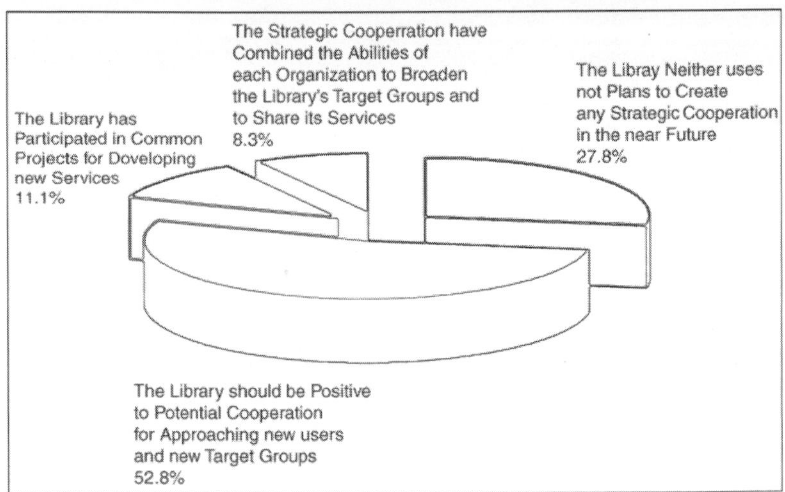

Fig. 10.5 Strategic Cooperation for Approaching New Target Groups

Nevertheless, half of the people that participate to library's events use the library, become members. The opposite valid also: the majority of the members are interested in library's events. That means that users' attitude is positive, but how many people use it? That's the crucial question. That's the main problem of libraries: not the whole people who need libraries use them.

THE QUALITY OF INFORMATION AS BASIS OF THE LIBRARY MANAGEMENT QUALITY

A great number of scientific, reference, educational, methodical and practical publications is devoted to the quality of library activity in Russia. One of the most characteristic tendencies is the active interest to management, especially quality manage-ment that explains the fact of formation of new management concept in the sphere of library science.

Modern management researches show a great significance of rational information processing for achieving strategic and operative aims. The quality of information defines the quality of management because information covers all spheres of management.

Being the most important function of management process, information must meet the following requirements: authenticity, accuracy and completeness, efficiency and regularity, its conformity with management level. Management of documen-tation as function of management is realised in the conditions of decision making process to achieve the aim. That is why documen-tation management is closely connected with the problems of management, organisation structures, the problems of design of information systems management, their implementation and operation, with automation of managerial procedures and processes.

Urgency of the problem consists in support of the processes of documentation information management due to more effective technologies of its processing including analytical components and the connection of management functions with documents, their servicing. The development of new management technologies plans systematic approach to the decision making process on the base of flexible information analytical integrated management system.

DOCUMENTS MANAGEMENT

The organisation of work with documents is a very important part of management processes and taking managerial decisions influencing efficiency and management quality. From the point of view of information technologies documentation information management activity and the management activity itself—as a subsystem of an integrated technological system of library. So, the library management is characterised as technological process that supposes regularity of management.

In management activity a document is a tool, means or method of management. The whole documentation is closely connected with the concrete management function for which it is created. It allows, in Larin's opinion with the help of systematic analysis to identify the content of managerial documents and to connect it with the definite management function.

Optimal system of internal legal regulation helps to provide successfully and realise substantially the local legal regulation of general principles of activity, some decisions and concrete aspects of library operation. The complex of internal regulated documents, being formed in each library objectively consists of a package of separate interrelated and mutually complementary blocks. The documents, included, reflect legal organisational and technological sides of professional activity, fix aims, order and conditions of library functioning as informational, educational and cultural institution.

Pilko suggests to classify the complex of documents regulating the activity of the library for convenience according to the following functions: organisational—administrative documen-tation, scientific—methodical documentation, normative documen tation and tcchnological documentation. At the present stage in the system of library management the whole range of documents concerning different types and kinds of documentation systems and being a part of documentation support of management.

INFORMATION MANAGEMENT SYSTEM

The use of information technologies in the sphere of management gives opportunities of more effective and rational organisation of information processes, increase of their flexibility and dynamics expansion of the range of analysed factors when making decisions. 'Perfect' information system of management must automate all or the majority of protective kinds of activity in the frames of integrated information space and in interrelation of automated functions.

It is more optimal to use the system which is the part of the architecture of the system of complex library automation that implies the use of joint technologies of management automation and documents circulation. The creation of the system of automated management of documents or service database in the library is a very complicated organisational technical task, administrative office automation being the main, basic platform within information library system. Designing database, one should orient on the use of standard management system of data and technology 'client–server' which allows to combine operative work with archiving documents.

Automated system in the library:

- Provides coordinated work of all departments;
- Simplifies work with documents, increases its effectiveness;
- Increases labour efficiency due to shortening time for creation, documents processing and search;
- Increases efficiency of access to information;
- Allows to delimit the competence of access of workers to information.

The implementation of such system in the library will optimize the activity of the library in whole, to get analytical information for using and taking important managerial decisions. Without any doubts, the system will influence on effectiveness of library activity as well as on increase of professional personnel training, the culture of the use of modern information technologies.

DATABASE OF REGULATING DOCUMENTATION

For solving intersystem tasks of the library one can suggest the module of service database of regulated documentation as foundation of effective library management. Designing technological project of database we relied on methodical basis and regulations considered by Pilko and Voroisky. The main source when forming database is regulated documents of library.

Database supports the main functions of documents processing on-line which include: documents development and custody; search of documents according to different parameters, input, support and custody of any kind of documents; control over implementation of documents; protection and management of separation of rights for access.

Database includes the complex of functional means realised as a programme modules helping to plan work, to get interim and resort valuation of separate operations, to control and, if necessary, to correct the plan or process. The idea of centralised storage of e-documents is also obvious: integrated database in server keeps documents safely, systematizes them and finds necessary information very quickly. Not the least of the features of the system is unification of the most widespread types and kinds of documents in management, development and use of patterns.

Database is corporate storage of regulating documents of the library. In includes the catalogue of organisational efficient, regulatory methodical and technological documentation, unified forms of documents, documents archive, office documents of departments or separate workers. Through interface of database, installed in all computers, the workers of the library get access to hierarchy of folders and operations concerning design and search of documents. The search of documents is realised through folders navigation.

Creating a new document a database offers users to identify its belonging to concrete theme by classifier and to use standard sheet, pattern. Information, formed by users in the process of selecting data, is displayed as a reference in matrix format, graphic material, fulltext document or pattern. Different functional and practical tasks are solved by the method of contiguous look of database modules and data selection or seriating. The tasks can be operational analysis of technological processes; valuation of resort support of processes; valuation of work content of library production.

Managers of a library, having full access to all documents, can control the process of creating office documents any time. The analysis of report documents formed in database, gives opportunity to correct the library activity, to improve organisational structure, character and content of implemented works, personnel, provision with financial, material and other resources.

6

The Digital Library Federation

GOALS AND PRIORITIES

The Council on Library and Information Resources (CLIR) is the outcome of the merger of the Council on Library Resources (CRL) and the Commission on Preservation and Access (CPA). CLIR's mission calls on the organization to identify the critical issues that affect the welfare and prospects of libraries and archives, to convene individuals and organizations in the best position to engage these issues, and to encourage institutions to work collaboratively to achieve and manage change.

CLIR pursues its mission out of the conviction that information is a public good and of great social, intellectual, and cultural utility. It has set its sights on a few targeted programs: the Commission on Preservation and Access retains its identity as a programme of CLIR, along with programs for Digital Libraries (the Digital Library Federation), the Economics of Information, and Leadership. As a fundamental principle of all its programs, CLIR will encourage institutions to achieve and manage change through collaboration, and collaborative action is particularly important within the preservation community.

The most striking evidence of this is the success of the ongoing effort to rescue through microfilming large portions of the deteriorating print-based collections in the U.S. and abroad. Since its inception, the Commission on Preservation and Access has worked to assure that knowledge produced by the scholarly communities of the world is saved and kept accessible and it will continue that role.

With advice from its standing committees and task forces, CLIR publishes materials that inform and instruct the preservation community, document the economic implications of establishing sound preservation environments for collections, frame the next set of issues to be considered within the changing definition of "preservation and access," and develop new strategies to sharpen the professional skills of individuals with preservation responsibilities.

A few examples of recent publications indicate the range of our concerns:

- "Digitizing Historical Pictorial Collections for the Internet"
- "Preservation and Archives in Vietnam"
- "Digitization as a Method of Preservation?"
- "Mass Deacidification: An Update on Possibilities and Limitations"

THE INTERNATIONAL PROGRAMME

Because few of the critical issues of preservation and access today can be addressed without an international focus, CLIR maintains an International Programme to help promote preservation awareness throughout the world. Through training seminars, workshops, translation projects, publications, and a policy of generous response to requests for counsel and advice from colleagues abroad, it continues to promote the long-term preservation and accessibility of information.

The International Programme has focused its efforts to date on Eastern and Western Europe, the former Soviet Union, China, and Latin America. Thanks to support from The Andrew W. Mellon Foundation, the work in Latin America will be extended, and CLIR will initiate new activity in Southern Europe (for example, in Greece) and in South Africa.

The Programme also hopes to expand in Asia and is seeking funds to develop new projects there.

Examples of activities that will be undertaken in the next several years include providing expertise for preservation-needs assessments in libraries and archives abroad; the development of cooperative filming and digitizing projects for specific collections; and designing strategies to increase the production and use of permanent paper.

Two Specific Examples

The International Register of Microform Masters: An international register of microform masters is essential if scholars and librarians are to know what has been filmed at locations throughout the world and to avoid duplication of effort. The Programme encourages libraries and archives to contribute records to regional nodes for the collection, organization, and distribution of information about reformatted collections.

It supports efforts to link these records to an emerging international register and to reach international consensus on the elements and the record structure for listings of digitized materials.

A successful example is the European Register of Microform Masters (EROMM) where through ten partners in nine countries, some 40 European libraries have so far contributed more than 400,000 records of microfilmed items to the database.

An exchange arrangement with the U.S. bibliographic network RLIN allowed the addition of another 1.9 million records to EROMM's database. Another example is the recently concluded project "Translation and Dissemination of Preservation Knowledge in Brazil." Access to information often means translation of professional literature into other languages.

An interinstitutional alliance of interested organizations in Brazil guided the project, which included the translation into Portuguese of 52 titles of preservation literature, from environmental control to digital conversion.

The translations (plus videos) formed the basis for workshops throughout the country. In the process, the project's coordinators collected valuable information about the state of collections in more than 1,400 libraries and archives.

During a recent meeting (Aveiro, Portugal) with librarians and archivists from Lusophone countries, we offered to make all these materials available in Portugal, Portuguese-speaking countries in Africa, and Macau. Since access to professional literature on basic preservation concerns for print, sound, and images is a top priority in most countries, the offer was received with enthusiasm. I mention support for traditional preservation efforts for print, images, and sound at some length since there is, particularly in developing countries, a danger of putting too much faith in digital solutions for the preservation of a country's heritage.

Librarians and archivists in developing countries are often unaware that digital storage for long-term archiving of information requires careful planning, that many organizational, technical, and organizational issues have not yet been resolved, and that digitization is not a means for preservation unless a long-term plan assures the survival of digitally stored information.

What is really disturbing is that in the general excitement about all things digital, many institutions have put on hold traditional and basic preservation activities. Also, preservation concerns did not start with digital information. There is a long tradition of preserving cultural heritage. The recognition that much of the printed documentary record is in jeopardy because of the introduction of acidic paper around 1850 led to a widespread preservation movement, similar to the one we're beginning to witness for digital information.

The preservation community, especially preservation managers and administrators, have much experience in selecting and preparing collections, and coordinating massive collaborative reformatting projects, mostly microfilming. Their experience is useful even though we're now dealing with an entirely new medium.

The Task Force on Archiving of Digital Information

An important contribution to the debate over long-term archiving of digital information came from the Task Force on Archiving of Digital Information, organized jointly by the Commission on Preservation and Access and the Research Libraries Group (RLG).

The Task Force, in effect, was asked to report on ways that society should work with respect to the cultural record it is now creating in digital form — not only through conversion from print to digital but, perhaps more important — through a record that is "born digital."

Consider that, by the year 2000, an estimated 75% of all U.S. Federal transactions will be handled electronically.

When President Clinton leaves office, it is estimated that his administration will hand over eight million electronic files to the National Archives; and these administration files are but a minuscule portion of the electronic record generated by the corporate world. Most of this information is born digital and there is no printed record to fall back on.

The Task Force's 1996 report argues that "the problem of preserving digital information for the future is not only — or even primarily — a problem of fine tuning a narrow set of technical variables." Rather, "it is a problem of organizing ourselves over time and as a society to maneuver effectively in the digital landscape.

It is a problem of building — almost from scratch — the various systematic supports, or deep infrastructure, that will enable us to tame our anxieties and move our cultural records naturally and confidently into the future". The Task Force's report is available in full at the website of the Research Libraries Group (http://www.rlg.org).

The Task Force was co-chaired by Donald J. Waters, now the Director of our Digital Library Federation. Among the report's conclusions and recommendations are:

- The Task Force recognizes that most of the challenges associated with digital preservation are organizational, not technical.
- The first line of defence against loss of valuable digital information rests with the creators, providers, and owners of digital information.
- Certified digital archives must have the right and duty to exercise an aggressive rescue function as a fail-safe mechanism for preserving digital information that is in jeopardy of destruction, neglect, or abandonment by its current custodian.

The final report focuses on three essential questions: What does digital preservation entail? How do we organize ourselves to do it? What steps should we take to move forward?

Time will not permit covering these questions in detail, but one major conclusion of the report cannot be emphasized enough: Our greatest challenges in the digital age are organizational rather than technical. Because we currently lack the infrastructure of practices, standards, and organizations needed to support preservation of digital information, the following elements of infrastructure must be considered:

- Legal bases for deposit and rescue. Nationally and internationally, legislation and agreements are needed to encourage legal deposit of electronic resources in archival repositories, to enable rescue of abandoned resources, and to facilitate access and use of archival files.
- Standards for description. Current library cataloging standards are not sufficient to describe access and contextual information about digital resources. Several efforts to address this issue are underway internationally. For example, existing registers of microform masters are examined for expansion to include digital items. In this context, see also the final report of the *RLG Working Group on Preservation Issues of Metadata* (http://www.rlg.org/preserv/presmeta.html).

There is more, and the need for sharing information about best practices across the wide spectrum of communities is overwhelming. Preservation of digital materials has emerged as a new, critically important field of interdisciplinary and international activity, and much work needs to be done.

Introduction to the film "Into the Future"

[Addressing our digital memory crisis begins with dialogue. CLIR prepared a discussion paper on digital preservation. Copies of the discussion paper are available, but first, if I may, I would like to show the documentary movie "Into the Future," on the preservation of knowledge in the electronic age. The movie was commissioned by the Commission on Preservation and Access and the American Council of Learned Societies.

Funding was provided by the Alfred P. Sloan Foundation, the National Endowment for the Humanities, and the Xerox Corporation. It was shown on U.S. national television last January and created much discussion. The mainstream press picked up on the issue and several thoughtful articles appeared on the subject of digital preservation. The discussion paper raises the question "Why should we be concerned?" "Into the Future" provides several answers.

Showing of the 1/2 hour version of "Into the Future."

After the showing: The movie sounds an alarm and raises questions; it does not provide answers. We hope that the answers will eventually be provided by groups such as represented at this conference, the Digital Library Federation (DLF) and its members, and other groups and individuals.

The Digital Library Federation (DLF) (For this part, I'm relying extensively on information provided by Donald J. Waters, Director of the Digital Library Federation.

The Council on Library and Information Resources is administrative home to the Digital Library Federation, which includes 19 members — university research libraries, the Library of Congress, the National Archives, and the New York Public Library. The primary mission of the DLF is to establish the necessary conditions for creating, maintaining, expanding, and preserving a distributed collection of digital materials accessible to scholars and a wider public.

Participants in the Federation are committed to a shared investment in developing the infrastructure needed for libraries of digital works. The infrastructure is intended to enable digital libraries to bring together, or "federate," the works they manage for their readers. The DLF has set the following programme priorities:

- DLF will focus on libraries of materials born digital. It is critical that the library community moves from conversion — except in specialized and well-justified cases — to organization, access, and preservation of materials born digital. A high priority is developing the archival mechanisms that preserve the integrity and usability of these digital works over a long term. The Federation is increasingly turning the attention of libraries to the numerous — and difficult — issues associated with works born in, rather than converted to, digital form.
- DLF will help integrate digital materials into the fabric of acadmic life. A critical focus for such integration is to define the circumstances under which conversion to digital form is justified. Conversion projects that facilitate the extension of higher education and promise to improve the quality and lower the cost of research and education deserve special attention.
- DLF will help stimulate the development of a core digital library infrastructure. The highest priorities for attention at the present time are the network and systems requirements and means of authentication and authorization, the means of discovery and retrieval, and archiving.
- DLF will help define and develop the organizational support needed for effectively managing digital libraries. Organizational issues requiring early attention include identifying institutional values and strategies for managing intellectual property in digital form, and creating the conditions for the development of the professional skills needed for digital library management.

CLIR and DLF Plans for Digital Archiving

As one of its primary agenda items, CLIR and the DLF aim to ensure the persistence of digital information, both born digital or created by conversion. Much has been written about the need to document digital information in order for it to serve the role of "record" in an archival sense, as well as about the need to "migrate" digital information to new media in order to prevent loss from media decay and obsolescence.

However, relatively little effort has gone toward answering the more fundamental question of how to ensure that digital documents will remain readable and understandable in the future. At this time, one might usefully distinguish the following strategies:

- Copying (no changes to the information)
- Migration (adpation to new hardware and software)
- Emulation (new platforms mimicking previous platforms)
- Archeology (doing nothing and trying to salvage neglected information when needed)

CLIR and the DLF commissioned Jeff Rothenberg, author of "Ensuring the Longevity of Digital Documents" (*Scientific American*, January 1995) to investigate approaches currently being considered to ensure the future accessibility and readability (i.e., longevity) of digital material. His preliminary findings challenge the concept of "migration." Since migration involves translation of each different type and format (text, images, sound video, animation, etc.), the process is highly labour-intensive.

If a document is accepted for long-term storage based on an assumed migration strategy, Rothenberg argues, it is impossible to give even gross estimates of what will have to be done to it in the future, when this will have to be done, how much it will cost, or how long it will be before the document is corrupted by inappropriate translation.

In his further research, Rothenberg will concentrate on emulation as a solution to the problem of digital preservation, one that is predictable and testable and eliminates repeated translation of documents "which must inevitably lead to their corruption and loss."

Others argue that "migration" is, at least for the shorter term, the only viable solution. Stay tuned.

Other Activities of the DLF that relate to Archiving are:

- Digital collections of licensed works. Libraries are pouring substantial resources into developing licenses for access to electronic journals, while still maintaining subscriptions to print copies of the same materials.

  Not all contracts provide for long-term access to the licensed materials, but terms in some licenses require the publisher to provide the library with a tape or CD-ROM containing a copy of the licensed work. The Copyright Division of the Library of

Congress is developing the means to accept archival quality versions of copyrighted works deposited there, but project work is needed to ensure that the tapes and CD-ROMS deposited with libraries and archives as archival copies can and will serve the fail-safe purpose for which they are intended.

- Institutionalizing digital information. Much scholarly information in digital form is currently being managed as a cottage industry by individual faculty on behalf of a particular discipline. The directors of the DLF institutions are considering how DLF can provide leadership in bringing products emerging from this cottage industry into a more stable, institutional environment.
- Cornell has developed a proposal that DLF will support, to explore the requirements and means for preserving materials converted to digital form in a subset of genres.
- Extension of reach: *Making of America* Phase III. Conversion, as the Library of Congress has demonstrated, is a significant means of extending the reach of library collections in the service of general education. One of the founding goals of the DLF is to find ways to aggregate the existing digitized collections. This effort will focus primarily at the level of descriptive metadata as a means of integration and provide a testbed for exploring intersystem searching methods.

There is another important dimension to the project: In several institutions (e.g., Yale and Cornell), large quantities of digitized Americana are inaccessible because the digital platforms on which the collections were built have become obsolete. *Making of America* Phase III thus affords the opportunity to develop and demonstrate migration techniques as a means of preservation of digital information. Perhaps we should add a fifth strategy to the four already mentioned — prayers.

James Gleick reported in *The New York Times* ("The Digital Attic: An Archive of Everything," 12 April 1998) that "the Daiho Temple of Rinzai Zen Buddhism held a `memorial service for lost information' in Kyoto and online." Gleick adds that "of course, the details are lovingly preserved, in English and Japanese, at its web site.

A look at the web site reveals that there is much common ground between this conference and the Rinzai Zen Buddhists (http://www.thezen.or.jp/jomoh/kuyo.html): "After the effort of transforming all this knowledge into electronic information has been completed, is it enough then to say that we are finished?

And from there, can we truly make effective use of that which we have created? Sometimes, the answer is 'no.' To provide an example, there are many 'living' documents and softwares that are thoughtlessly discarded or erased without even a second thought. It is this thoughtlessness that has drawn the concern and attention of Head Priest Shokyu Ishiko.

Head Priest Ishiko hopes that through holding an 'Information Service' and by teaching the words of Buddha, that this 'information void' will cease to exist." We will all have to help him.

7

Absolute Syntax and Structure of an Indexing and Switching Language

Switching from one information system to another would be convenient if the information languages – that is, the method of representation of subjects and other information content of discourse used in the systems are syntactically consistent, compatible with each other, and inter-convertible at a reasonable cost. In this connection, the development of an intermediate language through which the switching from one information language to another is an important consideration. An idea is a pattern, a gestalt, a form, a structure that one perceives. A subject of a discourse of an information source or of a user's query is a combination of ideas, that is, of structures; therefore, the structure of a subject representation that is, of a subject surrogate has a bearing on the user's 'perception' of the subject represented.

Some characteristic features of an information structure helpful to users, the problems of transformation of information structures, the linear structuring of subject surrogates, and some criteria for the choice of a 'standard format' or framework or model for such structuring are considered. Absolute syntax is defined as the sequence of the component ideas in a subject helpful and acceptable to a majority of users.

The helpfulness of structuring of subject parallel to the absolute syntax is indicated, together with supporting information based on postulations and research on deep structure of languages, biocybernetics, syntax of knowledge, common structure in preserving messages in a set of transformations, etc. The generalised facet structure of subject representation obtained on the basis of the general theory of classi- fication and the guiding principles for helpful sequence formulated thereof is found to be helpful and acceptable to a large number of users of information systems, and therefore, conjectured to parallel the absolute syntax.

Work done in this regard and in the development of specific schemes for classification and for the formulation of subject headings in different languages within the general framework is mentioned.

TERMINOLOGY

The following are the operational definitions of some of the technical terms used in this paper:

- *Idea*: An idea is a product of thinking, imagining, etc., got by the intellect, by integrating with the aid of logic, a selection from the apperception mass, and/or what is directly apprehended by intuition, and deposited in memory. Alternative term: Concept.
- *Entity*: An entity is any existent, concrete or conceptual that is, a thing or an idea.
- *Discourse*: A discourse is an expression of ideas, especially systematic or orderly expression in speech or writing.
- *Subject*: A subject is an organized or systematized account of a body of ideas, whose extension and intension are likely to fall coherently and comfortably within the intellectual competence and the field of inevitable specialization of a normal person.
- *Example*: A systematized account of "Conduction of heat" is a subject; and so may be deemed a systematized account of "Thermo-dynamics", and of the ideas in "Physics". But, not all the discourses embodied in the *McGraw-Hill Encyclopedia of Science and Technology*, taken as a whole can be deemed to be a subject; for, the totality of the subjects embodied therein cannot form an inevitable and convenient field of specialization of a normal person.

STRUCTURE AND PATTERN

The kind of pattern one perceives in a representation of an entity lies in the perceived structure. For instance, in a pictorial representation, the idea of "triangle" can be conveyed by 300 dots, or 30 dots, or 3 dots, as shown in fig. 6.1.

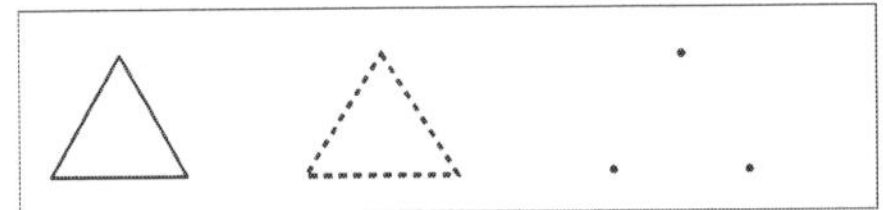

Fig. 6.1

Of these three representations, the last mentioned is deemed to be the most efficient, because it uses the fewest number of elements to convey the same amount of information as those using more number of elements.

This indicates the important role of structure of a representation in relation to the perception of its "meaning". Structure is the way in which the components of an entity are put together. Researcher defines the concept of structure as "effective patterns of relationships in any situation". In a general sense, structure denotes logical form. The content of a logical form may be physical, musical, psychological, temporal, or in some other way non-physical. Anything that has structure has parts, properties or aspects, which are in some manner related to each other.

Thus, in every structure one can distinguish the relations and the items which are related. The items may be qualities, values, or any conceptually distinguishable feature called elements of the structure. An idea is a pattern, a structure, a gestalt, a form, a kind of picture that one perceives. A subject is constituted out of a combination of ideas that is, a combination of patterns. In understanding a complex structure, the human intellect finds it helpful to identify the substructures and categorize them. Such pattern recognition, pattern formulation, and categorization have been found to be involved in the human learning process and information handling.

Library activities point out that the representation of knowledge-structures is an important problem in cognitive psychology:

- "what are the primitive symbols or concepts, how are they related, how are they to be concatenated and constructed into larger knowledgestructures, and how is this 'information file' to be accessed, searched and utilized. The choice of a representation is central, since how one handles this issue causes widespread effects throughout the remainder of his theoretical efforts. As computer scientists working on problem solving have known for years, a good structural representation of the problem already constitutes half of its solution".

Therefore, the structure of representation of subject that is, surrogate of subject has a crucial role in conveying information about the subject denoted.

REPRESENTATION OF SUBJECT

An information system handles discourses. A discourse may be verbal as expressed in a query of a user of an information system. It may be in a recorded form as in a conventional document such as, a book, an article in a periodical, and a technical report or on magnetic tape, film, etc., all of which may form information sources. Finding information and/or documents containing information co-extensively matching the subject of a user's query may depend, in a good measure, on the capacity of the system to identify and specify coextensively the subjects of discourses that is, subjects embodied in queries and those embodied in information sources.

The representation of subjects expounded in discourses for example, subject headings, class numbers, data structures, algorithms or other kinds or surrogates may provide the first point of entry into an information retrieval system. An information system of this sort may form a node or component of a hierarchy of increasingly larger network of local, national, regional and global information systems.

To facilitate the integration and collaborative functioning of the information systems developed in different contexts, it would be helpful if the "languages" used for representation of subjects in the different systems are syntactically consistent, compatible with each other, and inter-convertible at a reasonable cost. Thus, the representation of subject of discourses in the form of surrogates is central to the designing of information files for information storage and retrieval purposes.

PROBLEMS IN THE EFFICIENT USE OF THE LANGUAGE OF SURROGATE

The following are some of the factors which raise problems for the user of an information system in the efficient use of the language of the surrogate system. For various reasons, it may be difficult for the user to perceive precisely and express coextensively the subject of his interest at the moment. Therefore, the total semantic domain represented by the expression of the subject of his query may not be coextensive with the semantic domain of the subject of his interest as perceived by him.

The information scientist's perception of the semantic domain of the subject of interest of the user derived on the basis of the latter's expression of his interest at the moment, may not be coextensive with what the user purported to convey. A user may not and, perhaps, cannot be concentrating attention or work on at one and the same time on all the component ideas potentially falling in the subject of his interest, even if it be a narrow one. The recall value at the moment that is, the likelihood of being retained and recalled from memory for this component idea would be relatively greater than that for the other component ideas in the subject of his interest.

Therefore, he is more likely to bring up the name of this component idea in searching for information on the subject of his interest at the moment. The information scientists' knowledge and understanding of the subject of interest to the user may be inadequate.

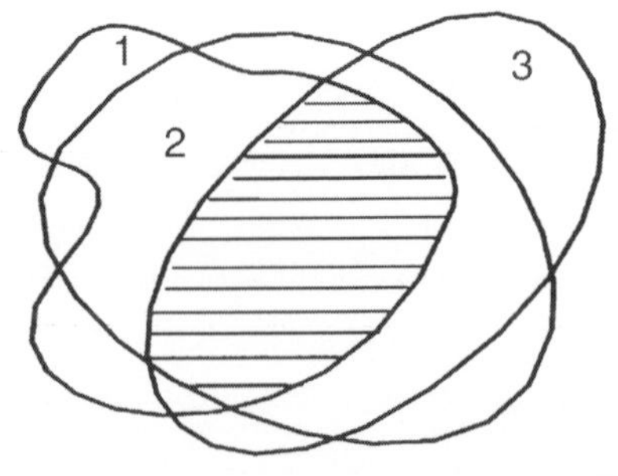

Fig. 6.2 Illustrates the Non-congruence of the Different Semantic Domains.

For various reasons, it would be difficult for the information scientist to perceive precisely and express coextensively the semantic domain of the subjects embodied in information sources.

Therefore, the surrogate system prepared by him for representing the semantic domain of subjects embodied in information sources may not be coextensive with the semantic domain of the subject(s) purported to be described by the author of the work.

- User's perception of the semantic domain of his subject interest-at-the moment
- Actual semantic domain of the subject as expressed by user
- Librarian/Information Scientist's perception of the semantic domain of user's subject interest-at-the-moment

MINIMIZING THE CONSTRAINTS

Helpful Features of an Information System

Some of the features of an information system that may help in minimizing some of the constraints and difficulties are as follows:

- Providing access to information on the subject of interest to the user by the name of the component idea(s) he may bring up in using the surrogate system.
- Providing facility for browsing and selection of information to compensate for the dissimilarity and non-coextensiveness between the subject perceived and expressed by the user and the at perceived and understood by the information scientist at the time of query negotiation or user-system interfacing. This may involve providing access to:
- Subjects greater in extension but subsuming the subject of the user's interest at the moment.
- Subjects greater in intension but containing a substantial portion of it devoted to the specific subject of interest to the user at the moment.
- Subjects in some other manner related to the specific subject of interest to the user at the moment.

Intersystem Connection and Compatibility

In order to facilitate switching over or movement from one information system to another with the longrange goal of establishing system interconnection on a global scale, there are at least two approaches.

These are:

- To use the same or very nearly the same information storage and retrieval language in all the information systems; and

- To use an intermediate language or switching language through or by which one moves from one information system to another.

FRAMEWORK FOR REPRESENTATION

Problems of Transformation

The second one is the more practicable at present stage in the development of information systems throughout the world. However, in either of the methods, an important consideration relates to the framework elements, relations, and structure to be used for the analysis and representation of subjects of discourses that is, subjects embodied in information sources and in users' queries. This stage mentions some of the suggestions about a common knowledge structure and framework for representation of subjects and discusses one such framework. There are various methods of representing subjects, such as, class numbers, subject headings or strings of words, multi-dimensional arrays, tree-structures, etc.

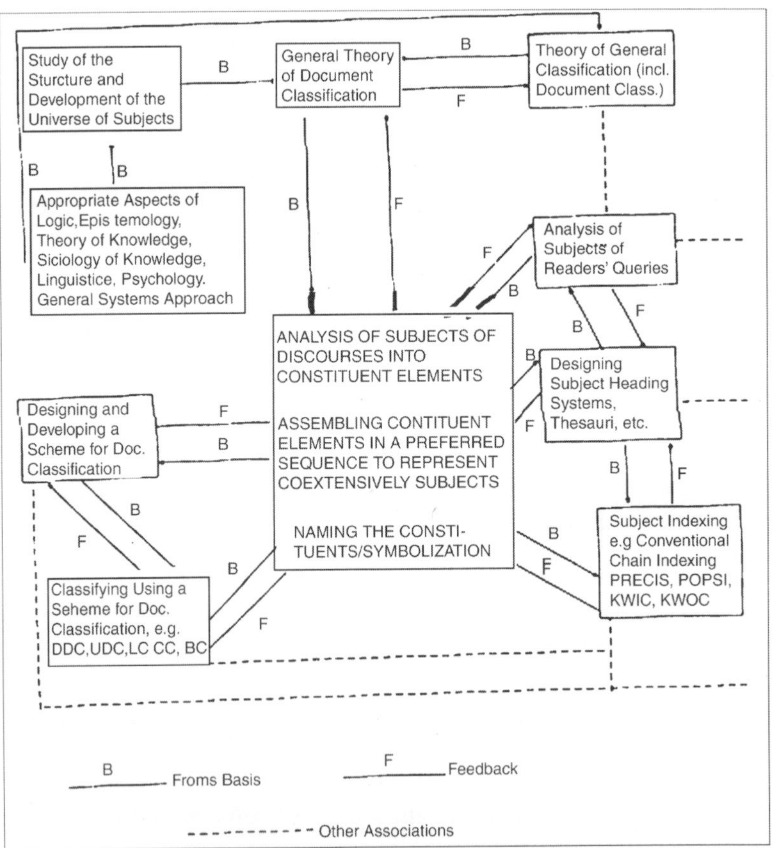

Fig.6.3 Interrelation Between Discourse Discourse/Subject Analysis, Classification, Subject Indexing, Subject Heading Work, Thesauri, etc.

These arise from the process of analysis of subjects of discourses into constituent elements; recognition of the relevant relations among the elements as they obtain in the context of the subject concerned; and assembling the elements in a preferred pattern so as to represent as coextensively as possible the subjects. Representation of subject by a subject heading or a class number is equivalent to transforming the n-dimensional configuration of the subject into a linear configuration. An arrangement of the component elements in each subject falling in a subject-field among themselves, in a sequence helpful to a majority of users requires keeping invariant every Immediate-Neighbourhood relation among all the subjects while transforming or mapping the n-dimensional configuration of subjects on to a line.

The number of subjects falling even in one subject-field is quite large and continues to increase rapidly such that it is difficult to arrange them in a helpful sequence consistently without the aid of guiding principles. In the transformation, only one of the many Immediate Neighbourhood relations can be kept invariant.

Determining which should this be, and which components should come respectively as remove 2, remove 3, etc., with respect to a reference component is a difficult decision. To depend, for this purpose, on the conjecture of different classificationists as to what is helpful to a majority of users may not yield a consistent pattern of arrangement of components of all subjects. But, such a consistency in pattern is helpful and necessary to the users, as well as the designers of the information system.

Criteria for Choice of Frame Work

The problem of transfer and trans- formation of knowledge-structures, are as follows.

- The long-term task is not merely to analyse the problems but to design methodological instruments for carrying out practical researches into problems of communication. These may be treated as problems of mapping. Given an original territory of factual phenomena how does this territory become mapped in the brain of the investigator? How does this map become transformed into a verbal or symbolic expression a linguistic map? How is this map transformed again into a language adopted to the needs of the ultimate recipient, the learner? Finally, how is this third map introjected into the learner's brain to form a pattern of knowledge? If we can establish a cartography for these maps, we can formulate "projective equations" leading from one map to the next. Each map will be a pattern of definable variables under appropriate controls and observing changes in the next map, the equations can be solved and laws of projection may be discovered.

Anderson and Bower have listed the following considerations deemed helpful in the choice of a "standard format" for representing information:

- The representation should be capable of expressing any conception which a human can formulate or understand.
- The representation should allow for relatively efficient search for and retrieval of information. That is, specific information should remain relatively accessible even when the data-files grow to encyclopedic proportions.
- The representation should saliently exhibit the substantive information extracted from a given input. It should not be influenced by the peculiarities of the particular natural language in which that information was communicated. This hope for language-invariance amounts to a wish for a universal interlingua in which any conception in any language could be expressed, but for which the format would not be specific to a particular language...
- For reasons of parsimony, the representation should involve a minimum of formal categories. That is, it should make a minimum of formal distinctions at the outset; more complex distinctions would be built up by the construction rules for concatenating primitive ideas.
- The representation must allow for easy expression of concatenation operations, by which "duplex ideas" can be constructed out of "simple ideas". This means, for example, that the representation should allow easy expression of conceptual hierarchies, or multiply embedded predications, or allow one to predicate new information on any old information- structure".

ABSOLUTE SYNTAX

A Postulate

At the International Conference on Scientific Information, S. R. Ranganathan suggested that. "to help in the establishment of a fairly longlived helpful scheme for classification, a team of epistemologists, psychologists, linguists, reference librarians, classificationists and statisticians should investigate the way in which the human mind thinks that is, the Syntax of Facets that will give the greatest satisfaction to the greatest number of readers".

In 1966, in his valedictory address to the Maryland Symposium on Relational Factors in Classification, Ranganathan postulated such a syntax of facets and named it as Absolute Syntax. Absolute syntax in the sequence in which the component ideas of subjects falling in a subject-field arrange themselves in the minds of a majority of normal intellectuals, for instance when they think and communicate about the subject. Ideas are largely products of intellection. Intellectual activity is known to be controlled by brain. There is considerable similarity in the structure and, therefore, in the functioning of the brain in a majority of normal human beings.

Thus, a majority of normal human beings have more or less a similar mode of thinking and learning that is, in forming ideas and in combining them to build knowledge-structures. It is further stated that biologically man has not changed to any appreciable extent since the emergence of Homo sapiens; for, the structure of the genetic material has not appreciably changed since then that is, for some 500,000 years although we have changed culturally. Therefore, the probability of a sudden change that is, a mutation in the mode of thinking and learning of a majority of normal persons in the immediate future is quite low. Hence, if the syntax of the representation of the component ideas of subjects is made to conform to, or parallel to, the Absolute Syntax, then the pattern of linking of the component ideas that is, the resulting knowledge structure is likely to be:

- Helpful to majority of normal intellectuals;
- Consistent in pattern in subjects falling in different subject-fields;
- Relatively more stable and continue to be helpful to a majority of normal intellectuals so long as there is no mutation in their mode of thinking;
- Free from the aberrations due to variations in linguistic syntax from the use of the verbal plane in naming subjects;
- Capable of representing and indication of subjects co-extensively with a minimum number of variety of component elements;
- Helpful in recognizing the less explored and unexplored regions in the universe of ideas; and
- Helpful in probing deeper into the pattern of human thinking and modes of combination of ideas.

Analogy from Search for Linguistic Universals

It was pointed out that the formulation of a generic framework for structuring subjects has a parallel in the search for universal linguistic forms such as that expounded, and the generative grammarians. Birnbaum suggests a multi-layered syntactic structure between the deepest of the deep structures and the surface structure. As a result of the general trend towards a generative semantic framework, a new slightly modified model of generative grammar seems now to be taking shape.

This model can be thought of as comprising three independent components:

- A Semantic Component which will define the relations obtaining between semantic units or, rather hierarchically ordered clusters of semantic features such as:

- (Thing),
- (Concrete),
- (Countable),
- (Animate),
- (Human),
- (Personal),
- (Male),
- (Adult);
- (Predication),
- (Agent),
- (Definite),
- (Action),
- (Patient – Oriented),
- (Time-Determined),
- (Aspect – Determined), etc.,

- A Transformational Component which will convert the semantic deep structure representations into surface structure representations.
- A Phonological Component.

Fillmore points out that "there may also be some psychological reasons that argue for the use of predication as a data-base language in a model of memory... Perhaps 'thinking' represents operations at the level of the semantic base structure, before it has been transformed into actual sentences through the application of syntactic rules".

The case categories suggested the following:

- "*Agentive* (A), the case of the typically animate perceived instigator of the action identified by the verb.
- *Instrumental* (I), the case of the inanimate force or object causally involved in the action or state identified by the verb.
- *Dative* (D), the case of the animate being affected by the state or action identified by the verb.
- *Factitive* (F), the case of the object or being resulting from the action or state identified by the verb, or understood as a part of the meaning of the verb.
- *Locative* (L), the case which identifies the location of spatial orientation of the state or action identified by the verb.
- *Objective* (O), the semantically most neutral case, the case of anything representable by a noun whose role in the action or state identified by the verb is identified by the semantic interpretation of the verb itself.."

Vleduts and Stokolova also propose structures – standard phrases at different levels for subject - representation in different disciplines. Leibniz's ideal language and the Whorfian hypothesis that "Every language contains terms that have come to attain cosmic scope of reference that crystallize in themselves the postulations of an unformulated philosophy.. such are our words 'reality, substance, matter' and.. 'space. time, past, present, future", are worth noting here.

Biocybernetic View

In his book on Systems Philosophy, Ervin Lazlo mentions about "basic modes of thinking".

- "..It is also becoming evident that all men, regardless of the culture they happen to belong to, have basically similar nervous systems, are equipped with analogous sense receptors, command like patterns of response, and use patterns of thought which obey very similar laws or regularities. In other words, there appear to be some "universal" traits underlying cultural cognitive relativities: Chomsky could locate "linguistic universals" and Kluckholn discovered a number of" universal categories of culture.
- "Finding such universals is rendered difficult if not impossible, by arguing out of one's own culturally or individually relativistic categories. In that light, every other world-model becomes but a special case of one's own, and is forced into the latter's structural scheme. But, in using the neutral frame work of a cybernetic mode, one is no more arguing out of his own culturecategories than out of that of a thermostat. Conceptualizing the cognitive process with such categories, we can reach universal structures, for we are not dealing with particular contents. Regardless of whether a person conceives a sensory pattern as trees, meaning "standing peoples, in whom winged ones built their lodges and reared their families" or interprets the very same pattern as obstructions to be cut down and burnt; he is using a construct which endows his perceptual input with meaning. And the development of constructs and gestalts obeys some general regularities, already manifest in biological evolution and set forth in cultural development".

Lazlo further points out:

- Regardless of the genetically and empirically induced differences, however, basic modes of thinking characterize all human beings, and indeed all higher biological species. These are rooted in, and explained by, the fact that all such organisms are self-maintaining open systems using a specific mode of reproduction, and forming part of some similarly specific social structure. The mental capacities needed to maintain such systems in their environments are adaptive functions; they crystallize as cognition in the more evolved species, and culminate in man.

The most immediately pertinent to human cognition make up an ascending ordering of categories, universally human in principle but variously evolved in different real individuals.

These categories may be listed as follows:

- Gestalt (invariant patterns with established meanings to which the input patterns are assimilated);
- Rational constructs (theoretic entities postulated through abstract reasoning and connected to the input patterns by means of some established rule of correspondence); and
- Aesthetic construct (non-discursive meanings discovered in the input and illuminating some part of the knower's "felt experience"). These are the types of constructs which represent the limits of human cognition, given the kind of perceptions, cognitive organizations and effective output channels at our disposal. I argue that many forms of human experience do not constitute disjunctive culture conditioned categories, but a set of universal structures which transcends individual and cultural differences and relativities, and accommodates as subclasses, the many varieties of cognitive patterns as environment mappings and constructions of natural cognitive systems on the specially human level of nature's hierarchy"

Syntax of Knowledge and Epistemics

Meredith suggests the existence of a "syntax of knowledge".

The argument runs as follows:

- "At a multi-lingual conference with a community of disciplines, experience and thought, the translators have no difficulty in transforming, virtually instantaneously, the most elaborate syntactic forms of one language into the quite different forms of another whilst reserving the essential structure of information and conceptualization in the speech.
- Thus, there is a 'syntax of knowledge' which, even if not entirely independent of the particular languages, can and does, in practice, follow its own course alongside the syntactic sequence of language. It may serve to sharpen the difference if, provisionally, we think of the latter as governed by temporal relations (by the sequence of words in the sentence) and the 'syntax of knowledge' as primarily a spatial structure only shredded into temporal filaments in order to conform to the sequential character of speech.

- "This is a big step forward. Even though the syntax of language cannot be entirely divorced from the syntax of knowledge, we can pragmatically separate them by treating the one as a temporal sequence and the other as a spatial pattern. But, it may be objected, what about the temporal character of knowledge itself? Our knowledge of history, our under- standing of sequential operations, of industrial processes, of astronomical events etc., all of which involve time. Two points may be noted here:
- Even though in a narrative the sequence of paragraphs normally follows the time-sequence of the events narrated, this correspondence scarcely holds at all within the limits of a single sentence. And what is called linguistic syntax is largely based on the analysis of the single sentence. 'The assassin shot the President at the end of his speech'. In the actual event, the speech came before the shot; in the sentence after it. Thus, 'epistemic time' and 'linguistic time' are partially independent.
- We speak a sentence sequentially, that is, at the beginning we have not yet spoken the end but what we are talking about even though it may be temporal event, is known to us throughout. 'Epistemic time' is in fact 'dead' time, the completed past history, fossilised, and hence not "time" at all in the linguistic sense. It has a discernible sequence but no flow. Our knowledge of it is a geometric knowledge of evidence spread out in space or held in memory".

Common Structure

Arturo Rosenbleuth postulates a "common structure" in preserving the message received through a set of transformations:

- "When a person hears a symphony, the messages sent by the orchestra reach the listener as air vibrations. These vibrations stimulate mechanically the receptors of the organ of corti, and these receptors set up nerve impulses along the fibres of the VIIIth nerve. It is clear that at this stage the physical events that are taking place are of an entirely different kind from those occurring in the instruments of the orchestra. Yet the message is preserved because there are similarities in certain features of the two series of events sounds emitted by the orchestra and nerve impulses traveling over the auditory nerves.
- The existence of these similarities of relations is precisely what is called a common structure. The mental decoding, which is the perception of the symphony, again preserves the corresponding relations. A common structure thus implies the quantitative preservation of the relations that exist between the independent

constituents of an event or message through a set of transformations".

Logic of Exposition and Linguistic Syntax

Rosenbleuth also comments on syntax of thought and linguistic syntax thus:

"As a further example of the fundamental difference between the mental events and the correlated neuro-physiological processes, let us consider the processes that would develop in my brain if I presented verbally a specific relatively complex, argument on three different occasions in Spanish, English, and French, respectively. Although the neurophysiological correlates corresponding to the logic of my exposition might be similar or identical in the three cases, clearly those corresponding to the selection of words and their syntactical organization, a very important aspect of the presentation of the argument would be absolutely dissimilar. If I should want to use dictionaries to translate from the language of the introspective data to that of the physical processes, I would need in this instance three different dictionaries, and more, if I were capable of using fluently other languages."

Concept and Conception

Suzanne Langer points out that the psychological context of our thoughts may be private and personal. Therefore, two persons talking about the same thing may perceive it in different ways. They are then said to have different conceptions. But, if they understand each other, then their respective conceptions embody the same concept. A concept is an abstracted form. Abstraction is the consideration of logical form apart from content.

GENERALIZED FACET STRUCTURE FOR SUBJECTS

Analysis into constituent ideas and structuring of several thousands of subjects in a variety of subject fields for the purpose of designing and developing of schemes for subject classification, preparation of feature headings and subject headings, and for indexing of subjects have helped in:

- Categorizing the constituent elements in a subject into three types: Facet, Modifier, and Relations.
- Sub-categorizing each of the three types of constituent elements into a few kinds.
- Developing a typology of Basic Subjects, the modes of formation of Basic Subjects, and the arrangement of Basic Subjects.
- Developing a typology of Modifiers for basic facet and for isolate facet in different subject-fields.

- Recognizing the relative strength of bond between the first context specifying element and other types of facets in subjects.
- Formulating principles for helpful sequence among
- Facet s of a subject
- Spectators to a facet
- Compound subjects falling in a particular subject-field
- Subjects falling in different subject-fields.
- Developing a Generalized Facet structure of subject, with specific models for different subject-fields.

The main developments are briefly outlined in a recent FID/CR report. Subject structuring obtained using the Generalized Facet Structure has been found to give a co-extensive representation of subjects and arrangement of subjects helpful to majority of users.

The chart in fig. 6.4 shows the interrelation between subject- structuring, designing a classification scheme, generation of subject indexes, etc. Depth classification schemes for over a hundred subject-fields have been designed and several hundreds of articles, technical reports etc., have been classified using these schemes in each subject-field. The structuring of subjects and the sequence in which the subjects get arranged have been found to be acceptable to a large number of users. In a small-scale experiment, subject-headings each with several components, structured in the manner, were presented to about a hundred persons for indication by them of the subject that each of them perceived in the structuring.

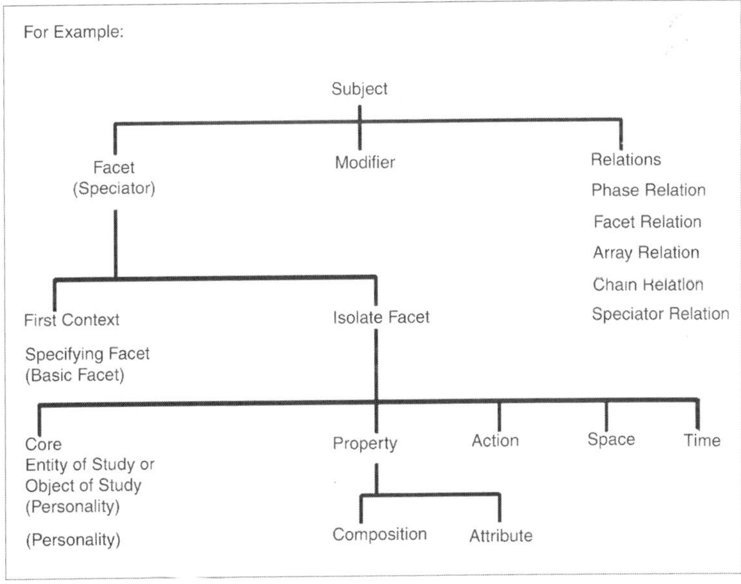

Although there were more than one way of representing each subject in the natural language, the subject perceived was the same in all the cases. That is, there was no homonym. Large scale experiments with other types of structuring of subjects has been planned. Translation of the subject heading terms into different natural languages did not give rise to any difficulty in interpreting the subject represented by persons knowing the language concerned. The facility of rearrangement of given terms into the preferred sequence and synthesis of class number given the descriptors, using computer, have been demonstrated.

These experiences indicate that the structuring of subjects conforming to the model developed according to the General Theory of Classification:

- Helps to secure a facet syntax parallel to that of the absolute syntax;
- Gives a "standard format" for representing information considered helpful by Anderson and Bower; and
- Provides a frame work for an intermediate or linking language that is helpful and consistent.

8

Library Movement in Washington

INTRODUCTION

The University of Washington Libraries has utilised a number of approaches during the past decade to assess the effectiveness of service programmes and library support of faculty and student research, teaching, and learning. Among the most valuable methods employed have been large-scale surveys of faculty and students conducted every three years beginning in 1992. Focus groups, usability and observational studies, targeted surveys, and interviews are also used to assess library programmes and services as well as user needs. Results from the triennial surveys have played a critical role in supporting the transition to a user-centred library and in creating a culture of assessment.

The large representative data sets generated by these surveys have also proven to be powerful information sources in the campus political environment. These surveys, though quite valuable, are expensive and time-consuming to design, administer, and analyse. Participation in the ARL-sponsored SERVQUAL pilot provided an opportunity to use a well- established survey tool with a different methodology, design, content, and delivery mechanism. It also afforded the chance for inter-institutional comparisons using a standardised survey instrument. Another attractive feature was the ability to gain experience with a Web based survey that might reduce survey costs associated with printing, mailing, and data entry.

This chapter will compare the UW Libraries' surveys with LibQUAL+ results from the University of Washington in such areas as response and representativeness of survey population, similarities and differences in results, and whether the right questions are being asked.

USER SURVEYS

Library user surveys have become widespread in academic libraries during the past twenty years. Surveys have often been used as a tool to assess service quality and user satisfaction. The Association of Research Libraries issued four Systems and Procedures Exchange Centre (SPEC) kits on user surveys and studies between 1981 and 1994. A substantial body of litreature has been developed on surveys and service quality, led by studies and reviews from such library educators/professionals as Hernon and McClure; Van House, Weil and McClure; Hernon and Altman; Nitecki and Franklin; and Hernon and Whitman. Library applications of the SERVQUAL instrument have been covered by Nitecki, and Cook and Heath, among others. Rapid changes in library services and operations, demands for internal institutional accountability, and assessment expectations by external accrediting agencies have contributed to further development and application of user surveys within academic libraries during the past decade.

User surveys can be designed and administered in a number of ways. Self-administered surveys are often employed to reach a large number of potential respondents with a minimum of direct contact and cost. Individuals are given or sent surveys to complete and return and the responses turned into data that can be analysed. Surveys can range from broad and comprehensive to those narrowly focused on specific services or activities. When properly designed and administered, user surveys can provide both quantitative and qualitative data directly from the target population.

UNIVERSITY LIBRARIES' SURVEY OF WASHINGTON METHODOLOGY AND DESIGN

The University of Washington Libraries began an active programme of assessing user needs, satisfaction, and the impact of library services and resources in 1992. Prior to this time, user input to the UW Libraries was generally informal and unsolicited through such channels as suggestion boxes and anecdotal comments from service desks. Other opportunities for user comment came through the Faculty Senate Council on University Libraries, a biennial meeting between subject selectors and faculty liaisons on collections-related issues and some earlier in-library surveys that focussed on specific activities within the library unit.

The catalyst for the development of a broad-based survey of faculty and students came from the UW Libraries' first strategic plan in 1991 that called for a user-centered approach to services. Specifically, the strategic plan recommended that the libraries: "Develop and implement a study to identify user populations, their information needs and how well they are being met".

The Task Force on Library Services was appointed by the Director of Libraries in late 1991 to design and implement a user survey that would provide information on the following:

- Determine who users and potential users are;
- How and why the library is used;
- What sources are used for library-related information;

- What faculty and students' library-related needs are;
- How satisfied faculty and students are with the libraries.

The litreature on academic library user surveys available at the time of the early 1990s revealed a wide spectrum of applications and uses.

Some common characteristics of these surveys were:

- Distribution within the library to users was more prevalent than mailed surveys;
- Focus on physical use of the library;
- Concentration on specific services;
- Interest in user satisfaction.

The task force designed the initial survey in 1992 in consultation with library staff and the University's Office of Educational Assessment (OM). The decision was made early in the design process to survey all user groups, distribute the survey through the mail in order to reach potential non-users, and provide similar survey content for each group to enable comparisons.

The survey would be sent to all faculty and a random sample of graduate and undergraduate students. While distributing the survey to all faculty would increase costs, it would also facilitate survey promotion and publicity, obtain sufficient number of responses to do analysis by academic subject areas, and foster positive political outcomes. Survey questions were similar for faculty and graduate students, with about 75 per cent consistency between faculty and undergraduates. Adequate space was provided for survey respondents to write comments. Content evolved with each subsequent survey in 1995 and 1998, and some aspects of survey design changed. Rapid changes in library services and programmes during the 1990s and usefulness of the data provided by some questions were prime factors in survey revision.

However, there was a core group of questions in each survey that dealt with:

- Information sources needed for research, teaching, and learning;
- Reasons and frequency of library use;
- Campus computer network connectivity;
- Use of electronic resources;
- Instructional needs and effectiveness;
- Library unit use;
- Satisfaction;
- Services availability or satisfaction.

The initial survey in 1992 was pilot tested in March with a group of faculty and students, revised, and then mailed mid-way through the Spring quarter to 3,900 faculty and a random, non-stratified, sample of 1,000 graduate and 1,000 undergraduate students. An incentive was offered to students who returned completed survey forms. Two weeks after the initial surveys were mailed, students were sent a second survey form, while faculty were sent a reminder notice. Completed surveys were returned to the Office of Educational Assessment (OEA) who arranged for data entry.

Data were made available in SPSS format and results were available in early September 1992. Subsequent surveys in 1995 and 1998 generally employed a similar methodology and design. Survey design work began in January of each year, pilot testing took place in March, and surveys were mailed in late April to early May.

The undergraduate sample was increased to 2,000 for 1995 and 1998, and the 1998 survey also included a specialised set of questions for faculty and graduate students in the biological and health sciences, and one for faculty and students in the fine arts. Focus groups were also held prior to the 1998 survey to provide input from users on their perception of issues and concerns.

The bookstore gift certificate drawing was extended to all groups beginning with the 1995 survey. Reminder notices were sent in 1995 but not a follow-up survey form. In 1998, a survey accompanied the reminder letter. Both the cover letter and survey form included the name, phone number, and e-mail address of a librarian as a contact person for questions or clarification.

The few questions received generally requested another survey be sent to replace a lost one. Sending this type of survey to nearly 7,000 faculty and students is not inexpensive. Direct survey costs in 1998 totaled $19,000, about $7 per returned survey. Survey costs in 1992 and 1995 were about $12,000.

The 1998 costs were distributed in the following manner:

- Printing 30 per cent
- Mailing 30 per cent.
- Data entry 30 per cent
- Other 10 per cent

Staff time for the 1998 survey was estimated at approximately 500 hours, including analysis and reporting.

LIBQUAL+

The UW Libraries was one of twelve libraries that participated in the ARL-sponsored LibQUAL+ pilot administered in Spring 2000. Survey design and methodology were handled primarily by a team from Texas A&M where a SERVQUAL based library survey had been used several times. In addition to the twenty-two basic SERVQUAL questions which covered the standard dimensions of accountability, assurance, reliability, responsiveness, and tangibles, nineteen additional questions were added to test two additional dimensions: access to collections and the library as place.

Thus, there were forty one questions that used the SERVQUAL three-column response format of minimum, perceived, and desired. Another fourteen behavioural questions, two on frequency of library use, and an overall ser- vice quality question were also added which used just one response column. The survey also collected demographic data.

The survey team at Texas A&M determined that the survey be administered to a random sample of 600 faculty, 600 graduate students, and 900 undergraduates at each institution based on an anticipated return of 200 surveys from each group. The UW Office of Educational Assessment extracted the sample from the faculty and student databases, and e-mail ad- dress lists created for each group were sent to the UW Libraries.

The UW Libraries systems office created separate mailing lists for each group. A cover letter from the director of the UW Libraries was sent by e-mail to each participant. The letter included information about the survey and the university's reasons for participation, and also provided a URL address where respondents could complete the survey. The initial message was sent May 2 and a reminder notice was sent on May 11.Almost immediately after the initial e-mail notification was sent, there was a steady stream of messages back to the director and the local survey coordinator.

LibQUAL+ implementation at the University of Washington ultimately generated more than fifty e-mail messages, most coming from faculty members. The messages fell into two basic groups: technical problems trying to complete the survey, and comments, usually negative, on survey design and content. Direct expenses were $2,000 for the UW Libraries paid as a participant in the ARL project.

This worked out to be about $5 per completed survey. Library staff contributed about 150 hours to the project, including responding to e-mail messages, analysis, and report writing.

SURVEY RESPONSE AND REPRESENTATIVES

Survey return rates for the 1992, 1995, and 1998 UW Libraries' surveys and the 2000 LibQUAL+ survey are shown in table.

Table. Surveys Distributed and Returned

Survey		Faculty		Graduate Students			Undergraduates		
Year	Sent	Returned	Rate	Sent	Returned	Rate	Sent	Returned	Rate
2000	600	128	21.3 %	600	131	21.8 %	900	137	15.2 %
1998	3750	1503	40.1 %	1000	457	45.7 %	2000	787	39.4 %
1995	4400	1359	28.4 %	1000	409	40.9 %	2000	489	24.5 %
1992	3900	1108	28.4 %	1000	561	56.1 %	1000	422	42.2 %

A second survey mailing appeared effective in raising the response rate as seen in the 1992 return rates for students and for all groups in 1998. The number of faculty surveyed varied according to criteria used to define the faculty pool, but all surveys included tenure track and research faculty as well as full-time lecturers.

The overall response rate as shown is slightly understated as undeliverable surveys were not subtracted from the total sent out. Undeliverable survey rates ranged from approximately.5 per cent of faculty to 2 per cent of undergraduate students. Response rates to the LibQUALt survey were substantially lower.

The definition of faculty was the same as used in the UW Libraries' 1998 survey. LibQUALt response rates were calculated by matching the number of completed surveys against the number of e-mail addresses to which the survey message was sent. Approximately 1percent of these messages were undeliverable.

REPRESENTATIUENESS OF SURVEY RESPONDENTS

The large number of responses to the UW Libraries' surveys generated correspondingly large data sets, especially for the faculty survey.

Table. Faculty Population and Respondents by Academic Area, 1998 and 2000 In Percentage

Academic Area	2000 LibQUAL+ Respondents n=128	1998 Faculty Population n=3750	1998 Survey Respondents n=1503
Health Sciences	43.0	48.6	44.7
Sciences/Engineering	25.8	26.2	27.1
Humanities/Arts/ Social Sciences	31.2	21.0	24.4
Other (non- Health Sciences)		4.2	3.8

As table 7.2 shows, the faculty survey respondent population in 1998 was reasonably representative of the population as a whole when grouped by broad subject areas.

Faculty in the Health Sciences were slightly underrepresented, while those in the Humanities/Social Sciences/Fine Arts group were somewhat over-represented compared to the actual population. Response rates by academic schools ranged from 31 per cent in Business to 54 per cent in the Social Science departments within the College of Arts and Sciences. Graduate student responses were similar to the faculty with Health Sciences respondents again lower than their percentage of the actual population while those from Humanities/Arts/Social Sciences were slightly higher.

Response rates by academic schools ranged from 24 per cent in Dentistry and 28 per cent in Education to 62 per cent in Nursing and '72 per cent in Social Sciences. Health Sciences does have a larger proportion of faculty and graduate/professional students located away from the main UW campus, and this may be a factor in the under representation of respondents from those areas.

Table. Graduate/Professional Student Population and Survey

Respondents by Academic Area In Percentage

Academic Area	2000LibQUAL+ n=131	1998 Graduate Population n=8183•	1998 Survey Respondents n=457
Health Sciences	22.1	30.4	26.0
Sciences/Engineering	28.20	29.4	30.2
Humanities/Arts/ Social Sciences	45.0	40.3	43.8
Other (non- Health Sciences)	4.6		

- Law was not included in the 1998 survey, 1998 graduate population with Law is 8,785, Law is 69. per cent to total.

Determining how representative undergraduate respondents are is more complicated. Undergraduates in earlier UW Libraries' surveys appeared to identify with certain academic majors before they were actually accepted into those programmes, thus skewing responses by academic areas. Year in school appeared to be a more reliable measure. Table shows undergraduate population and respondent population by year in school.

Again, the respondent population is reasonably similar to the entire population. Freshmen were somewhat underrepresented in the 1998 survey and sophomores underrepresented in the LibQUAL+ survey.

Table 7.4 Undergraduate Student Population and Survey

Respondents by Year In Percentage

Class	2000LibQUAL+ n=137	1998 Undergraduate Population n=23413	1998 Undergraduate Respondents n=787
Freshman	22.6	19.0	14.4
Sophomore	13.9	18.3	17.0
Junior	27.7	26.3	26.9
Senior	35.8	32.9	33.9
Other (including 5th Year		3.4	7.8

Compared to the population as a whole, and UW survey respondents in 1998, the LibQUALt respondent pools, although significantly smaller than those generated by UW surveys, appear reasonably representative when grouped by broad academic areas for faculty and graduate students, and by class for undergraduates.

The under representation of Health Sciences and overrepresentation by those in the Social Sciences mirrors the respondent population achieved in the large-scale UW Libraries' surveys.

This is probably reflective of the way faculty and students in these areas use libraries as well as the larger proportion of the Health Sciences population located away from the main Seattle campus.

SURVEY RESULTS

Results from the UW Libraries' surveys provide an effective record of changes in the way that students and faculty used library and information resources during the 1990s.

These results also documented significant variations within groups and between groups in some areas. Information from these surveys has been used extensively by the University of Washington Libraries to revise existing programmes and services and promote new ones.

Survey results showed:

- High satisfaction levels;
- A shift towards remote use and increased importance of electronic re- sources;
- Continuing importance of libraries as place for students;
- Increased complexity of finding and using information for teaching, learning, and research.

Although the University of Washington Libraries' surveys and the LibQUAL+ survey differs substantially in design and content, it is interesting to compare results where questions were similar.

The large respondent pool for the 1998 UW Libraries survey can serve as a benchmark for viewing the LibQUALt results based on a much smaller sample. For example, UW Libraries' surveys results revealed that faculty generally viewed the libraries through a collections-related focus, while undergraduate students placed a high value on the library as a place.

Even though the questions and design in these surveys differ, would LibQUAL+ results also show similar responses? Results from the UW Libraries' survey in 1998 and the LibQUALt survey in 2000 will be compared in the areas of overall satisfaction, opening hours, collections importance, the library as a place, and remote use of library services and resources. These areas are often barometers of service quality.

OVERALL SATISFACTION

Responses to overall library satisfaction questions on the 1998 survey showed faculty had the highest satisfaction while undergraduate students the lowest.

Table 7.5 Overall Satisfaction: UW Libraries 1998 Survey and Libqual+ 2000 Survey by Group In Percentage

Level	Libqual+ Faculty	1998 Faculty	Libqual+ Grad Students	1998 Grad Students	Libqual+ Undergrads	1998 Undergrads
Very satisfied	78.0%	91.3%	80.9%	84.9%	72.9%	78.5%
Satisfied	21.2%	7.8%	18.3%	13.5%	24.0%	19.9%
Not satisfied	0.8%	0.9%	0.8%	1.6%	3.1%	1.6%
Mean Score	7.17	4.33	7.13	4.11	6.88	3.99

The LibQUAL+ survey phrased the questions as overall quality of services but still produced similar results although the difference in Likert scales can lead to a different type of response. For LibQUALt, the differences between undergraduate scores and graduate and faculty ones were significant at the.10 level using t-tests.

LIBRARY HOURS

The 1998 survey asked whether libraries were open when needed on evenings, weekends, summer, and interim periods. Graduate students had the lowest satisfaction with hours while faculty had the highest, as shown in figure. Undergraduate student satisfaction had slipped from 1995 when it was similar to faculty satisfaction.

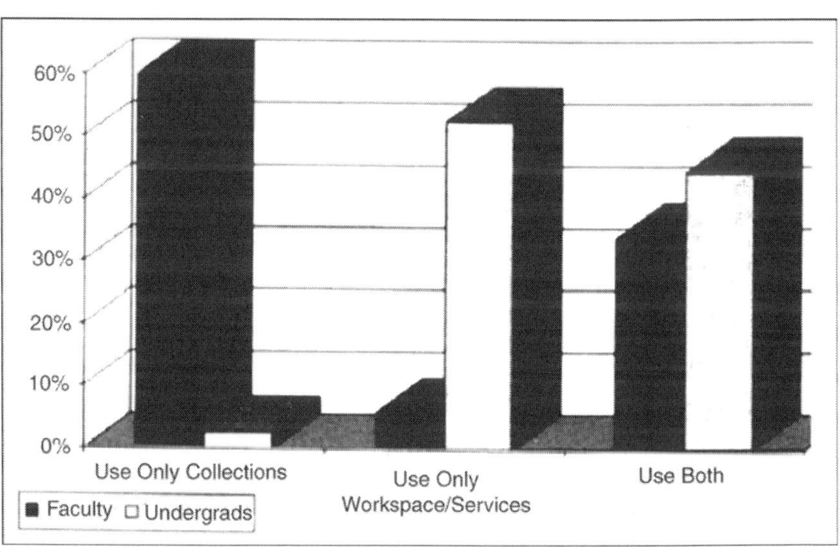

When asked to choose from a list of priorities, more than 37 per cent of graduate students and 42 per cent of undergraduates chose increased library hours as a priority compared to 17 per cent of faculty. Graduate students also wrote more comments about hours than any other group. The LibQUAL+ question was concerned about expectations and perceived level of service related to whether the library had convenient business hours.

Table 7.6 LibQUAL+ Convenient Business Hours

	Faculty Minimum	Faculty Perceived	Grad Minimum	Grad Perceived	Undergrad Minimum	Undergrad Perceived
Convenient Business Hours	6.45	6.56 (.11)	6.68	6.63 (-.05)	6.50	7.13 (.63)

As table shows, graduate student minimum expectations for convenient business hours exceeded their perception of library performance. Faculty minimum expectations were lower, and the gap between expectations and performance, while small, was positive. Undergraduate students had both the highest perceived value and most positive gap. One likely reason for this positive response in LibQUAL+ was the Undergraduate Library's move to 24 hour opening in autumn 1998.

COLLECTIONS

A valuable part of each one of the UW Libraries' surveys is asking users to identify their library priorities from a list of ten to twelve choices. The list of potential priorities is compiled from comments provided on the pretests as well as areas the libraries are interested in.

The first survey in 1992 showed that all three groups had the same priorities in their top three choices, while in 1998 the top three priorities for undergraduates were different than those for graduate students and faculty. Faculty, in particular, showed an almost exclusive focus on collections/information resources-related areas as shown in table.

Table 7.7 1998 Survey: Library Priorities by Group In Percentage

	Faculty	Graduate Students	Under-graduates
Maintain quality of print collections	69.6%	52.3%	28.2%
Deliver full-text to your computer	60.4%	55.8%	34.4%
Deliver bib databases through the web	52.1%	40.0%	17.7%
Provide reserves electronically	18.8%	36.6%	50.8%
Add more computers in the library	8.6%	20.1%	54.5%
Provide training in use of web/ library resources	28.3%	27.4%	47.5%
Increase library hours	17.0%	37.5%	41.9%
Preserve library materials	40.0%	34.9%	24.7%
Add group study/seminar rooms			35.5%
Provide consulation on how to do library research		13.3%	39.8%

The LibQUAL+ survey reinforced the primacy of collections and information resources for faculty. This was the only area where faculty had negative gap scores. Faculty minimum expectations were generally higher as well. Graduate student results also showed high expectations for collections-related questions and negative gaps for full-text delivered electronically and complete journal runs. Undergraduate students had lower expectations and positive gaps in all collections related areas. Reviewing mean scores for six collections-related questions on LibQUAL+ showed higher mean scores for faculty and graduate students in minimum expectations.

Table 7.8 LibQUAL+ Collections Expectations/Perceptions

Question		Faculty Minimum	Faculty Perceived	Grad Minimum	Grad Perceived	Undergrad Minimum	Undergrad Perceived
10.	Resources added on request	4.23	6.10 (-.13)	6.04	6.27 (.23)	5.97	6.37 (.40)
17.	Timely document delivery/IIL,	6.41	6.82 (.41)	6.61	7.22 (.61)	6.31	6.88 (.57)
23.	Full text delivered electronically	6.32	5.84 (-.48)	6.20	6.16 (.04)	5.96	6.24 (.28)
27.	Comprehensive print collections	6.30	6.64 (.34)	6.65	6.65 (.02)	6.14	6.98 (.84)
36.	Interdisciplinary needs addressed	6.89	6.44 (.55)	6.24	6.55 (.31)	6.05	6.65 (.60)
37.	Complete journal	6.52	6.40 (-.12)	6.77	6.58 (-.19)	6.22	6.61 (.39)

However, the differences between undergrads and faculty were not significant at the.05 or.10 level according to t-tests. There were differences at the.05 level between grad students and undergraduates in complete runs of journal titles and comprehensive print collections, and at the.10 level for timely document delivery and interlibrary loan.

LIBRARY AS PLACE

A consistent theme revealed through each of the UW Libraries' surveys has been the different perspectives of faculty and students on the library as a place. Faculty use of the library is primarily collections driven, while students view the library as a place to do work, including finding and using information resources.

This difference shows up dramatically in responses to a 1998 survey question on reasons for visiting the library as well as other questions dealing with priorities and needed services. LibQUAL, clearly showed similar differences between faculty and students on the library as a place.

Table 7.9 LibQUAL+ Library as Place

Question		Faculty Minimum	Faculty Perceived	Grad Minimum	Grad Perceived	Undergrad Minimum	Undergrad Perceived
14.	Comfortable and inviting location	6.08	6.12 (1.04)	5.72	6.12 (.40)	5.98	6.73 (.75)
21.	Secure and safe place	6.77	7.51 (.74)	6.81	7.26 (.45)	6.80	7.23 (.43)
22.	Center for intellectual interaction	5.61	5.31 (1.15)	5.20	5.97 (.59)	5.75	6.24 (.49)
29.	Space for group/individual study	5.57	5.94 (1.34)	5.90	6.07 (.17)	6.20	6.78 (.58)
30.	Haven for quiet and solitude	4.74	6.02 (1.28)	6.12	6.08 (-.04)	6.53	6.46 (-.07)
40.	Space that facilitates quiet study	4.69	5.75 (1.06)	6.23	6.30 (.07)	6.52	6.62 (.10)

On seven questions related to the library as place, the differences in minimum expectations were significant at the 0.01 level except for 'safe and secure space.' With the exception of 'secure and safe space," faculty minimum expectations were generally below 5 and gaps between minimum and perceived were larger than 1.O. While graduate student expectations were higher than those of faculty, they were still lower than those of undergraduates. Both student groups were concerned about quiet study areas.

REMOTE USE

The 1995 UW Libraries' survey revealed for the first time that more were' going so remotely than physically visiting the library. This trend continued in 1998, and table shows degrees of remote use among all groups both in the 1998 survey and LibQUAL+.

Table 7.10 Type and Frequency of Library Use among Faculty and Students who Use Library at Least Weekly In Percentage

Type of Library Use	Visit in Person	Visit Remotely Using Computer
LibQUAL+ Faculty	54.5%	81.1%
1998 Faculty	47.3%	73.4%
LibQUAL+ 1998 Grad	77.0%	80.2%
1998 Grad	77.9%	66.1%
LibQUAL+ Undergrad	66.7%	48.8%
1998 Undergrad	70.3%	45.5%

Responses to other survey questions in 1998 revealed that more than 97 percent of faculty had access to the Web through a desktop computer. While remote use is not itself a measure of service quality, this information is critical for planning and delivering electronic services and resources. In general, LibQUAL+ results tended to correlate with results from the libraries' surveys which had a much larger number of respondents for each group, especially faculty. Differences between groups, especially faculty and undergraduates, that were evident in earlier UW Libraries' surveys, were also found in the LibQUAL+ results.

SUB-GROUP ANALYSIS

One of the benefits of a large respondent pool is the ability to do analysis on differences within the group. While there may be a set of similar characteristics that define a group, there may also be significant variation within that group. Academic user communities are not homogeneous in the way they use libraries nor in their needs for library resources and services. In addition to differences between faculty and students, there may also be significant differences between those in different academic areas or by gender or some other demographic component.

These have important implications for identifying user needs, concerns, and issues that may be missed in analysing aggregate results. The number of respondents to the UW Libraries' 1998 survey, especially for faculty, was sufficiently large to examine the degree of variation within the group and between subject areas.

The sample size and response rates of the LibQUAL I survey generally precluded analysis by academic area and made it difficult to find differences among demographic characteristics. Increasing the LibQUAL+ sample size and the response rate would provide larger data sets that could be used to examine variation within and between groups.

Factors related to the low response rate for LibQUALt include survey length, complexity, perceived redundancy, technical problems, behavioural issues associated with Web-based surveys, and how related survey content is to actual library use and issues of the respondent. While the LibQUAL+ sample appears representative of each group as a whole, it is not large enough to perform sub- group analysis.

How important is it to have a respondent pool large enough to do analysis at the subgroup level? UW Libraries' surveys have consistently shown significant differences in how faculty from different academic areas use libraries and in their needs for library resources and services.

They also show surprising uniformity in areas such as connectivity arid remote use where differences might be expected based on traditional use patterns. Although graduate student response numbers are lower, they were similar to faculty in the same academic areas. Satisfaction responses, while showing some variation, generally do not differ significantly by academic area. Priorities, on the other hand, clearly do as shown in figure.

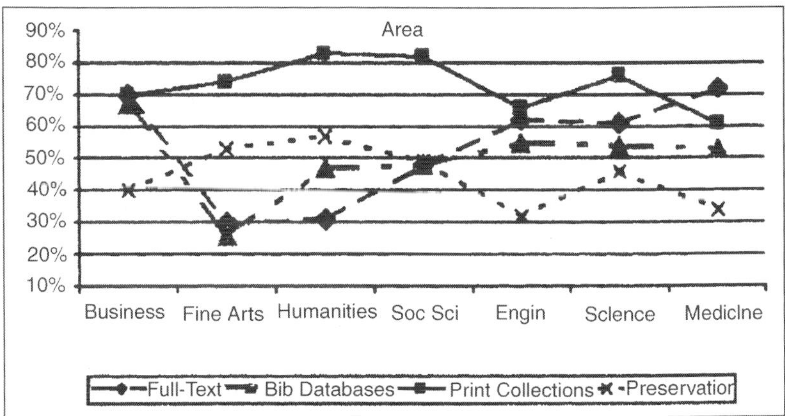

Fig. 7.1 1998 Survey. Faculty Top Priorities by Academic Area

The 1998 results showed significant variation among academic areas in the top four overall priorities, especially for de- livery of full text to the desktop and preservation. Variation within undergraduate responses to the UW Libraries' 1998 survey were more difficult to determine. There were some gender differences, especially in areas related to computer access and library instruction as well as differences by class year.

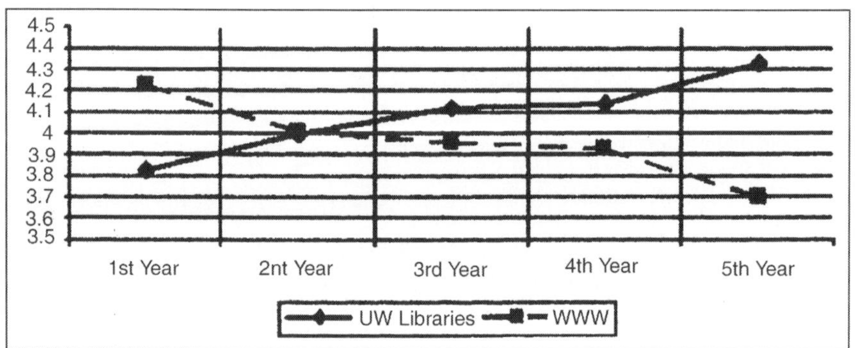

Fig. 7.2 1998 Survey. Importance of World Wide Web and UW Libraries by Undergraduate Class (Scale of 1 not important to very important)

Figure shows the importance of UW Libraries and the World Wide Web to the work of undergraduates by year in school. The differences between first year and upper division students were significant at the.05 level using a simple t-test. However, LibQUALt survey results did not show any statistical differences in responses either by gender or class year.

The importance of different resource types such as journals, books, bibliographic databases, and foreign language materials also showed significant variation between academic areas. When asked to rank these re- source types on a scale of 1 to 5, faculty in all academic areas ranked journals as very important. A large number of responses also enables analysis within smaller sub- groups. For example, the 1998 faculty survey had 241 responses from those in science departments.

Table 7.11 1998 Survey (Faculty). Importance of Resource Types

Department (Responses)	Books	Journals > 1980	Journals < 1980	Bibliographic Databases
Chemistry (36)•	4.28	4.83	3.92	4.39
Geology-Geophysics• (22)	4.54	4.91	4.27	4.18
Math-Stat (37)••	4.89	4.89	4.57	3.51
Physics (39)•	4.21	4.56	4.08	3.69
Psychology (24)	4.13	5.00	3.75	4.42
Zoology (27)	4.11	5.00	4.30	4.63
All Science (241)	4.26	4.76	4.09	4.05

Table 7.11 shows mean scores by department on responses to questions dealing with type and frequency of library use and importance of resource types.

Only departments with at least twenty responses were included. While current journals are important to all groups, the importance of books, earlier journals, and bibliographic databases showed variation within each group. Understanding the importance of these resource types to different subject areas is useful in allocating the collection-development budget as well as making decisions on what matcrials to house on-site or in storage.

There were also significant differences in the frequency of physical visits to the library by science faculty. Perhaps it is not surprising that distance from the library appeared to play an important role. Not only did the departments located closest to their primary library visit those libraries more often, the frequency of their physical visits exceeded the frequency of library use from an office computer.

A comparison between large-scale user surveys done by the UW Libraries and the LibQUALt survey administered to UW faculty and students shows good agreement in population representation and in broad result categories at the group level. However, the ability to do subgroup and intra group analysis can provide valuable results and efforts to increase the number of responses if the Web based LibQUAL+ survey should continue.

ASKING THE RIGHT QUESTIONS

Whether the survey results are statistically reliable, representative, valid, or significant, doesn't necessarily mean that they provide information that can be used to assess and improve library service quality. It is also important to examine whether these surveys are asking the right questions in the right way to the right group.

Survey design is a complex and evolving process that requires substantial interaction between the surveying group and the surveyed population. At many large academic research institutions, user communities are diverse and differ in their needs for library resources and services.

It is essential to recognise that these differences exist when designing and administering surveys. Undergraduate students, based on their understanding or experience, may respond quite differently from faculty to some questions, making it difficult to do cross group comparisons. It is also important to remember that surveys are just one method of acquiring user input. While surveys offer the prospect of obtaining quantifiable data from large populations at reasonable costs, they need to be employed in the right situation. Surveys should be de- signed from the user perspective. Questions should be short, simple, and clear to the user. Complex issues may be better addressed using other techniques.

There should be sufficient motivation for faculty and students to take the time to complete a survey. The evolution of SERVQUAL to LibQUALt is a positive step. The ability to move away from the twenty-two question

SEKVQUAL core pack- age to a design that provides a library focus, and perhaps a simpler format, is welcome. Grounding the survey based on user-provided information on library needs and use is critical to maintain currency and relevancy. Such qualitative data obtained at regular intervals enables the library to keep on top of user issues and concerns.

The library and information environment is changing rapidly. The continued growth in remote use of library services and resources and in user self-sufficiency calls for new ways to measure user needs and library performance that can be done quickly, inexpensively, and flexibly enough to catch environmental changes. The ARL New Measures Initiative plans to provide libraries with tested tools that can help provide information that will assist in meeting these challenges. The underlying concept of developing a standard instrument to mea- sure service quality across libraries is a powerful one and certainly one deserving institutional support.

However, it cannot supplant local efforts to work closely with faculty and students to assess user needs and library collections and services. There are local issues at each institution that probably cannot be effectively addressed in a standardised survey tool. The University of Washington Libraries expects to continue both its participation in LibQUALt as well as utilising a variety of ways to assess user needs and library performance, including the deployment of locally based large-scale user surveys.

9

The Change of Libraries: Movement in German

HOW TO MANAGE A LIBRARY

Library management involves functions such as planning, organising, leading, and controlling. Planning is about systematically making decisions about the library goals. Organising is about assembling and coordinating human, financial, physical, informational, and other resources needed to achieve library goals. Leading is about functions that involve efforts on the part of the librarian to stimulate high performance by employees, and controlling about monitoring various library operations and services. These four management functions are highly integrated, but libraries that excel in organising material resources and in leading their human capital are known to give better performance. Keeping in view the fact that libraries in adult education set ups are, by design, small budget libraries, confined to one room space, and adult education staff manages them manually on part time basis, these four management functions would occur in varying degree. In such a typical set up, the functions of organising and controlling would receive greater attention compared to other two functions.

For managing a library you may take the following step-by-step approach:

- *Step 1:* Defining library policies for collection development
- *Step 2:* Defining library authority and library advisory committee
- *Step 3:* Define procedures for library organisation and administration
- *Step 4:* Defining library space, equipment and tools for library operations and services
- *Step 5*: Defining procedures for maintenance of library collections

STEP 1: LIBRARY POLICIES FOR COLLECTION DEVELOPMENT

Step 1 includes the following task:

- *Define the Objectives of your Library:* State clearly the purpose of its existence;

- *Define your User Community and their Information Needs:* This requires complete knowledge and understanding about library stakeholders. This may include adult education teams, extension workers and adult education professionals, local community members and those who provide funds for the library. Their information needs can be assessed through library surveys, personal interviews, and informal discussions with all stakeholders;
- *Define Library Policy for Building Collections:* The policy states the guiding principles and procedures under which collection development activities, including the selection, maintenance, and weeding of print, electronic, and media library materials will occur. This would also mean specifying subject areas of interest to library stakeholders, their languages preferences, and formats of published and unpublished material. Non-print material could include films, slides, transparencies, photographs, maps posters, charts, etc. The policy must also define the limits in terms of collection size, keeping in view the users strength in a given subject, space available within the library premises, and annual budget earmarked for the purpose. The policy may also specify the subject areas in which the library is going build its archival collection, if any. Such a policy statement on the part of the library ensures continuity and consistency in selection and revision of materials for the library collections;
- *Define what Different Collections are Required to be Developed and Sustained Keeping in View Users' Information Needs:* The possible options include books collection, reports collection, pamphlet collection, multimedia collection, and reference collection (comprising dictionaries, yearbooks, directories, who's who almanacs, general and subject encyclopaedias), etc. The library may decide on developing some of these collections keeping in view the users' information needs.
- *Define your Book Selection Policy:* State the distribution of library budget by subject and by collection. The policy may also state guidelines for acquiring multiple copies of books, guidelines for accepting books from donors, and guidelines for weeding out material.

STEP 2: LIBRARY AUTHORITY AND LIBRARY ADVISORY COMMITTEE

Libraries in adult education setups are, by design, small budget libraries, confined to one room space, and managed manually on part time basis by adult education staff. The person incharge of the library should be the library authority, responsible for organisation and management of the library. He/she should play a dominant role in decision making, should enjoy the authority to

The university library will continue the process of the qualitative transformations during the following period, but in different ways. The aim is at using efficiently the strategy, as management instrument and at developing mechanisms that should allow the continuous control and improvement of the library performance through systematic actions. To this purpose, in a first stage there was carried out the diagnostic analysis of the management system of the library, whose conclusions are presented as follows, synthesized in strengths and weaknesses.

STRENGTHS

- There is a strategy of the library, harmonized with that of the university. The mission of the library and the system of values are published on the site. The objectives are realistic, measurable; the accent is laid on improving the performance, in order to contribute to ensuring the quality of the educational and research services carried out by the university. There was set as priority axis of research the implementation of a system of quality management, through which there is created the framework for the continuous improvement of the quality.
- The university and library management has the capability to professionally approach the changes, evinces competences as regards the ample perspective and its concretization in valid strategies of development, the settling of the plans for further action and the provision with the resources necessary for accom-plishing the change projects, the optimization of the structure, the implementation of modern methods of management.
- Human resources: the library has 52 employees, among which 32 with higher education and 11 with higher education in the field. The staff benefited from training and of mobility exchanges in the country and abroad.

WEAKNESSES

- *Control of the Performance*: The library achieves the assessment of the performance every year; however the criteria and the indicators which are used do not reflect the qualitative aspects of the activity, the effects of the library services upon the educational and scientific research processes.
- There is no management system that should measure the costs of the services/activities realised by the library.
- *Control of the Processes:* There has begun to be implemented the management through processes, however the action is in an incipient phase of analysis and description of the key processes through procedures.

- *Human Resources*: Staff's evaluation is done in compliance with the law, however the insufficient resources used in this process make the evaluation not always relevant. The participation of the staff in solving the problems is unequal and the rewarding system is non-stimulating.
- *Organisational Culture:* There is no culture of the quality, there are insufficiently promoted values such as team work, staff's implication, opening towards change.

Taking into account the submitted situation, the priority axes for the development of the capability of the library to continuously improve its performance are the following:

- *People:* The continuation of the process of staff training in quality management, with accent on achieving behavioural changes, on raising the degree of implication in solving the problems and on team work.
- *Users:* Orientation towards the customers, definition of the requirements and evaluation of their satisfaction. This implies in the first place the improvement of the system evaluating the library performance, through the introduction of criteria and indicators that should better reflect the effects upon the quality of the educational and research processes.
- The control will be also extended upon the costs of the services and of the activities realised by the library.
- *Processes:* Development and implementation of instruments and also of working and control procedures that should ensure the optimization of the processes and their continuous improvement.

The achievement of the change processes will be coordinated by the Management Council of the library. Both the initiation of the projects and their unfolding will be largely promoted in the framework of the library, for obtaining the feedback and for attracting the people in realizing the changes. The financing of the projects will be done from its own funds, but there will be likewise accessed funds from the Operational Programmes.

CASE STUDY: 'A SMALL LIBRARY WITH BIG GOALS' THE LIBRARY FOR GERMAN LANGUAGE AND LITERATURE, UNIVERSITY OF TARTU

BRIEF HISTORY OF THE UNIVERSITY OF TARTU

I will start my presentation with a small overview of the University of Tartu as our library is a part of the university and it is not possible to observe them apart. The University of Tartu is the oldest university in Estonia and communicate freely with groups across the organisation, and enjoy financial and administrative powers for managing library operations and services smoothly.

The financial and administrative limits of the library authority should correspond to staff of equivalent status in the organisational hierarchy. The library authority should be reporting to the top management in the organisation. There is a need to set up a Library Advisory Committee, which would perform the role of advising the library on its growth and development.

It will also act as interface between the library management and the top management in the organisation and between the users groups, for ensuring smooth functioning of the library operations and services without compromising on policies set out for library development. The Committee should comprise members mainly drawn from the organisation, and representing various user groups on the Committee.

Its terms of reference could be worked out on the following lines:

- To formulate policy for developing library resources for reading, reference and projects;
- To develop a general programme of library services to suit the interests and requirements of different categories of users;
- To frame, review and approve library rules;
- To recommend suitable budgetary provisions for the library and resource centre;
- To make recommendations for proper functioning of library as knowledge centre.

STEP 3: PROCEDURES FOR LIBRARY ORGANISATION AND ADMINISTRATION

In any larger set up, library organisation tasks involve assembling, forming logical units of works, defining hierarchical structures, identifying staffing requirements, assigning tasks and responsibilities, coordinating human, financial, physical, informational, and other resources needed to achieve library goals. Administration is another activity required to be undertaken for performance and achieving library goals. It is defined as the process of getting things done through men and materials within the organisational framework.

Library organisation and library administration are closely related to each other. The distinction between the two is very subtle. Organisation comes before administration. The latter starts when the organisation ends. One lays down theoretical principles, whilst the other puts those principles into practice. In the adult education set up, wherein libraries by design are small and are going to be managed on part time basis by adult education staff, not much needs to be done in so far as library organisation is concerned.

In such flat hierarchical structures, the staff has no option but to perform multitasking operations such as administration, technical functions, service support, and library maintenance. For effective performance, it is advisable for the library to opt for outsourcing of library maintenance operations such as stack maintenance, catalogue card maintenance, photocopy services, library up keep, stock verification, gate security, etc. It may also consider outsourcing classification and cataloguing operations if circumstances so warrant.

The libraries in adult education set ups need to undertake planning activities such as strategic planning (*i.e.* identifying library goals, objectives, methods, resources needed to carry out methods, responsibilities and dates for completion of tasks), budget planning (for document collections, library equipments, library furniture, library stationery, media library equipments, if planning for a multi-media library), and library promotion planning. These are not perennial activities and are required to be undertaken once in year.

The extent of budget planning activities would depend upon the size of adult education programmes, network linkages, and staff deployed within the organisation, etc. For building a library from the scratch, it must begin with a small annual budget of ₹100,000/-during the first three years. In the subsequent years, budget requirements may be reviewed and decided based on collection already built and actual requirements. It is a good practice to undertake budget planning exercise in consultation with the Library Advisory Committee for developing collections, library equipments, library furniture, media equipments, etc. It is also a good practice to formulate library plans for promoting and popularizing library services.

STEP 4: LIBRARY SPACE, EQUIPMENT AND TOOLS FOR LIBRARY OPERATIONS AND SERVICES

Bureau of Indian Standards provides that a library should have a stack room, a Librarian's room and a Reading Room having seating capacity of 40 to 120 chairs. The stack room should be big enough to accommodate between 6,000 and 10,000 books. The library-in-charge would need to plan actual library size and seating capacity of 'reading room' keeping in view the optimum number of members in an adult education setup, the variety of library services it is planning to offer, and the members of the adult community who would be coming to visit the library for social interactions. The library equipments and tools like furniture, fittings and accessories should of standard pattern and design, so that users feel comfortable in using them.

The following is the list of essential furniture and fittings for an adult education set up:

- Reading tables
- Chairs for pupils

- Librarian's table
- Circulation or charging desk and chair
- Librarian's shelf list trays
- Card catalogue trays
- Card catalogue cabinet
- Bulletin board and notice board
- Book supporters
- New arrivals display case
- Dictionary stands
- Periodicals display stand
- Newspaper display stand
- Storage cabinet for work room
- Filing cabinets
- Atlas stand
- Wall clock

Besides, the library may acquire radio and television set, tape recorder/ player, VCR and VCP, slide and film projector, overhead projectors, computers with internet connection, Xerox machine, etc.

STEP 5: PROCEDURES FOR MAINTENANCE OF LIBRARY COLLECTIONS

You will find that the following procedures help in maintenance of library collections.

Preservation of Library Material

Proper care of library collections is necessary with a view to prolong its life. This requires preserving and protecting books against decay and deterioration. As preventive measures, dusting and cleaning of books and shelves must be carried out on regular basis. Books must be exposed to adequate air and sunlight for a short time in case the library room does not get sufficient sunlight. Avoid keeping books is in damp places. Pest control treatment may be got done on periodic basis. Books and other reading material may be got bound from time to time. Besides, book supporters may be used to keep books upright on the shelves. Reference books such as dictionaries, encyclopedias, directories and picture books are costly and heavy in weight. They must be handled with care.

Organising Reading Materials on Shelves and Their Rectification

Normally, books and other reading display of new books and other reading material received in the library, preparing stack room guides, and shelving volumes returned after use, etc. Library may also perform stock verification on periodical basis, with a view to weed out books, as per its policy, and writing off books, etc.

THE METHODOLOGY OF ACHIEVING ORGANISATIONAL CHANGES

Recent years were for the libraries a period of faster, greater and more dramatic changes than has ever before been experienced. The omnipresence of the new technologies, the ever-increasing cooperation, the globalization as premises of the evolution towards the *Global Information Society,* the emphasis on quality, the diminution of the financial resources are the main agents imposing the change of libraries.

Implementing the necessary changes for the academic libraries is no easy job as it requires a differentiation between changes to ensure the coherence of actions within the available resources. It is also important to use planning and control methods that contribute to reduce the span of the change process and to optimize the use of resources. Finally, it requires suitable structures, staff training and overcoming the resistance to change. All these respects are subjects of change management—a distinct discipline whose key-aspects-in point of increasing the success and the efficiency of organisational changes—we present. The concept of organisational change, as defined by the management theories, is a significant, extended, important change that affects the entire organisation or parts of it.

Such changes do not occur naturally, they are changes whose implementation is the task of the management team. The methodology of achieving these changes is one of the main issues of change management and it is treated in very different ways by management theoreticians. The best known approach is the one proposed by Kurt Lewin and E. H. Schein that identifies three essential stages in the process of organisational changes, stages somewhat similar to chemical processes: unfreezing—the trial to create the reasons for change; moving/implementing change—identifying solutions adequate to circumstance and applying them; freezing—a new equilibrium is crystallizing.

From the point of view of implementing changes in the university library, the methodology presented by Popescu, M. has the advantage of a pragmatic approach that defines two major stages of the process of starting and implementing change: identifying the need of change and achieving change. Identifying the need of change aims to establish the favourable changes that may add value to the organisation. In the authors' opinion the important changes must be implemented from a strategic point of view; this means that, when establishing the changes that must be done and their order, the mission and the strategic objectives of the organisation are kept in mind.

This way one can avoid the risk of starting complex and expensive processes that can not be financially supported or that have little or no effects upon the performances of the organisation. Several studies discussing changes in libraries develop the above idea.

Thus, Troll, A.D. underlines that the evaluation activity usually carried out in libraries is not enough in order to plan changes: without knowing the external and the internal context and the library's strategy, such an evaluation is of no help in understanding what changes are relevant and can assure the accomplishment of the library's mission. It's necessary to define clearly the strategic objectives and the main lines of change that sustain planning changes in the library. To complete this idea we state that, once the strategy is elaborated it has to be communicated; making public and discussing the mission, the policy and the general objectives of the library are means of communication through which the top management acknowledges everyone concerned its view on the future of the library and obtains their support. Communicating, informing and involving the staff are elements that contribute to overcome the resistance to change which is normal in the case of any major change. The bigger the changes, the greater the resistance to change and ignoring this is the source of many failures as shown in many studies on this topic. Achieving change, the second stage, is a complex process having clearly stated beginning and ending points and, between, a sequence of three activities:

- The preliminary study or the planning–it's goal is to define change, to evaluate the achieving conditions and the expected results;
- Projecting the change–it refers to defining solutions and including them in specific documents;
- Implementing and checking the results–it is a stage that, paradoxically, often raises difficulties because of the resistance to change.

These three activities are intricately interconnected: change is achieved progressively, but the process is not linear, solutions adopted in one stage are often rectified in a following one.

The amount of innovation the solutions bear, the fact that change by definition involves contouring and implementing new solutions—what causes it to seem unique and risky—the important quantity of resources involved, the participation of many specialists and actors from different structures are characteristic elements that render complex and difficult the achieving of organisational changes.

The solution is to approach them as projects, in the manner proper to project management. The scheme in figure synthesizes the methodology for accomplishing the organisational changes, whose application ensures: on one hand–the coherence of the actions, through relating to the strategy of the organisation, on the other hand, advantages determined by approaching the change as project, by using the project as 'vehicle for the change', which means, implicitly, applying the principles and methods specific to project management.

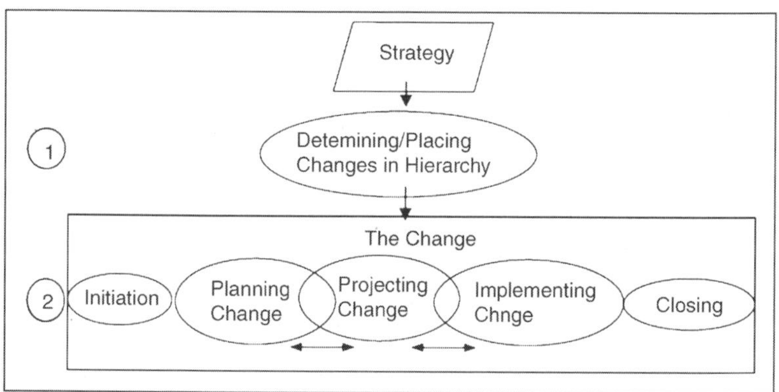

Fig. 11.1 Stages of the Process of Achievement Organisational Changes

CASE STUDY: LIBRARY OF TRANSILVANIA UNIVERSITY

The case study realised at the Library of Transilvania University of Brasov sets out to analyse the changes made during the last decade within the university library, from the perspective of the change management, to present the change priorities inscribed in the library strategy along the years to follow and to identify the key factors on whom there depends the success of the change projects. *Transilvania* University of Brasov is an institution of higher education and research, which enjoys high prestige on the local, national and international level. It is an extended university, with 16 faculties—8 are of technical profile and 8 of university profile, with more than 22.000 students at the university degree, master's degree and doctorate cycles, full time and distance learning. In the context of globalization, of Romania's integration within the EU, the University achieved important changes in all fields of activity and structures, in view of harmonizing with the new requirements and in view of assuring the quality of the services of education and research.

The Library is a structure of *Transilvania* University of Brasov, an entity without its own judicial personality, subordinated to the top management of the university. The mission of the university library is to ensure the documentary and information basis necessary for the education process, to enhance and to communicate them, as well as other services, to the benefit of the information users, facilitating the diversified and rapid access to all categories of sources.

The documentary patrimony of the Library of *Transilvania* University of Brasov includes: books, serial publications, manuscripts, cartographic documents, printed musical documents, audio-visual documents, graphic documents, electronic documents etc. The collections of the Library are constituted and developed through acquisition, transfer, national and international exchange, donations and sponsorship. The endowment is ensured through financing from the university management, as well as through transfers, donations and sponsorship.

Table 11.1 Organisational Changes from the Library of Transilvania University of Brasov

Objective of the Change	Description of the Change, Period
Concentration of the library activities and improvement the working conditions and documentary storage	The movement of the Library in a new, large building centrally placed, easily accessible to of the users and also to the staff. In 2006 of the there was set up the new free access room collection and in 2007 the central deposit for the loan of publications.
Automation of the processes document management	Provision with computers, linked in network of and connected to the Internet; and communication implementation of the Library integrated software Liberty 3, the fourth in chronological order, used since 2007.
Access to digital information: electronic documents, data-internet resources the year 2003).	The acquisition of electronic documents and the subscription to on-line magazines (since bases, the end of the '90-ies) and databases (after
Improvement of the system evaluation	Making up reports with respect to the of activity publication circulation and to the user frequency at the free access room; Users' statistic evidence and that of the publications made up by the loan service; improvement of the data collection for making up the official statistics required by the local and central authorities. They are realised partly automated, the tendency being of generalizing the automated means of quantitative evaluation.
Development of the human in the library	Employment, professional training, life-long resource education of the staff.
Improvement of the management structure	Redefining the compartments and the posts taking into consideration the new strategy of the library.
Optimization of the processes	Analysis, optimization and description through procedures of the key processes.

The organisation and the functioning of the Library observe the provisions of the specific legislation elaborated on the national level, as well as the internal regulations of the university. The Library has its own strategies and plans of activity whose approval by the Senate of the University ensures the integration in the general strategy of the institution. Like the university it is part of, the library achieved a series of changes in order to improve its performance. The synthetic situation of the important changes within the library, achieved during the last decade is presented in table.

Seen from the perspective of the results, the described actions display a series of defaults.

For instance:

- The relocation of the library became a strategic objective during the year 2005 after the finalization of a building with another initial destination. The placement of the Library in this building ensured the concentration of the activities and the amelioration of the working environment, however the adaptation costs were high, without ensuring the perfect compliance with the needs of the library;
- The automation of the processes of document management and communication is likewise questionable under the aspect of the adopted solutions, taking into consideration that the used software requires expensive hardware resources, and the results with respect to the performance of the processes were not up to the expectations;
- The efficacy of the actions undertaken within the library for the access to digital information may be appreciated as reduced, because of the lack of correlation between the equipments in the structure of the informatics system, as well as of the insufficient training with respect to the users' access to these resources. These resources did not benefit from an adequate promotion among the users who, to a too great extent, ignore their informative value and even their existence;
- The modernization of the evaluation system is slowed down by the lack of an adequate evaluation model and also by the generalized delay of the automated means for collecting and processing the data, and the efficiency of the evaluation is also affected by the persistence of the non-trained and disinterested staff in accomplishing this activity.
- The endowment with sufficient, stable and qualified staff is hindered by the still low number of librarians with specialized studies from the geographical area, by the unattractive level of the wages, by the rooting in certain posts of non-efficient employees, refractory to the new.

The outlined deficiencies are, at least in part, determined by the manner in which change management was implemented in the university library, both as regards planning the changes and settling the solutions, and as regards their implementation. It is to be observed especially the neglecting of the social aspects with respect to the staff's training, the resistance to change etc.—as factors which have negatively influenced the efficacy and the efficiency of the change processes.

9

The Change of Libraries: Movement in German

HOW TO MANAGE A LIBRARY

Library management involves functions such as planning, organising, leading, and controlling. Planning is about systematically making decisions about the library goals. Organising is about assembling and coordinating human, financial, physical, informational, and other resources needed to achieve library goals. Leading is about functions that involve efforts on the part of the librarian to stimulate high performance by employees, and controlling about monitoring various library operations and services. These four management functions are highly integrated, but libraries that excel in organising material resources and in leading their human capital are known to give better performance. Keeping in view the fact that libraries in adult education set ups are, by design, small budget libraries, confined to one room space, and adult education staff manages them manually on part time basis, these four management functions would occur in varying degree. In such a typical set up, the functions of organising and controlling would receive greater attention compared to other two functions.

For managing a library you may take the following step-by-step approach:

- *Step 1:* Defining library policies for collection development
- *Step 2:* Defining library authority and library advisory committee
- *Step 3:* Define procedures for library organisation and administration
- *Step 4:* Defining library space, equipment and tools for library operations and services
- *Step 5*: Defining procedures for maintenance of library collections

STEP 1: LIBRARY POLICIES FOR COLLECTION DEVELOPMENT

Step 1 includes the following task:

- *Define the Objectives of your Library:* State clearly the purpose of its existence;

- *Define your User Community and their Information Needs:* This requires complete knowledge and understanding about library stakeholders. This may include adult education teams, extension workers and adult education professionals, local community members and those who provide funds for the library. Their information needs can be assessed through library surveys, personal interviews, and informal discussions with all stakeholders;
- *Define Library Policy for Building Collections:* The policy states the guiding principles and procedures under which collection development activities, including the selection, maintenance, and weeding of print, electronic, and media library materials will occur. This would also mean specifying subject areas of interest to library stakeholders, their languages preferences, and formats of published and unpublished material. Non-print material could include films, slides, transparencies, photographs, maps posters, charts, etc. The policy must also define the limits in terms of collection size, keeping in view the users strength in a given subject, space available within the library premises, and annual budget earmarked for the purpose. The policy may also specify the subject areas in which the library is going build its archival collection, if any. Such a policy statement on the part of the library ensures continuity and consistency in selection and revision of materials for the library collections;
- *Define what Different Collections are Required to be Developed and Sustained Keeping in View Users' Information Needs:* The possible options include books collection, reports collection, pamphlet collection, multimedia collection, and reference collection (comprising dictionaries, yearbooks, directories, who's who almanacs, general and subject encyclopaedias), etc. The library may decide on developing some of these collections keeping in view the users' information needs.
- *Define your Book Selection Policy:* State the distribution of library budget by subject and by collection. The policy may also state guidelines for acquiring multiple copies of books, guidelines for accepting books from donors, and guidelines for weeding out material.

STEP 2: LIBRARY AUTHORITY AND LIBRARY ADVISORY COMMITTEE

Libraries in adult education setups are, by design, small budget libraries, confined to one room space, and managed manually on part time basis by adult education staff. The person incharge of the library should be the library authority, responsible for organisation and management of the library. He/she should play a dominant role in decision making, should enjoy the authority to

The university library will continue the process of the qualitative transformations during the following period, but in different ways. The aim is at using efficiently the strategy, as management instrument and at developing mechanisms that should allow the continuous control and improvement of the library performance through systematic actions. To this purpose, in a first stage there was carried out the diagnostic analysis of the management system of the library, whose conclusions are presented as follows, synthesized in strengths and weaknesses.

STRENGTHS

- There is a strategy of the library, harmonized with that of the university. The mission of the library and the system of values are published on the site. The objectives are realistic, measurable; the accent is laid on improving the performance, in order to contribute to ensuring the quality of the educational and research services carried out by the university. There was set as priority axis of research the implementation of a system of quality management, through which there is created the framework for the continuous improvement of the quality.
- The university and library management has the capability to professionally approach the changes, evinces competences as regards the ample perspective and its concretization in valid strategies of development, the settling of the plans for further action and the provision with the resources necessary for accom-plishing the change projects, the optimization of the structure, the implementation of modern methods of management.
- Human resources: the library has 52 employees, among which 32 with higher education and 11 with higher education in the field. The staff benefited from training and of mobility exchanges in the country and abroad.

WEAKNESSES

- *Control of the Performance*: The library achieves the assessment of the performance every year; however the criteria and the indicators which are used do not reflect the qualitative aspects of the activity, the effects of the library services upon the educational and scientific research processes.
- There is no management system that should measure the costs of the services/activities realised by the library.
- *Control of the Processes:* There has begun to be implemented the management through processes, however the action is in an incipient phase of analysis and description of the key processes through procedures.

- *Human Resources*: Staff's evaluation is done in compliance with the law, however the insufficient resources used in this process make the evaluation not always relevant. The participation of the staff in solving the problems is unequal and the rewarding system is non-stimulating.
- *Organisational Culture:* There is no culture of the quality, there are insufficiently promoted values such as team work, staff's implication, opening towards change.

Taking into account the submitted situation, the priority axes for the development of the capability of the library to continuously improve its performance are the following:

- *People:* The continuation of the process of staff training in quality management, with accent on achieving behavioural changes, on raising the degree of implication in solving the problems and on team work.
- *Users:* Orientation towards the customers, definition of the requirements and evaluation of their satisfaction. This implies in the first place the improvement of the system evaluating the library performance, through the introduction of criteria and indicators that should better reflect the effects upon the quality of the educational and research processes.
- The control will be also extended upon the costs of the services and of the activities realised by the library.
- *Processes:* Development and implementation of instruments and also of working and control procedures that should ensure the optimization of the processes and their continuous improvement.

The achievement of the change processes will be coordinated by the Management Council of the library. Both the initiation of the projects and their unfolding will be largely promoted in the framework of the library, for obtaining the feedback and for attracting the people in realizing the changes. The financing of the projects will be done from its own funds, but there will be likewise accessed funds from the Operational Programmes.

CASE STUDY: 'A SMALL LIBRARY WITH BIG GOALS' THE LIBRARY FOR GERMAN LANGUAGE AND LITERATURE, UNIVERSITY OF TARTU

BRIEF HISTORY OF THE UNIVERSITY OF TARTU

I will start my presentation with a small overview of the University of Tartu as our library is a part of the university and it is not possible to observe them apart. The University of Tartu is the oldest university in Estonia and one of the oldest in the Northern countries. On 30 June 1632, King Gustav II Adolf of Sweden signed the Foundation Decree of *Academia Dorpatensis*, which marks the beginning of our university's history. We can distinguish five periods when we speak about the history of the University of Tartu:

The students were mostly Swedes and Finns. We are proud that our university is so old but in fact the university, established during the Swedish period, was not one of the best reconized universities in Europe. The university in Tartu functioned with the Faculties of Philosophy, Law, Theology, and Medicine, enjoying the privileges similar to those granted to the University of Uppsala. The University of Tartu was closed in 1710 after the Swedish army had surrendered to the Russian forces after the defeat in the Northern War. The second period of the history of the university was 1802-1918 'reopening of the university'. This period can be characterized as the prosperity of the university. The Baltic Germans needed the university to educate their children. After the French Revolution studying abroad was not allowed. Russia also needed its own university. So in Tartu the European science and the Russian state met. The Germans wanted to have a small Heidelberg or Göttingen and somehow they succeeded in it.

The official language at the university was German and the religion was Lutheran. The 19th century was the period of prosperity of the university, the scientists K. E. von Baer, J. W. Struve and many others show us the level of scientific research in Tartu at that time. The teaching of Germanic languages also goes back to this period and has long traditions. Already in 1865 the Department for German Language at the University of Tartu was established. The first professor at the department was Leo Meyer, a linguist from Göttingen who stayed in Dorpat for 33 years. The number of students increased every day, Rutiku and Kegelmann.

OVERVIEW OF THE FOUNDATION OF GERMAN LIBRARY

I concentrate my attention on the fifth period which begins in 1991 while at that time our library was established. After the collapse of the Soviet Union the situation in our country was changing. We had to build up new society, a new educational system. The example of our library illustrates the developments in Estonia very well. In many areas we had to start from scratch. When learning foreign languages, it is natural that the dictionaries, lexicons and scientific literature are at students' disposal, but in Tartu it was not so.

The first German DAAD—Professor in Tartu—Claus Sommer-hage—started establishing a library. Among the many names the DAAD-Lecturer Claus Sommerhage should be emphasized. In 1992-1997 Dr. Claus Sommerhage was Guest Professor at the Department for German Language and Literature, 1997-1999 Extraordinary Professor. He innovated new curricula in teaching German literature, especially Modern German Literature.

Since his coming only the overview courses had been taught. He started with analytical literature seminars, Rutiku and Kegelmann. The most important thing he did for the department was establishing our library. He knew that without a library teaching literature was impossible. As Sommerhage had said we had a couple of copies of the novel Aula by Hermann Kant on our shelves. He was right. He started looking for funds in Germany and Switzerland, he used his own connections and personal charm. Without intensive support of the German and Swiss funds our library would not exist today.

FINANCING, PROGRAMMES, FUNDS

Our library is unique because until 2003 there was no budget for it. Nevertheless, it was increasing with every day. At the beginning many books were donated to our library. Tartu is an old university town and professors and lecturers had their own very good libraries. Many professors and lecturers decided to give their German books to our library. The theatre 'Vanemuine' liquidated its library in 1999 and we received all their books in the German language. From there we have our 23-volume complete works of Dostoevsky from 1922 which is considered to be the best Dostoevsky translation since then.

The oldest book in our library dates back to 1780. We also received books from our German friends. More than 15 years Professor Norbert Nail from the University of Marburg equipped us with every kind of books and journals about the German language and linguistics. Since 2001 our library is in the project of Gebert Rüf Fund-the Swiss Baltic Net for the Swiss Libraries and Swiss Literature in the Baltic States. We can order German Swiss literature every year for 1000 ChFr. The sum is not big but very valuable for our library. The project also coordinates the work of Schweizer Lesezimmer in the Baltic States. We meet every year in Lithuania, Latvia or Estonia to present our annual work and discuss our problems. These meetings are always useful and interesting. This time the meeting takes place in Vilnius In 2005-2007 our library was involved in the programme 'Menschen und Bücher', an initiative of the Goethe Institute for Central and Eastern Europe.

For our library it was a great privilege to be involved in the programme because our financial resources have always been limited. This time we could order books necessary for us and all our lecturers were involved in the ordering process. So we could efficiently enrich our library and every lecturer could order books for his or her course. The budget was 15,000 EUR and we could also invite a German author to Tartu.

DEPARTMENT LIBRARIES AT THE UNIVERSITY OF TARTU

Since 2003 the University Library has pursued the policy of supporting department libraries. Until then the status of a small department library was obscure. At the Department for German Language and Literature the library policy was always clear. We needed a well equipped library for students and lecturers, we were for the open access. Since 2002 our books are in the library system INNOPAC, which makes every process with books very easy and transparent. Sometimes the department libraries are in a bad state, the books are available for very few readers but our policy was different from the very beginning. When we do have a book, people must know about it, they must have access to it.

IMPORTANCE TO THE STUDENTS AND LECTURERS

One of the priorities of our library is its closeness to students and lecturers. We are informed of every need very quickly and for the students it is comfortable that everything about one subject is concentrated at one place. Since 1999 the Department for German Language and Literature has its own rooms in the former printing-house in the centre of the town, opposite the university main building. The renovation of the building had been contributed by different foreign embassies. It houses Departments for German, French, Spanish and Scandinavian Languages and is called 'Paabel'.

For our library it gave a possibility to expose all the books better, to create a real library system, to create a room where people like to work. The rooms for the German library in this new building are next to the seminar rooms. The students can use library early in the morning and between the lectures and seminars during the day. Our users are the students of the Department for German Language and Literature, the students of the Language Centre of the University, the Master's course students who study translation and interpretation. Every reader who possesses the university library card is welcome in our library. Closeness also means that we always consider the requests of the students.

In the last years when we received our budget, we have ordered books for the students who need them for writing their Bachelor's or Master's theses. The priority of our library is to be of high scientific quality. This is the direction Claus Sommerhage gave to our library and we still hold on to it. It is sometimes difficult because of our insufficient financing, but we always choose books carefully, ask advice from our German patrons and friends, try to be informed of the newest scientific literature. So we can affirm that our library has been created by professionals and it fulfils its tasks. One of our main tasks is to support the study process. At the Department for German Language and Literature the main research areas are linguistics, sociolinguistics, contact and text linguistics as well the Swiss literature and the German literature by women writers and the Baltic-German literature. Some subject areas in our library are very well presented, for example German linguistics, literary science, German history, German language history. In the last years the collection of our dictionaries and lexicons is almost ideal. As translation and interpretation are taught at our university, the collection of these books is almost excellent. We also have a good collection of German language textbooks. We have a sufficient number of copies thanks to 'LUKKA'—EU supporting programme. At our department teaching of modern Swiss literature has long traditions. Associated Professor Eve Pormeister has taught it already for 20 years and even wrote her Doctoral thesis on this subject. She has connections with the Embassy of Switzerland, Swiss Funds, Pro Helvetia. Her special interest is the reason why Swiss literature is so well presented in our library.

PLEASANT MEETING PLACE, NICE INTERIOR

Last but not least, in a small department library, the milieu plays a big role. There are people who never go to the main library of the university. They do not like too big bleak rooms without cosy corners, with too many strange people. Our library is a kind of a social gathering place for the students who study the same subject, have the same problems and pleasures. The nice and comfortable interior plays an important role here. As our rooms have interesting architecture, it is possible to establish exhibitions and that is what we regularly do. The last exhibition is from our student who studies art as her minor. She was happy to have an opportunity to show her paintings to her friends and fellow-students. We all can enjoy her colourful and interesting works.

CONCLUSIONS

The existence during the last decades of the university libraries has been characterized by ample changes, a process that will continue. The achievement of the changes is an issue of the management library, whose results may be considerably improved through a professional approach, based on the methods of the change management. The case study developed by the authors presents the first sequences of the change programme that will be achieved during the years to follow at the library of *Transilvania* University of Brasov, with reference to the methodology of change elaboration and implementation.

Bibliography

A.K. Gupta: *Digital Library and Education*, Pearl Books, Delhi, 2012.

Ajay K. Srivastav: *Digital Library Environment and Networking*, Sree Publications, Delhi, 2006.

Bharti Sharma and Jayanti Singh: *Serial Management in Academic Library*, Manglam Publications, 2011.

Brian Mathews: *Marketing Today's Academic Library: A Bold New Approach to Communicating with Students*, Ess Ess Publications, Delhi, 2010.

C Praveen Singh: *Library Automation in Modern Age*, Alfa Publications, Delhi, 2008.

G.K. Sampath Kumar: *Digital Library and Information Technology: Changing Concepts*, Altar Publications, 2012.

G.K. Sampath Kumar: *Digital Library Automation Planning Designing and Development*, Akhand Publications, Delhi, 2012.

G.K. Singh: *Principles of Digital Library Development*, Shree Publications, Delhi, 2004.

J. Sridevi and Vijay Laxshmi: *Model of Digital Library*, Shree Publications, Delhi, 2004.

Jagadeesha S. and Mahesh V. Mudhol: *Library Automation Using Foxpro 2.0*, Ess Ess Publications, Delhi, 1998

K. Nazeer Badhusha: *Digital Library Architecture*, Ane Books Pvt. Ltd., Delhi, 2008.

K. Rajasekaran, R. Raman Nair and K.M. Nafala: *Digital Library Basics: A Practical Manual (With Software CD Inside)*, Ess Ess Publications, Delhi, 2010.

Kusum Verma: *Digital Library and Information Developments*, Vista International Publishing House, 2008.

Kusum Verma: *Digital Library Preservation Strategies*, Akansha Publications, Delhi, 2005.

Kusum Verma: *Metadata and Digital Library Systems*, Akansha Publications, Delhi, 2004.

Manohar Nanda: *Library Automation*, Anmol Publications, Delhi, 2006.

N.R. Satyanarayana: *A Manual of Library Automation and Networking*, New Royal Book

Co, Lucknow, 2003.

Omesh Aadhavan: *Development of Digital Library*, Oxford Book Company, Jaipur, 2010.

Omesh Aadhavan: *Management of Digital Library*, Oxford Book Company, Jaipur, 2010.

P. Balasubramanian: *Library Automation and Networking*, Deep and Deep publications, Delhi, 2011.

Prabhat Pandey: *Recent Advances in Library Automation*, Mahamaya Publications, Delhi, 2010.

Pramod Kumar Singh: *Library Automation*, Shree Publications, Delhi, 2005.

Purushotham Tiwari: *Digital Library*, APH Publications, Delhi, 2014.

Purushotham Tiwari: *International Encyclopaedia of Library Automation, Vols. I to IV*, A.P.H. Publications, Delhi, 2011.

R.K. Singh and C.K. Sharma: *Library Automation and Total Quality Management*, Shree Publications, Delhi, 2011.

R.K. Singh: *Basic Facts of Digital Library*, Shree Publications, Delhi, 2004.

R.S. Aswal: *Library Automation for 21 Century*, Ess Ess Publications, Delhi, 2006.

R.S. Kochar and K.N. Sudarshan: *Library Automation*: *(Issues and Systems)*, A P H Publications, Delhi, 2010.

Raghunath Pandey and M.N. Velayudhan Pillai: *Digital Library*: *Trends and Prospects*, Jnanada Prakashan, Delhi, 2011.

Rajan Nagia: *Making of Software Packages for Library Automation*, Cyber Tech Publications, Delhi, 2012.

Rashmi Upadhyay: *Digital Library Management*, Alfa Publications, Delhi, 2011.

S. K. Sangma: *Manual of Library Automation and Networking*, Centrum Press, Delhi, 2013.

S. Yadagiri and R.K. Pavan Kumar: *Library Automation*: *Perspectives and Challenges*, Swastik Publications, Delhi, 2013.

S.C. Dwivedi: *Digital Library (2 Vols-Set)*, Shree Publications, Delhi, 2005.

S.P. Singh: *Library Automation and Acquisition System*, Omega Publications, Delhi, 2009.

Savita Mittal: *Digital Library Resources*, Ess Ess Publications, Delhi, 2005.

Shiv Ram Verma: *Academic Library System*, Shree Publications, Delhi, 2005.

Shri Nath Sahai: *Academic Library System*, Ess Ess Publications, Delhi, 2009.

V.K. Jain: *Information Technology for Digital Library Management and Automation*, Atlantic Publications, Delhi, 2009.

Index